VALUES
SHIFT

VALUES
SHIFT

Recruiting, Retaining and Engaging the
Multigenerational Workforce

John B. Izzo, Ph.D. and Pam Withers

FAIRWINDS
PRESS

FairWinds Press
PO Box 668
Lions Bay, BC
V0N2E0
t. 604-913-0649 **f.** 604-913-0648 **e.** info@fairwinds-press.com

ORDERING INFORMATION

Quantity Sales: Special Discounts are available on quantity purchases by corporations, associations and other groups. Please contact us directly.

Individual Purchases: Please visit your local bookstore, online bookstores or visit FairWinds Press at www.fairwinds-press.com to order

Orders by Canadian and US book trade: Please visit www.fairwinds-press.com.

Library and Archives Canada Cataloguing in Publication

Izzo, John B. (John Baptist), 1957-
    Values shift : recruiting, retaining and engaging a multigenerational workforce / John B. Izzo, Pam Withers. — 2nd ed.
First ed. had different subtitle.

Includes bibliographical references.
ISBN 978-0-9780974-0-0

    1. Work ethic. 2. Organizational change. 3. Personnel management.
I. Withers, Pam II. Title.

HD4905.I99 2007   658.3'14   C2007-901694-4

 Please Reuse and Recycle.

SECOND EDITION
10 09 08 07 06 05 04 03 02 01
Development Editor: Leslie Nolin
Cover and interior design: Leslie Nolin
Cover and interior layout: Jill Voges
Research and editing: Julie Bertinshaw

"To turbo charge retention, you must first know the heats and minds of your employees and then undertake the tough rewarding task of sculpting careers that bring joy to both."

Harvard Business Review

"If you want a good overview of why business is so different today from what it has been in the past and what to do about it—this book is for you! Well written and informative!"

William Bridges, Author
Managing Transition, Jobshift and *You & Co*

" John and Pam offer a thought provoking, compelling and practical book on the shifts that need to occur to bring lasting renewal in organizations today. This book is an important contribution for leaders who are committed to reshaping their workplace."

David Irvine, Author
Simple Living in a Complex World

"Wise leaders know how to listen. This book not only tells you what your people expect from work, but it helps teach ways to deliver it."

Peter Urs Bender,
author of the national best seller,
Leadership from Within
(1952—2005)

"This book provides realistic strategies businesses will need to win commitment from workers who are demanding more balance among work, family, health, community, and their own personal growth."

Rex Weyler, author *Greenpeace,*
Co-author, *Chop Wood, Curry Water*
Co-founder, **Hollyhock Seminar Center**

"This book is filled with timeless wisdom and practical insights on the essence of true leadership"

Robin Sharma, LL.B LL.M.
author of *The Monk who sold His Ferrari*

"This book was long overdue! Values Shift provides a blueprint of the future, as no longer is it sufficient for managers to just recruit talent to their organizations but more importantly, managers must find innovative ways to retain the workers then need to achieve their corporate goals!

George Madden, President
Pinton Forrest & Madden
EMA Partners International
Management Search Consultants

media that paid attention to this book

Bloomberg TV

CNN

ABC World News

Business Week—Online

HR Magazine

HR Executive Magazine

Employment Relations Today

Compensation & Benefits Magazine

Association Executive

Training Magazine

American Management Association Magazine

Entrepreneur Magazine

Life@Work Magazine

Investor Business Daily

The National Post

The Globe and Mail

The Vancouver Sun

Los Angeles Times

FAST Company

INC. Magazine

And many, many more!

For those companies and leaders
for whom creating a great place to work
is an end in itself.

CONTENTS

PART ONE:

Winning the Changing Workforce 1

CHAPTER ONE:

The Retention Game: Why Bother With Values? 3
Retention: the new game 9
Hard time fining good people? Get used to it! 12
But are these shifts new? 16

CHAPTER TWO:

Forces That Have Changed How We See Work 18
FAMILY
Changing parenting and family patterns 20
The affluence factor 22
Changing family structures 24
THE ECONOMY
Now that work is like, it had better be a good one 29
SOCIETY
Consumerism and spiritual hunger 30
Democracy and the Internet 33
TECHNOLOGY
Putting it all together 36

CHAPTER THREE:

**Understanding Demographic Differences
in Work Values 37**
The age issue: A tale of three generations 40
The gender gap 50
Diversity 53
Values 57

PART TWO:

The Six Expectations of the New Work World 63

CHAPTER FOUR:

The Expectation of Balance and Synergy 65

Extreme flextime 67

A balanced "diet" 73

Responding to the shift toward balance 79

Roots of the balance revolution 82

More than time 86

What does the desire for balance mean for your business? 87

Responding 91

Assessing your company for balance 97

CHAPTER FIVE:

The Expectation of Work as a Noble Cause 101

What business are you in? Mission statements that inspire loyalty 108

Demonstrating the connection 112

The new corporate citizen 118

Altruism on company time 120

Why people are drawn to values driven companies 124

Assessing your company for noble cause 128

CHAPTER SIX:

The Expectation of Personal Growth and Development 131

Learning new skills 133

Training is a philosophy, not a class 140

Helping people manage their careers 142

Discovering oneself at work 147

Promoting growth or pay the price 150

Assessing your company for development 156

CHAPTER SEVEN:

The Expectation of Partnership 159

Communication above rank 163

Open books 172

Performance-based pay 174

The practices of partnering leaders 177
Vigilance and attention to symbolism 182
Assessing your company for partnership 187

CHAPTER EIGHT:

The Expectation of Community at Work 190
Is the expectation of community new? 193
It all begins with values: The new company town 195
Creating a place where people feel connected 197
Building community across rank 203
Making fun a priority 205
Community: It can't be left to chance 206
Assessing your company for community 210

CHAPTER NINE:

The Expectation of Trust 212
The aftermath of downsizing 215
New-style loyalty 220
The ingredients of trust 223
Assessing your company for trust 238
Leadership Values Self-Assessment 241
Generational reference guide 247

PART THREE:
Getting Started 257

CHAPTER TEN:

Leading In the Wake of the Shifts 259
Retention is a philosophy before it's a strategy 261
Will the shifts shift? 264
The first step: An honest assessment 268
The second step: Transferring the knowledge 271
Where to start the knowledge transfer strategy 272
Imitation: The worst form of strategy 274
Doing something us more important that waiting for perfection 276
A final benediction 277

ACKNOWLEDGEMENTS

To Leslie Nolin-Izzo, my partner in business and in life, whose hard work, often with little visibility, has made my first book as well as this book a reality. She is indeed the unseen presence behind all of my good work and one of the brightest and most supportive people I've ever met. She continues to push me to the greatness I write about.

To my co-author Pam Withers whose openness to feedback and willingness to give are the mark of a true professional. To my children to sacrificed times with me so that I could write this but interrupted me enough to play basketball, golf, and bug watching to keep this work in perspective. to our researchers, Janet Freeman, Julie Bertinshaw and Olivia McIvor. To the many companies and leaders who have taught me/us by example about what it means to create a great workplace. Special thanks to Synovus Financial and TD Industries, two companies that remind me of what heights can be achieved at work. To Pete Mackowski and Paul Rushforth for their own leadership and ongoing personal support. To Jeremy Ball who continues to be a trusted friend and believer in this work. To my grandfather Henry Turpel, who in myth and reality served as an example of how to live and work. To my mother, Irene Izzo who as a single mother did her best to ensure I wanted to make a difference in the world too. To the leaders and companies who gave freely of their time so that we could get their perspectives on the changing ways we see work. As always, to my clients, who have always taught me as much as I have taught them. To the millions of North Americans who go to work each and every day desiring what my grandfather called a "good tired."

— John Izzo, Ph.D.

Above all, I'm indebted to my co-author for his vision, accessibility and professionalism, not to mention his talent for modeling every one of the concepts in this book. I'd like to give special thanks to our researchers, Janet Freeman and Julie Burtinshaw. They're worth acknowledging again because without them, this book would never have made its deadline. Julie in particular went above and beyond the call of duty in grasping the concepts and giving us a rich amount of data from which to work. I'd also like to salute Bonnie Irving, editor of BC Business magazine, for her support and friendship over many years, and for her generous permission to use material from my past BC Business magazine articles for this book. I'm grateful to Robin Roberts and Sue Dritmanis for their moments of "sushi sanity," and to my clients, who put up with my "leave of absence." Thanks to Leslie, Alison, Nicole de Montbrun, Peter Frost and George Madden. And on a personal level, to Heather Pringle and Tish Sears. Last but by no means least, I am deeply appreciative of the patience and support my husband and son have given me through the months of being rather too attached to my keyboard. It has been a journey worth taking!

Pam Withers

FOREWORD

For the last twenty years I have been advising companies on creating great workplaces, helping them attract and retain their people. When we wrote the first edition of this book in the year 2000, many people were just waking up to the shifts occurring in the values of people at work. What's more, most people were framing the shift as mostly a "generational shift" where younger workers (Gen X and Gen Y) were different from their baby boomer and traditionalist colleagues. This book was groundbreaking because Pam Withers and I suggested an alternative hypothesis, which was that values were changing at and about work across all of the generations still at work. We suggested that there were generational differences but that there were six shifts which were held in common.

Since the year 2000, I believe the research suggests that we were correct in our hypothesis. It turns out there is a thin line of difference between the twenty something who does not want to do overtime and the baby boomer who wants to retire from full time work early. The mid-lifer who leaves a large company to join a smaller, younger company with less bureaucracy (where she can have a say) is not much different than the new college graduate who makes the same choice. Still there are differences, some of them significant, and we have tried in this edition to clearly identify those differences (and help leaders understand the practical implications.)

In the time since that first edition and this new one seven years later, it has become more apparent both that what we want from work is changing and that employers are recognizing that the key to retaining people is to respond to these shifts. It has been exciting to see these new values embraced and recognized by so many companies. Among these are: The desire for balance as a key expectation at work now being a given amongst employers; efforts by employers to "advertise" the nobel purpose of their enterprise to prospective employees; and an increasing number of companies taking career development seriously as a retention strategy.

At the same time, the values we identified in the first edition continue to evolve. For example, as the baby boomers approach traditional retirement age it is becoming apparent that they plan to re-define retirement. Unlike their parents, most of who left the workplace for good to play the golf courses and cruise ships, these baby boomers will demonstrate that one size no longer fits all. Some of them will retire early and volunteer, others will work long past the traditional retirement age, while others will work part-time as long as they are physically able to do so.

Younger workers continue to demonstrate a bold willingness to live their shifting values at work, often walking when these values are not honored. Generational differences and the challenge of managing a multi-generational workforce has become a common subject of conversation amongst the managers and human resource leaders.

Events such as September 11th and the Enron disaster, forced employees to ask even more questions about the place work plays in our lives and the importance of choosing employers who are trustworthy.

When it came time to write a second edition, we had two goals in mind. First, we wanted to update some of the research. Seven years is not a great deal of time but we wanted to provide more recent data to both support the ongoing shift of values and how companies are responding to them.

The second goal for this edition is that while the first edition focused primarily on helping companies understand these shifts, we felt this new one had to be even more practical. Since 2000 we have been conducing training sessions with leaders all over North america on understanding these shifts, responding to them and managing a multi-generational workforce. We have created some practical tools for understanding and managing each of these generations as well as managing these generations together at work. This edition includes some of what we have learned including practical tips for incorporating these shifts in recruiting and retaining employees.

Whenever I speak to a group about these shifting values I ask for a show of hands as to how many people have seen "values" at work shift during the last ten-fifteen years. Almost every hand goes up. Now that we widely recognize that values are changing, I hope this book continues to deepen our understanding of how they are changing, why they are changing, and how organizations can retain people by responding to them.

John Izzo, Ph.D.

PART ONE

Winning the Changing Workforce

CHAPTER ONE

the retention game: why bother with values?

"As boomers retire, employers find they're fishing for talent in a puddle instead of a pool"

SEATTLE POST INTELLIGENCER

Thirty years ago, when job-hopping was frowned upon and employees tended to stick with one employer for a lifetime, hardly anyone knew, let alone cared about, the term "employee retention". No one needs to tell today's leaders that the workforce is now engaged in an entirely different game, one that involves revolving-door employment and never-ending recruitment at all levels.

Some are far too quick to chalk this up to an new economic approach (empowered workers in a flatter, faster organization), and to demographics (more openings than qualified candidates) as boomers retire. But there's a third, much less explored phenomenon, and that is a fundamental shift in workers' values and expectations. Why and how are employees changing? Let's begin with a quick summary of how the workplace has been put through the wringer.

Over the past two decades, workers have gone from secure jobs, life-long careers, and predictable ascents up corporate ladders, to a world of temporary jobs, lifelong learning, and highly competitive industries in which they're only as good as their last gig, regardless of rank or experience. All this has triggered a deluge of words on how workers had better adapt or die. But even as career counselors scurried to re-educate the masses, two more powerful changes sneaked up from behind. First, workers began seeing work through a new shade of tinted glasses. By that we mean that, virtually unnoticed by corporate leaders, work itself has been devalued in the bigger picture of life as seen from the eyes of today's talent. And second, a growing skilled-labor gap has begun to put applicants in the driver's seat and to turn employers from confident recruiters into groveling pursuers desperately holding their fingers in the dike of employee turnover. Baby boomers' impending retirement officially starts in 2011, but given the likelihood that they'll retire early (fifty percent by the age of sixty-two, and seventy percent by the age of sixty-five), the skilled-labour gap will begin building to a crisis starting in 2008. And that means either the current economy will start to suffer for the lack of skilled labor, or workers fifty-five and over will have to increase their labor-force participation by twenty-five percent just to maintain a constant employment-population ratio. In other words, forward-thinking companies must implement creative ways to retain skilled mature workers.[1]

The hunter has become the hunted-not yet in all industries or regions,

[1] Source: U.S. Census Bureau, 2000 data (www.census.gov/Press-Release/www/2001/tables/dp_us_2000.PDF, accessed Feb. 22, 2002); 2005-2025 data (www.census.gov/population/www/projections/natsum-T3.html)

but with gathering force. Nor, as we'll explain many times in this book, is this a temporary phenomenon. And even if it were, the workplace and worker have changed too much to go back to where they were. Today, the secret to winning the loyalty of professionals is understanding their shift in values. Fortunately, that concept is easy to grasp if one takes a quick journey back into the annals of modern business history.

Twenty years ago, much of the business world was taken by surprise when the proverbial work pyramid was up-ended. Suddenly, customers were on top, and a flattened hierarchy placed the responsibility on frontline workers to study, understand, and satisfy the customer's every whim. Keeping the customer satisfied was now more than a mantra; it was a matter of corporate life or death. The roots of the customer service shift are well-known to everyone: speeded-up business cycles, increased international competition, and a growing assertiveness on the part of customers.

Today, we're poised for the natural sequel to that revolution: It's time to focus on keeping the worker satisfied — or at least, engaged in his or her work. The factors triggering the pyramid's final meltdown may even sound familiar: warp-speed business cycles, a borderless world, and a degree of employee assertiveness that makes demanding customers of the 1990s look docile.

For years, analysts have freely acknowledged the following:

- Work processes are changing at a frantic speed to keep pace with ever-faster business cycles. This puts tremendous pressure on workers *at every level*, which in turn invites a degree of burnout previously known only to top executives and entrepreneurs.

- "Worker motivation" has become an antiquated and paternalistic concept. Today, workers at every level must be more responsible, autonomous, and self-motivated than ever before, with the authority to make quick and important decisions. They work across time zones, often connected only by e-mail for short periods before joining a new team. Of course, the entrepreneurial qualities they need to succeed are precisely those that tempt them to leave their company and start their own enterprises.

• Top-flight contract workers and consultants that leaders wish to attract are even more slippery to hold onto than employees.

• Workers, salaried and otherwise, are becoming ever more certain and demanding about what they want from the work experience. Ranking highest on their wish list — regardless of age, gender, or culture — are a work/life balance, constant personal and career development, exciting work, and a sense of contributing to their community. Responding to such values, previously considered "fuzzy" or extracurricular, is in some respects a greater challenge in our electronically-linked, revolving-door workforce than it was in the old economy. (In other ways, it's easier.)

Put these together and the message is clear: Worker motivation now ranks evenly with customer service as the key to holding market edge. Never has it been so important to see the workplace through workers' eyes and to cater to their beliefs and needs, which represent nothing short of a sea change from worker values of even ten years ago. Besides, there's a frequently overlooked link between employee retention and customer service. As the director of human resources at Kinko's Inc. put it, "Our customers told us they wanted to see a familiar face taking care of them."

How content are workers these days, and how likely are they to stay put? Although surveys show that most people like their jobs, this has little to do with whether they'll stay. Two-thirds of North Americans say they are actively thinking of leaving their present company. In our own engagement and retention assessments, we have discovered many companies where employees are satisfied with their jobs but still plan to leave. Understanding what drives people to stay and what drives them to leave is more critical than ever.

A recent CareerBuilder.com survey showed that thirty-eight percent of directors, managers, supervisors, and team leaders were considering changing their jobs in 2004. Yet employees don't want to change companies so much as their position within their company. To keep these restless employees, corporations need to provide new internal challenges.

For instance, at Intel, ten percent of employees change jobs internally each year, and seventy-five percent telecommute each day. And if an employee stays for seven years, he or she receives an eight-week paid sabbatical!

When consultants like Tom Peters first started suggesting that the "search for excellence" aimed at customers would drive results, his inverted pyramid was controversial. Now people take the link between customer service and profits for granted. This book suggests that a similar and equally profound shift is happening. The work experience will now have to be organized around the worker, and not vice versa. Converting a company to be worker-driven is a daunting but unavoidable task for every forward-thinking organization. Fortunately, it becomes less daunting as you read on.

Albert Einstein once said, "History has changed everything except our way of thinking." This book is about how, in the world of work, history has now changed everything, *including* how individuals think. A new set of values is emerging, a new way of thinking about work and what employees want from it. These shifts cut across generations, and gaining an understanding of them is fundamental for any leader or company wanting to attract, keep, and maximize the performance of the changing workforce. What's more, understanding the shifts is not enough. So this book also helps readers *respond* to them in practical and tangible ways.

Tumultuous change at a speed unprecedented in history is the definition of today's workplace. In a business world that shrugs off international boundaries, where companies live or die by their ability to keep increasingly fickle and demanding customers satisfied, old-fashioned values like loyalty, patience, and deference to one's elders have been tossed overboard like excess baggage. Newer competencies, including intuition, risk-taking, and mercenary résumé-building, are today's currency. And yet, precisely because they must live life in the express lane, great employees learn early on when and how to pause and refuel. Baby boomers, missing the irony of what their own era has taught younger workers, often look askance at younger workers' determination to add balance to the mix, chalking it up to slackness or unreliability. In truth, a work/life balance is just one of several items that has graduated from an asset to a survival tool in this new era.

Perhaps least-recognized and most significant of all the changes the economy has wrought is the abrupt end of the employer's "buyer's market," which has existed (with the exception of occasional war-induced shortages) since at least the mid-1800s, the dawn of the Industrial Revolution. In other words, for more than 150 years, there have always been more workers than positions available, which means there was never any doubt as to who set the rules and who was in control. Even where desired skill sets failed to match applicants' experience, there was plenty of time to train them — in contrast to today's hit-the-ground-running environment.

The triad of a global economy, the information age, and skewed demographics (ninety-eight percent of population growth is occurring in countries that do not have a strong education system) has changed all that. Now, not only do skilled workers increasingly have their pick of employers; they've learned to negotiate salaries and benefits with all the aplomb of yesterday's executives. Candidates with the right stuff are being head-hunted by firms that once filled only corner offices. In contrast to their less skilled workmates, skilled employees are also being granted regular access to the training they crave. As the self-serve economy extends into every corner of life, today's job applicants are even able to conduct highly efficient comparative research on prospective employers' corporate culture and benefits by Internet, and once in the door, design their own benefit packages by Intranet.

retention: the new game

Here is the paradox of employee relations for the new century: Companies need good people more than ever, and yet loyalty as we know it is dead or hardly breathing. According to a report from August 2004, even the U.S. job market continues to grow, so do Americans' dissatisfaction with their current employment situations and work/life balance. It is clear that workers are ready and willing to make a change. According to Monster's 2004 Work/Life Balance survey, eighty-two percent of Americans are unhappy with their work/life balance — (up from eighty percent in 2003) — and seventy-two percent work more than forty hours per week, up from seventy-one percent in 2003. Some eighty-nine percent of workers hope to change jobs in the next six months, despite the fact that eighty-four percent say the economy has hindered their ability to change jobs in recent years

In other words, workers today feel strongly that they have the skills necessary to compete in the new century. That's evolution and adaptation within a very tight timeframe. It is also a reflection of new worker values.

Unfortunately, many of today's employers don't "get it." They don't believe their buyer's market has ended, or they believe the current situation is very temporary and restricted to a few elite industries. They don't want to pander to spoiled kids with quirky notions of benefits, like the team of young stars that demanded, in absolute seriousness, that they be located beside a certain cookie-franchise outlet to enhance the sugar-highs of their breaks — and were granted their desire. Wizened companies are in a bending-over-backwards contest, barely able to keep up with the new limbo positions demanded as the bar slowly falls. Human resources issues — staffing, recruitment, retraining, and morale — have leapfrogged to employers' No. 1 concern, notably ahead of sales and growth, profits and cash flow, macroeconomic issues and competition. And justly so, for a skilled labor shortage in a knowledge industry means that those who catch and keep the best will thrive; the rest will shrivel and die.

When the high-tech balloon deflated in 2000, many employers stopped catering to "demanding" or "spoiled" employees. But current figures from the Bureau of Labor and Statistics show that the job recession

> **JAMES GOODNIGHT,** founder of SAS, saw the recession as an opportunity to recruit valuable employees who had been laid off from SAS's competitors. In an interview with Inc. magazine, he recently said, "We decided there were so many people looking for jobs that we should take the opportunity to bring in some really first-class people. We accepted that our profits would be down, but that we would build for the future."

is over. In January 2004, 112,000 jobs were created — a substantial increase from 2001. Suddenly, dissatisfied, overworked, and unappreciated employees are able to look for new and better jobs — and employee retention is at front and center of employer concerns.

The proportion of people currently unemployed who left their last job voluntarily is at its highest in almost ten years. Yet, most of the companies on the Fortune 100 Best Places to Work (2004) are well below this figure. The average job tenure has shrunk even though the cost of losing and replacing an employee can reach between 100 and 250 percent of the salary of the leaving employee — or more: Taco Bell's research found that their outlets with the lowest employee turnover produced up to fifty percent more in sales.

Not long ago, co-author John Izzo was present when the CEO of a company that had been receiving all kinds of accolades for its products and services reviewed the returns of an employee survey. He looked stricken, as if someone had plunged a dagger into his heart. Especially given that his company is not part of an industry for which professionals are highly sought after, he could hardly believe his eyes: Employees had indicated that they liked their jobs for the most part, and believed in the company, but more than fifty percent of them were actively looking for another place to work!

"Screw it," he muttered.

Welcome to the new world of retention, and to a set of workers with a whole new outlook on work. In the old days, a growing company with relatively happy employees could count on most of them staying. But today's workers bring a new set of profound, if at times unrealistic, expectations of what work should be like. Here are two bold guesses: A lot more of your people are thinking about leaving than you think. And by taking to heart the strategies outlined in this book, you can help stem that tide.

As *Inc.* magazine has proposed, "Smart companies don't think only about filling jobs anymore. Nor do they add one perk here, one perk there, ending up with a patchwork approximation of what their competitors are already doing. Instead the companies immerse their employees in an experience they'd be hard-pressed to find anyplace else."

We call it a *values match*.

hard time finding good people?
get used to it!

Is the current retention scare temporary? Decidedly not. Sixty percent of large employers say they are having difficulty attracting workers now, but the struggle has only just begun. As much as thirty to forty percent of the managerial workforce is currently on the verge of retirement, prompting a rising panic to retain some of these graying leaders for a smoother transition, as outlined in Beverly Goldberg's *Age Works: What Corporate America Must Do to Survive the Graying of the Workforce*. Research shows that baby boomers, by far the largest pool of workers plan to stop working full-time much earlier than did their parents. To entice some of these workers to stay longer, workplace observers have suggested various strategies. An article in Harvard Business Review offered the following suggestions: create a culture that honors experience; offer training to older workers; offer flexible work (off-site, job sharing, telecommuting); and introduce flexible retirement by changing some of the regulations around pensions that inhibit workers from accepting flexible work arrangements.

According to a study by International Data Corporation, western Europe faces the same growing talent gap: About 510,000 full-time information technology jobs are vacant, a number expected to grow to 1.6 million by 2002. Given that by 2006, half of all workers will be employed in information technology positions or within industries that intensively utilize information technology, products, and services, this shortfall presents a crisis. According to the Future of Work organization, by 2010 there will be a shortfall of about ten million knowledge workers in the US. In other words, companies are shortest on help in the fastest-growing sector, one that promises to swallow other sectors whole. Training will help, but how can it help fast enough? What about importing professionals? Although the US Congress raised the number of visas from 1999 through 2001 for skilled technology workers by 142,500 — a seventy-three percent leap — it then cut back on the program for foreign-trained high tech and other specialized workers by two-thirds in 2003 in response to the recession and unemployment in the Silicon Valley after the dot-com bust. Regardless of what governments do about raising the number of visas for skilled technology workers, the stark truth is that birthrates have fallen below replacement level in countries that stress education. Also, as we said earlier, most population growth is occurring in countries where education is not widely available.

Meanwhile, Western-style consumerism is racing to establish itself in every corner of the globe, a process that requires a skilled workforce. Clearly, only companies that excel at retaining skilled workers can compete in this race; those that also manage to "engage" the hearts and souls of their workforce will come out at the head of the pack.

The concern for "intellectual capital" is new and pervasive. John recently arranged a major consulting project, involving an employee retention strategy, on his car phone during a fifteen-minute initial conversation. The client had never even met John face to face. It was almost as if the simple words, "This could help you attract and keep people," were sufficient unto themselves. It's not that the client was completely convinced a retention strategy would help. It was more like a dying person was requesting a drink of water: The need was greater than the rationale. Such is the world of business today. People are the only real asset, and they are harder than ever to find and keep.

At a Fortune 500 company's corporate event, John spoke about the need to organize business around the changing worker. Afterwards, an executive approached him to comment, "Ten years ago, we'd have laughed you out of the room. But today, everyone was riveted." Such is the shift in today's workplace: from requiring the worker to organize around corporate needs, to a place of more equality, where a company ignores the deepest needs of workers only at its peril.

The shortage of skilled workers is beginning to reach much further into the workforce than a few years ago, when only high-tech industries were affected before the dot-com crashes. In a 2001 study by the National Association of Manufacturers, more than eighty percent of respondents reported a "moderate to serious" shortage of qualified job applicants.

So, demographics, the global economy, and the information age together dictate that the overturning of the employer's "buyer's market" is far from a temporary situation. Only companies that have moved their human-resources staff front and center into strategic planning will survive this trend. Success in this new environment relies on three simple premises: Know your employees' needs and desires. (This book reveals what they are.) Meet their needs and desires. (We show you how.) And never assume you know what they want.

For example, companies have found they can increase productivity, revenue, or both by twenty percent simply by implementing a work/life balance program for staff. Likewise, it's possible to reduce turnover by as much as fifty percent by introducing any of the following: dependant care leave, childcare subsidies, eldercare programs, counseling and referral, and flexible working hours.

Here's the bottom line: The era of analyzing economic changes in terms of how workers must adapt to survive is over. Instead, this book explores how companies must adapt to keep workers, and how economic and societal shifts have literally changed the way workers see work.

The economy and society have changed what people want from jobs and employers, and what they want rests on changing values. Values are the primary source of energy driving behavior. Inwardly, we know our values as beliefs. Outwardly, they are manifested as behaviors and choices. When our values and work drift apart from one another, we experience a commitment crisis. When they're tied neatly into a bundle, we put our hearts and souls into our work.

Values Shift identifies six major expectations, all based on those changing values, and all of which affect what workers of several generations now want from work. We also help leaders by suggesting practical strategies for winning commitment from the changing workforce. This new outlook represents a force to which organizations must respond if they want to attract, motivate, and keep talented people of all ages and backgrounds. We help forward-looking organizations and leaders understand exactly what it takes to maximize people performance in today's economy.

The six trends discussed throughout the book, which apply to workers of all demographics, include:

1. An expectation of personal growth and development

2. An expectation of partnership in a collapsed hierarchy

3. An expectation of a work/life balance and synergy

4. An expectation of work as a noble cause

5. An expectation of community at work

6. An expectation of trust

but are these shifts new?

Some business leaders will suggest that the "shifts" we discuss in this book are not, in fact, new. When we interviewed Paul Hollands, chief operating officer of A&W Canada, for this book, he commented, "These are the things people have wanted since human beings have been around." Wanted? Yes. But in a position to demand? We think not.

As we move deeper into the new century, "wants" are becoming "expectations." Just as workers' attitudes towards work have changed radically in key areas — their view of authority, their more entrepreneurial orientation, and their attempts to achieve a work/life balance, to name a few — so too have their values. The two are clearly intertwined, each impacting on the other.

These value shifts are the result of several decades of change in the family, society, and work itself, as explained in the next chapter. What we are saying is simple: The six expectations outlined here form a template for companies that want the best employees to flock their way. Companies that align themselves with the new worker values will achieve great things. Knowing how people see work is critical. Knowing their dreams and highest hopes is paramount.

A tongue-in-cheek Monster.com advertisement a few years ago illustrated this shift in values. The ad featured young children talking about what they wanted to be when they grew up. Through a series of vignettes, the kids said they wanted to be a brown-nose, a yes-man, a middle manager in a large organization, a downsized employee. The ad ended with the poignant question, "What did you want to be?" It strikes a timely chord in North America because our views of work and what we want from it have changed dramatically (although not as dramatically as the kids' lines would have us believe!). Monster.com, of course, is a Web presence devoted to helping people — maybe your people? — find employers highly tuned to workers' shifting dreams.

Years ago, sociologist Studs Terkel wrote *Working*, a collection of interviews with people about work. In talking with people who laid bricks and cleaned floors, Terkel quickly discerned that work was not just about earning a living; for these folks, it was about making a difference, making a contribution. Echoing that insight, eighty percent of North Americans today say they would continue to work even if they won the lottery. Why? Because work has never been just about pay, and in a society relatively satiated with material goods, pay means ever less.

Study after study on employee retention shows that while money is often a factor in an employee's decision to leave, it is rarely the primary reason. So, we'll say it once more: Knowing what *else* today's workers expect from work is sure to keep your business competitive. But before we talk about the six shifts, let's explore the forces that have changed the way we see work and what we want from it.

CHAPTER TWO

forces that have changed how we see work

"Rather than thinking of the economy as something that operates independently of our culture, history and community values, think of them all as interwoven."

– ANGUS REID, SHAKEDOWN

In a finely polished boardroom, the senior executives of a large chemical manufacturing firm have gathered to ponder an uncomfortable question: What can they do about the increase in turnover at their research facilities and the growing difficulty in recruiting the kind of talent they need? During the heated discussion, the senior vice-president of human resources draws vigorous nods of approval when he says, "Look, employees today want exciting work, a corporate buzz. They want to believe in our products and services."

"No, they're not willing to stay in one place for long no matter what we do," someone else objects. "Not even for a secure job."

Now the CEO, who has been tapping his fingers impatiently, speaks. "Once things get slow, people will just want a paycheck again," he asserts.

If only it were so simple. Depending on what industry they're in, some leaders and business owners are tempted to see the shifts in worker values as temporary responses to labor market upswings. But the economic slow-down between 2000 and 2004 proved this to be a myth. Today, more than ever, discontented employees are on a constant lookout for new jobs. Four broad forces have been at work for a number of decades to shape a brand-new work ethic. We'll discuss those forces momentarily. For now, suffice it to say that long-term loyalty is long gone, and attracting, retaining, and motivating skilled workers has risen to a new art form. It's an art we guar-antee you can master by the end of this book, and one that promises more payback than any other business investment you could make.

The trick is to put away all those personnel department how-to-hire manuals, and head into the realms of sociology and psychology. Values are not just the fancy of academics. Rather, the underlying values of a society and its workforce shape the contours of business strategy. Put more simply, understanding the core values people have about work is the key to win-ning their commitment. And acting on that understanding is far more pow-erful than learning a series of recruitment techniques. In the end, it is the fit between an individual's values and the perceived values of his or her company that determines how long that company and worker will stick together and whether the worker is putting in time or giving her all to move the company ahead.

This chapter identifies four fundamental forces that together have reshaped what workers want from their work and the workplace. Understanding these shifts and building your company around the needs that they have spawned are the keys to attracting and retaining people.

FAMILY

Today's leaders underestimate changes in the family at their own risk, for this is where each and every one of us forms our values. As author and speaker Stephen R. Covey says, today's economy needs leaders in every rank, and leadership abilities may have more to do with how we were raised than with our training, or how we were mentored early in our careers. While Covey is perhaps ahead of his time — still a voice in the wilderness on the family/leadership link — the Western world's tendency to draw a strict divide between work and home is relatively new in historic terms. Indeed, it is still unusual worldwide, as we discuss in greater depth in Chapter Four. Turning our backs on the work/life connection is also ironic given that technology is increasingly blurring the distinction between home and work time.

Leaders must recognize that over the past thirty years, the family has undergone major changes that have reshaped the values of workers from baby boomers to the so-called Net generation. Here, we describe some of those changes and how they have affected what we want from work.

changing parenting and family patterns

Now that most married couples are dual-wage earners, and a large contingent of employees are single parents, it's no longer possible to pretend that childcare considerations never impinge on work. Today, half of women with *young* children work, while seventy-one percent of all women with children work. And as of 2002, the workforce has achieved equal numbers of men and women.

Family size, structure, and values have all changed markedly in recent decades. Essentially, smaller families and a more egalitarian and permissive parenting approach have contributed to individuals' sense of autonomy and the decline of rigid hierarchies and paternalism. Anyone who visits the local supermarket will find aisles filled with young children debating with their parents about everything from cereal to acceptable behavior. This new style of parenting, combined with smaller families, has helped spawn a ferocious distaste for hierarchies and paternalism at work, as Chapter Seven discusses. At the same time, rising divorce rates, dual-worker couples, the latchkey experience, and a lack of time with hardworking parents have introduced a feeling of insecurity, which in turn is contributing to workers' desire for a more personal relationship with bosses than would previously have been acceptable. The need for recognition has made a steady rise up the list of workers' reasons for job satisfaction, as reflected in human resources surveys over the past decade, in part due to such changes in parenting approaches.

"Generation X feels robbed of time with their parents. Managers inherit life issues that weren't resolved in families. The manager now becomes the parent," writes Claire Raines in *Beyond Generation X*. The successful leader accepts this new, if not always comfortable, role while learning to garb himself or herself in the same protective gear that more professional listeners — such as therapists — have learned to wear. Peter Frost's book, *Toxic Emotions at Work: How Compassionate Managers Handle Pain and Conflict*, recently dubbed such leaders "toxic handlers." Warning: Special training is required to avoid encouraging dependency or burning oneself out in the process of trying to help.

Ironically, these changes in the family have created significant paradoxes in winning workers' loyalty. More time spent alone and less experience with a hierarchical parenting style has created workers who are fiercely independent and resent being told what to do. At the same time, all that time spent alone has created a hunger for mentoring, recognition, and a deeper experience of community at work. Is it any wonder many managers have expressed to us their bewilderment at how to win workers? These are issues tackled in Chapters Six and Eight.

the affluence factor

Societal changes have altered family values in other ways, too. Decades of commercials enticing us to buy unnecessary goods on impulse have taken a toll on society, especially on families with more money than focused parenting time. The bombardment has intensified over the years: Americans were exposed to roughly six times as many advertising messages in 1997 as in 1971. Baby boomers can be seen as the first truly post-materialistic generation. They came of age in a time of rising affluence and expectations. Most of them assumed that they would be better off than their parents, and many of them are. This shift to an expectation of affluence led many boomers to see work as more than a paycheck. Work became an expression, if not the central core, of their identity. But that was only an interim stage. With the shift to knowledge work and their basic material needs met, a growing number of baby boomers came to expect even more from work than a salary and self-identity. As it turned out, the rise of affluence and hard work had not bestowed upon them the requisite sense of fulfillment. So they've since focused their sights on a life/work balance, meaningful work, a sense of community, and more. Meanwhile, the next generations are crowding the workforce and bringing their own values, formed in part from watching the boomers' overemphasis on work and materialism, and the undignified manner in which both boomers and younger workers were downsized during economic downturns in the 1980s' and late-90s' dot-com bust.

Thus, the Information Age, into which boomers and Generations X and Y have moved, has been characterized by a dual focus-on materialism and soul. Today's workers arrive at work daily with that subconscious paradox. On the one hand, they have been indulged with material things all their lives, a situation that has bequeathed to them a distorted sense of "entitlement." Highly educated Generation Y (also known as the Net generation) workers have this in concentrated form, having arrived at the work world's doorstep at a unique time in modern history, when companies are so desperate for highly educated workers that they greet them and treat them like royalty. What twenty-something's head *wouldn't* swell?

But remember, these same workers were raised by parents who often felt demoralized by the blessing and bane of high salaries that came without deep fulfillment. Both Generations X and Y, having taken the boomers' often unspoken ambivalence to heart, move through the workforce focused on wealth, but with a deeply held belief that work should offer something more meaningful. Yet, however much boomers, Xers, and Yers may crave a soul/work connection, they remain inclined to see work as demeaning and pointless, say family therapists John C. Friel and Linda D. Friel, authors of *The Worst Seven Things Parents Can Do*. Turn them around on that score with all the patience, tough-love attention, and positive reinforcement that a skilled mentor would engage, and they're yours. Social workers in at-risk teen programs do it all the time. They slowly win the respect and loyalty of individuals suffering from an inner clash of fierce independence, cynicism, and insecurity. A skilled leader does what it takes, including boning up on parenting texts to help finish an unfinished job.

Robert Bly, author of *The Sibling Society*, added the following theory to this discussion: The turbulent period of adolescence (marked by insecurity and a lack of impulse control) has more than tripled in length since before the Industrial Age, now extending well into one's twenties. The reasons may be partly physical and partly cultural, Bly posits; the cultural aspect is best explained by consumerism, a growing lack of intimacy with one's parents (due to diminishing family time), and little contact with grandparents, who have traditionally offered youth a steadying hand. This trend, Bly and others have warned, offers serious repercussions for each succeeding generation, as relatively immature adults become parents. Top that with the fact that the percentage of twenty-somethings living with their parents has doubled since 1960. Are current demands in the workplace for more balance a natural attempt to readjust this scenario?

If there is a silver lining to a pampered or demanding employee, of course, it is that they have an intuitive understanding of today's increasingly pampered and demanding customer base. Regis McKenna had much to say on this in *Real Time: Preparing for the Age of the Never Satisfied Customer.*

changing family structures

If today's employees are riddled with insecurities because of gaps in how they were parented, business leaders need to understand that this has created a backlash against workaholism. The last two decades have taken a measurable toll on family life, and today's workers are trying to take a stand against that toll. Half of Generation X comes from divorced families, and the divorce rate has shot up since they were growing up in the 1970s. Time and family are now the gold of the new millennium worker, regardless of age or professional status. Now that they're in the driver's seat, job candidates can and will decline work where the company has a reputation for burning out practitioners in six months. Lest you think that such a reputation could not possibly belong to your company, or that dissatisfied ex-employees could not broadcast their feelings very far, check again. The Internet is full of sites that do nothing but let people with too much time and angst vent their spleens. These freedom-of-speech sites cost little to host, and can be discovered from anywhere in the world with as little as one keyword...like your company's name perhaps?

The point is that today's workers have witnessed firsthand what an over-focus on work can produce. Consequently, they come to the workplace with their guards up and often with a personal pledge not to fall into the same pattern. A recent survey of graduating MBAs showed that a large percentage has vowed never to let their work life overwhelm their personal life, a clear backlash against an over-devotion to work.[2]

Did you know that Gen Xers as a group are more likely to contribute to their companies' pension plans than are boomers (twenty-nine percent of Gen Xers versus 200 percent of boomers)? And that Gen Xers aspire to more loyalty than their older counterparts? Only twenty-three percent of boomers say they want to work for the same company until they retire, but almost half — forty-seven percent — of Gen Xers voice that hope.

The Census Bureau recently noted a decline in the number of women returning to work within a year of having a baby, and, since 2000, a sharp increase in the number of families with a single income-earner. Surveys of Gen X moms show that what they value most is significant amounts of family time.

At the same time, that family-first, career-second approach poses a financial challenge. Gen Xers "are struggling with debt." Because of the run-up in real-estate prices, Gen Xers' housing debt is sixty-two percent higher than it was for boomers at the same age, contributing to debt levels a staggering seventy-eight percent higher than was the case for boomers at comparable ages. Top that off with the fact that Gen Xers have less confi-

[2] *Fortune*, August 2004, Anne Fisher; These findings come from a fascinating study by Boston-based marketing strategy firm Reach Advisors (http://www.reachadvisors.com).

dence in secure employment prospects and it's no wonder their debt level makes them both anxious and fiercely frugal.

What does it all mean in the workplace? Well, for employers, it means meeting Gen Xers' desire for shorter hours and more requests for time off, as well as respect for their less ambitious career-mindedness, and their appreciation of raises.

THE ECONOMY

The economy has influenced workers' values in two primary ways. First, finding satisfactory work and building a career have had to become constant concerns; no longer can these issues be placed on autopilot. Second, with work having become so all-encompassing and the number of hours individuals are working having risen dramatically, employees are looking to the workplace to meet needs they once fulfilled elsewhere.

Thanks to global competition, mergers, downsizing, upsizing, and longer and more demanding work hours, today's workers understand that if they are not growing and learning, they can quickly become obsolete. When they do have a job, it now seems to follow them around everywhere. Witness the back seat of their car filled with work they intend (intend being the operative word) to do in their leisure time. As we mentioned in Chapter One, forty percent of employees always have their résumés up-to-date. The same study found that sixty percent have taken courses to upgrade their skills in the last year alone.

Contrast all that with the experience of John's grandfather, a Nova Scotia shipbuilder who settled in New England during the 1930s. For thirty-five years, he worked at the same shipyard, weathering occasional layoffs and furloughs, but never questioned the concept of a lifelong job that began each day at nine and ended at five, when the whistle blew. He never had to change careers, and as far as we know, never even considered it. His work days generally ended on time, and weekends were always his.

John's son, Carter, on the other hand, came home from elementary school one day and announced that he would have to tackle four to five careers during his lifetime. Children are being indoctrinated very early in the realities of a new economic approach. Not only is this boy correct in anticipating constant change, but already he understands the importance of learning as a pursuit for a lifetime.

What does all this have to do with workers' values? It means that career development and résumé enhancement are now a way of life. Regardless of their age, nearly all workers today regard the notion of hitching their wagon to one company for life as an unrealistic if not unwise career choice. Companies are lucky to keep an employee for the current average of three and a half years (men, 3.9; women, 3.4), and some say the Net generation's average is closer to two years.

Today's youngest workers learned from their parents' layoff experiences that corporate loyalty is nearly obsolete in a global environment. The boomers learned it firsthand when security guards showed them the door during the 1980s' "reengineering." So, the worker as mercenary is now a natural part of the landscape, as we'll discuss in Chapter Six.

But while today's economy has bred mercenary workers, it has also created new and more human desires among workers. Thanks to mergers and acquisitions, and the growth of super-large companies, we're seeing two opposing trends: more small and home-based businesses, and more mega-corporations. Both of these trends have spelled longer and more intense work hours, shorter career ladders, and shrinking buying power.

Nearly two-thirds of full-time workers reported that their job responsibilities increased in the six months heading up to 2004. One-third said they were working longer hours, and sixty-two percent had not received a pay raise.[3]

Even with greater job flexibility, this scenario creates a need for something to make all the stress worthwhile: work-sponsored socializing, career-building courses, and community causes. The all-encompassing nature of work today means we want more from it. Ideas rather than tasks are the currency of today's economy, and the workers who can work anywhere and anytime often feel compelled to work everywhere, all the time. Again, a level of burnout once reserved only for business owners has been passed on to the entire workforce, along with a dare to shoulder the risks of decision-making in a high-speed business environment. No doubt that's why three-fourths of employees believe today's worker has more on-the-job stress than did workers a generation ago.[4]

COMPUTER ASSOCIATES INTERNATIONAL Inc. in Islandia, New York, is planning a child-development center for four hundred children.

The good risk-taker is served up every day with large portions of ambiguity, uncertainty, and vulnerability, and too much of this diet eats away at one's sense of character. One's sense of character, which includes values, can be built back up only through leisure, family time, and comradeship, all of which can and should be openly supported by the employer who wants to retain and inspire valued staff.

[3] (2004 Labor Day Survey Harris Interactive® study, sponsored by Kronos® Incorporated (Nasdaq: KRON)

[4] (Princeton Survey Research Associates, 1997, Labor Day Survey: State of workers. Princeton, NJ)

now that work is life,
it had better be a good one

Before modernism, we lived in the country, worked largely in crafts with our family in close quarters, and were deeply religious. When a new age of economics shoved us into city factories with strict supervisors, we felt depersonalized, but at least we still had income and an after-work life. At five p.m., we could leave work and experience life through the traditional means: church, family, and geographical neighborhoods. As mobility further loosened our ties with family and neighborhood, however, and as divorce rates rose and work began claiming us for longer and longer hours, work and self-identity fused. The result: Social behavior is now affected primarily by chosen interest groups (for instance, sports or environmental). For better or worse, we're now free to create our own lifestyle group identity. With so many of the traditional sources of fulfillment outside of work crowded out by longer work hours and the dual-worker family, people seem to be focusing on work as a primary source of personal fulfillment. This is a role that the workplace did not have to meet in previous generations, as we discuss in depth in later chapters.

Today's employees work eleven percent more than did workers as recently as 1975.[5]

So is it any wonder that workers want and expect the workplace to meet needs it never had to meet in the past? Business leaders ignore this trend at their own risk of high turnover and waning performance. Wise companies understand that their role, like that of society, has shifted, and that the word *values* no longer needs to be whispered in the cloakrooms.

5 (State of Working America, 2004/2005]

Ninety-three percent of corporate and human resources executives believe that a strong corporate values system has a positive impact on financial performance, but only sixty-four percent report that values are part of their companies' performance management systems. Only forty-six percent involve senior management in developing companies' values, and only nineteen percent tap their full employee base when determining company values. Can anyone say "ENRON"?

We'll bet the farm on this: Companies unafraid of tackling the values shift, unafraid of fully embracing the new responsibility for employees' greater welfare — with employees' input — will be around in the next decade. And they will discover that this approach offers more than one kind of payback.

SOCIETY

Societal values, like everything else, have shifted with the times. Let's begin with two that have had particular impact on *work* values.

consumerism and spiritual hunger

One of the ironies of the new century is that in North America, we are wealthier than ever and yet less at ease. The signs of our angst are everywhere, and they profoundly influence our view of work. Since the mid-1960s, there has been an unprecedented increase in clinical depression in advanced and rapidly advancing economies, generally attributed to individuals' increasing lack of friends or confidantes (or quality time spent with them). People born after 1945 are ten times as likely to suffer from depression as people born fifty years earlier, in a less materialistic era. The most prescribed drugs in North America treat depression and ulcers, and since 1960, there has been a steady downward trend in the percentage of respondents who say they trust most people. Meanwhile, the global economy's consumption rate of material goods has doubled in the past twenty-five years.

Simon Zadek of the New Economics Foundation believes consumerism and loneliness are linked: "The market in general and rage to consume in particular have crowded out or undermined friendship," he wrote in a fascinating book entitled *The Good Life*, from Demos, an independent think tank in London, England.

Two-thirds of experts at the Open University's Futures Observatory in England believe that materialism will be replaced by ethics within twenty-five years, and three-quarters believe that organizations in general will stress ethical values within twenty years. The following chart, measuring students' definition of success over two decades, agrees:

Primary measures of success

(according to graduating MBAs of Duke University)

1989	1991	late 1990s
power	successful relationships	marriage
prestige	a balanced life	health
money	leisure time	ethics

Source: Making a Living While Making a Difference, p. 3.

Regardless of whether the experts are right, it's certainly true that the old paternalistic, controlling, and bureaucratic system is neither necessary nor tolerated in an age of educated masses and instant information — especially when serving the customer means being empowered to make fast decisions, often as part of an ever-changing team.

Meanwhile, more independence and customer focus has, for some, uncorked a longstanding desire for the freedom to be one's true self at work. As the Duke University and other surveys show, our society is shifting towards a focus on things of the spirit. For instance, what of the plethora of books, magazine columns, and Internet chat groups about "bringing one's soul to work"? A quick review of recent bestsellers in North America is strong evidence of this movement. From the proliferation of converts to Zen Buddhism (now the fastest growing religion in North America, according to *Time* magazine), to the phenomenon known as "Chicken Soup for Every Kind of Soul," to the remarkable popularity of the anti-advertising magazine *Adbusters*, there is a backlash happening against modern consumerism. Call it shifting values.

English poet David Whyte, popular on corporate speaking circuits for this topic, has written, "Work is not and never has been the very center of the human universe…. Continually calling on its managers and line workers for more creativity, dedication and adaptability, the American corporate world is tiptoeing for the first time in its very short history into the very place from whence that dedication, creativity, and adaptability must come: the turbulent place where the soul of an individual is formed and finds expression." Without encouragement to contemplate what spirituality is and how it might be connected to work, he says, workers experience a "dehydrated workday."

This growing desire to respect things of the spirit (discussed in

Chapters Five, Six, and Eight) is having a profound impact on how we see work. As Michael Hammer declares in *Beyond Reengineering*, "It is thrilling to be part of a revolution that replaces meaningless work, petty bureaucracy and dead-end jobs with a workplace to which people enjoy coming, knowing they will be challenged and appreciated." What leaders must understand is that people are looking for these things on work time, not just on vacation time!

democracy and the internet

All over the world, there is a nascent democratization happening, albeit punctuated with backslides into dictatorships. The Internet is part of this shift in societal values, proving that information and decision-making are not the realm of a privileged few, but the right of all. (On a recent trip to the mountains of Costa Rica, John was taken aback to see a lineup of Internet cafés bearing witness to this trend.) Thanks partly to the instant accessibility of information, we've moved closer to a "direct democracy" than ever before. According to a study conducted by the University of Zurich, the ability to have a say in how one's region is run ranks right up there with a giant hike in income for ensuring personal happiness. Certainly, speaking one's mind — to parents, bosses, or co-workers — is tolerated far more now than in previous times, for better or worse — and the Internet has proven a highly popular vehicle for soapboxing. A quick Google search reveals 8,520,000 hits for Web forums.

This worldwide shift towards democratization and access to information, coupled with more permissive parenting and teaching styles, has accelerated the values shift against hierarchy. Here's a simple way to frame it: "If I can speak to anyone in the world via the Net, and even the Berlin

Wall can't stand up when the people want it to come down, I surely should be able to challenge my boss."

TECHNOLOGY

Technology has both changed the workplace and made it easier for people to stoke a long-held desire to leave and work for themselves. Technology has become so integral a part of our society that expenditures for it in the United States grew from five percent of total capital spending in 1970, to nearly fifty percent in 1999. In 2001, 56.5 percent of American households had computers, more than half of those accessing the Internet.[6]

Technological innovations have brought us faster product cycles; changing work processes; a smaller, more skilled, and internationally competitive workforce; and seemingly inescapable communication devices. Those devices contribute both to efficiency and to burnout. In our worship of the former, we often drive ourselves blindly into the latter. According to a 2004 article in *Fast Company* magazine, Americans "now clock more time on the job than any other worker on earth," They are working 163 hours (about one month) longer per year than they were in 1969, and work 500 more hours per year than the Germans and 250 more hours per year than the British, although the British are also working longer: just over one-third work on weekends, and fifty-four percent work into the evenings. Americans are even outworking the notoriously workaholic Japanese: 1,966 hours per year in the US compared to 1,889 in Japan.

By 2010, one in five American workers will telecommute. In Britain,

[6] Source: NTIA and ESA, U.S. Department of Commerce, using U.S. Census Bureau Current Population Survey Supplements.]

roughly one-quarter of employed Britons telecommute, a sixty-five percent rise from 1997.

Although telecommuting has been hailed as a positive technological development, a less welcome result, as far as employees are concerned, is electronic monitoring and surveillance. It has sent all the advances that a more democratic and open work environment seems to offer are sent reeling. Employers can now check out job applicants' Web surfing to examine their hobbies, interests, and attitudes. British companies are discussing implanting microchips in employees to monitor their whereabouts and for timekeeping. Employers can read their employees' e-mail, access their computer files, track their Internet traffic, and listen to their voice mail. They *can* do all this, but when and how often *should* they? Do technical advances in this arena endanger the trust on which employee motivation sits? We discuss this issue in Chapter Nine.

> **A RECENT SURVEY** conducted by the National Manufacturers Association found that 48% of respondents were concerned that their workers would be unable to read and interpret drawings and diagrams.

Much has been written about the effect of the Web on society's values. The Internet has also had a huge impact on how we conduct business, from the ease of accessing information about a company by its customers to the speed of dealing with inquiries leading to a sale.

"Customers have become empowered, engaged, and actively integrated into the business organization's decision-making process," Richard W. Oliver stated in *The Shape of Things to Come*. We say *workers* have also become empowered, engaged, and actively integrated into this process.

Technology is helping to change our values, especially when it comes to our workplaces.

putting it all together

Although workers naturally become more demanding when times are good, our thesis is that this shift goes much, much deeper. The values underlying these demands — the very way we see work — is what has begun to shift. And only by understanding the forces that have shaped the shifts can one begin to see how robust they will remain, even when the economy slows down.

Change has become the watchword of the twenty-first century. We are living in a world that is radically reshaping the human experience. From biotechnology to information technology, from the way we work and the way we shop to the way we connect with one another, no traditions from the past can be taken for granted any longer. Families, the economy, society, and technology have all undergone radical change — unquestionably the most profound upheaval since the Industrial Revolution. The values of today's workers are changing along with that upheaval, and in the chapters that follow we focus on how companies can respond to workers' changing needs.

CHAPTER THREE

understanding demographic differences in work values

"There is a thin line between a twenty-something 'slacker' and a forty-something convert to 'voluntary simplicity.'"
— BARBARA MOSES, *CAREER INTELLIGENCE*

As we've said, there are six clear shifts in the way workers see work, and these shifts cut across age and gender lines. The latter first became obvious to John when individual listeners approached him after his talks to corporate audiences about what younger workers want from work. In his lectures, he emphasized younger workers' desire for community, constant development, integration between personal and work life, and a higher purpose to work. Afterwards, young employees would bound up to him and say, "Hey, bang on, you really know us! Thanks for helping these old guys understand us." More intriguing, however, was the response baby boomer listeners would offer: "You know those things you said younger workers want? Well, I want them too."

After months of such feedback, John was able to determine that while there are demographic differences in why and how workers arrive at these goals, the similarities are stronger than the differences. That is why we have chosen to spend six full chapters on the shifts that are universal to workers of all ages, genders, and ethnicities — shifts that matter if an organization wants to attract and keep good people.

But before we launch into those chapters, we've chosen to pause and reflect on some of the demographic differences that are worth paying attention to. First, there's the age factor: Different age groups have somewhat different views of what the ideal work life looks like. Next, there's the gender gap. Clearly, men and women have different takes on how to improve the workplace experience. Finally, there's the cultural diversity factor: workers of differing cultures define workplace issues differently.

Everyone knows that today's North American workforce is more racially and ethnically diverse, and comprises more women than the workforce of twenty years ago. But are they aware that far more Generation X than baby boomer workers are toying with the idea of starting their own business (fifty-four contrasted with thirty-six percent). That's a *generational* issue. To employers concerned about losing young talent or facing competition from ex-employees, surely that means catering to younger workers' more searing need for independence and flexibility. We call it the search for partnership. Boomers want partnership, too, but in different ways and for different reasons, as discussed in Chapter Seven.

How many employers know that far more boomers than Gen Xers (born 1963 to 1977) identify their jobs as "an expression of themselves" (fifty-six compared with forty-six percent). While all workers are putting the desire for balancing work and personal life near the top of their lists, there are real generational differences in the role work plays in one's life.

Work is central to the self-identity of boomers and Netters, perhaps because, unlike their Gen X cousins, they came of age in times of economic prosperity.

Of course, the age gap is only one aspect of diversity. When it comes to the *gender* gap, knowledge of different perceptions about work is no longer a luxury. For instance, both women and men identify balance as an important issue for them at work, but survey after survey shows that this balancing act is the *overwhelming* concern for working women, especially when they become parents. Addressing balance in a way that allows women, and a growing number of men, to deal with family and negotiate the "opportunity" ladder is critical to retention. This means flextime, job sharing, no glass ceiling installed during maternity/paternity leave, and tackling the childcare issue with more enthusiasm (ideally in the form of on-site facilities).

The late Ellen Gee, professor of sociology at Simon Fraser University in British Columbia, Canada, said that employers looking for optimum performance need to pay particular attention to the young female employee's requirements. Whereas early boomer career women sought flexible hours and daycare, when such perks were not forthcoming they often hired nannies or dropped out of the workforce. Many Generation Xers and Yers aspiring to motherhood — and women remain the primary parents — have less relative income, pricier housing, and no dropout option. They are delaying parenthood significantly longer than boomers did. For some, lack of flexibility in the workplace is causing them to sacrifice the parenting experience altogether — or it's heavily affecting employee loyalty and the health of the next generation's children.

"They need not just flexibility, but recognition by the employer that there is this family/work conflict," said Gee. "They need provisions for when a child gets sick. They need not to be punished attitudinally." Mortgage assistance plans and paternity leave are also on Gen X's and Y's wish lists.

Finally, awareness of the *cultural diversity factor* means understanding and communicating across different frames of reference, and tailoring rewards to the context and culture of individuals — not according to traditions based on a more homogenous workforce. Building a more diverse workforce and training staff in intercultural sensitivity pays, and with ever greater dividends in our increasingly interlinked world, as numerous studies have shown.

the age issue: a tale of three generations

Three generations of workers currently dominate the halls of the work world: the baby boomers (born 1947 to 1966), Generation X (born 1963 to 1977) and the newest graduates from adolescence, often known as Generation Y or the Net generation (born 1978 to 1998). Boomers total more than sixty million Americans, Xers make up forty-seven million, and the Net generation has roughly twelve million so far in the workforce. The major differences between generations — each with potential for conflict — involve work ethic, technical competence, company loyalty, and people skills.

To understand the unique differences in attitude that define generations, we need to contemplate the concept of "value imprinting" — the notion that our experiences between late childhood and early adolescence have a particularly strong influence on how each of us continues to view the world, especially in relation to cultural values. Value imprinting has ensured some sharp differences between how the three generations view work today, although it's crucial to note that the generalizations we make here do not necessarily apply to workers raised outside of North America — a fast-growing segment, to say the least.

Baby boomers received their value imprint during a time of great optimism; the 1960s saw significant economic expansion in North America. Jobs were plentiful and opportunities abounded, most of them nestled within the corporate structure. Due to the sheer size of their segment, boomers were focused on and doted over. Alongside the youthful questioning — the sexual revolution, the bra-burning stage of women's liberation — old values stood their ground. As youngsters, boomers largely experienced stay-at-home moms, and dads who finished work at five o'clock. In their early careers, the sense of long-term rewards for company loyalty was still intact. A deep respect for the longstanding institutions of society — church, education, corporations, and government — was under challenge but not dismantled. Hence, baby boomers still see public service as a legitimate career choice, whereas a recent study by the Nexus Group in Toronto found that public service is not even on the radar screen as a preferred career option for the Net generation.

The baby boomers were imprinted with a few contradictions: Question authority but climb the corporate ladder. Think for yourself but the company will take care of you. And above all, affluence is your destiny. What did not imprint was the notion that finding a job could be a problem.

The views of today's boomers reflect these values: They rebel against authority but instinctively desire it. Deep down, they believe companies should be loyal, and they feel betrayed that this appears to be no longer the case. And after years of working to achieve the good life, they find that the definition of the good life they bought into appears to exclude what they valued most as children: family and leisure time. Having hit midlife, they feel guilty about what their work has done to their home life, and they feel a tug towards the ideals of their youth. They are focused on defining and achieving a work/life balance, a new priority induced by work burnout and/or the sense that they can now afford to rebel against long hours.

The boomers' dilemma is in direct contrast to younger workers' determination to achieve balance for the sake of family and health, even if it means taking a hit in terms of career and earnings so that they don't turn out like their out-of-balance parents and older siblings. (Besides, they've correctly assessed that two-way corporate loyalty and long-term payback is no longer there.)

Finally, baby boomers in the United States also experienced the civil rights and anti-war movements, the birth of the Peace Corps, and the "save the world" activism that these movements spawned. Boomers often have a nascent desire to be involved in pursuits more profound than the bottom line. Many feel that they "sold out" on several fronts, and want to correct that before it's too late.

When it comes to imprints, Generation X, on the other hand, got a rough start. They were imprinted at the height of a brutal recession in the late 1970s and early 1980s and took dead-end jobs outside their field, or entry-level positions with promises, but few prospects, of moving up. This early work experience confirmed or strengthened that imprint. Corporate cost cutting ensured them lower pay than their predecessors received for many years. Underemployment was their middle name, living at home their nightmare. They delayed long-term relationships and parenting, watched their pre-boomer parents get downsized with no regard for a lifetime of loyalty, and observed older boomer siblings working sixty-hour work weeks with little job security and less life to show for it. Again, this early imprint formed the tendency toward what boomers often describe as cynicism. (Perhaps it's actually a reality check.)

Then there is the Net generation. By the time they arrived at their imprint age, a new world of work was emerging. Many grew up in single-parent or blended families, and their mothers were very likely to work outside the home. Time spent alone and independently was common to these latchkey children, who observed the dawn of the entrepreneurial age and, unlike boomers, viewed corporate loyalty as a thing of the past.

Like John's elementary-school son, the Net generation accepted from a young age that they would have to learn and fend for themselves. They glimpsed the formation of a two-tier system, one that treated skilled workers like gold and all but discarded those without technical skills. By the time they entered college, a college degree had the same value as their parents' high school certificate. Throughout their growing-up years, technology was a favored companion. When the game got boring, they simply pressed reset. Likewise, since yesterday's big issues — the ozone hole, global warming — had become so big that no individual could be expected to change them, they learned to focus on local issues and tune out grand schemes.

Indulged by their wealthy and materialistic boomer parents as children, the Net kids have less experience than Xers of deferred pleasure and deferred career attainment. This has given them both more confidence and a sometimes overblown sense of entitlement. Also, while Gen X was the first generation to experience an epidemic of parental divorce, Netters learned to view various family configurations as normal. They're also more apt than any previous generation to embrace cultural diversity and flattened hierarchies as the norm. This in itself may heighten their sensitivity to age-related issues, especially subtle X-Y divisions that boomer bosses may fail to see or address.

Members of the Net Generation, like their older boomer coworkers, share a world of contradictions. All their early independence has made them averse to rules and hierarchy, yet they long for mentoring, community, and recognition. They want the benefits of community-belonging — without its bane (rules, procedures, and structure).

How do all these generational differences determine retention strategies that work? Above all, establish flexibility in the workplace, through and through. That's No. 1. It speaks to all three generations, albeit for different reasons. A policy that says, "This is the schedule. Take it or leave it," worked for boomers years ago, but as more of them reach the option of early retirement, they may just leave it. Generations X and Y are even more likely to leave it, or to feel "less engaged" with their assignments in such a regime.

The No. 2 retention strategy should be attempting to bond this disparate workforce. Multigenerational conflicts, like multi-ethnic tensions, must be addressed proactively, through policies that promote mutual respect. From circulating magazine or Web information on the topic, to encouraging discussion groups or departments seminars, there are many options for heightening generation-gap awareness and meeting the challenge head-on.

Ensure that teams are multigenerational, and that one segment is not inadvertently trampling on the others' potential input. Keep in mind that Gen Xers tend to see boomers as making decisions and then calling for a pseudo-discussion to secure a stamp of approval. Further, Xers' history and their sense of detachment from a company's long-term plans make them reluctant to speak up at all, let alone in multigenerational meetings. Why should they waste time on a done deal, and why should they care if they're only investing a year or two in the company to grab some experience before setting up their own business? Perhaps the boomers' tendency to "over discuss" and the Net generation's cockiness and naive belief that they can change the world annoy Xers. Perhaps they feel outnumbered, outranked, or sandwiched between an army of oldsters and post-teens. Perhaps, like Netters, they'd be more vocal in an intranet discussion group, or through e-mail.

On the other hand, boomers may feel that no one pays attention when they offer an opinion, especially if it involves a high-tech issue. They may feel discouraged that no one else seems to care, and stop offering valuable input as a result. They may resent reporting to the increasing number of supervisors younger than themselves, an issue that can be dealt with through good leadership (see Chapter Seven). Boomers may hanker for a full team effort accomplished through face-to-face brainstorming meetings, while X and Y employees prefer to puzzle things out through a series of e-mail discussions, or each take away a portion they can call all their own, and bring it back resolved, in an entrepreneurial fashion.

We reflected earlier on the irony of younger workers possessing both hard-edged cynicism and a fire to change things. Here's a boomer manager, quoted in *Civilizing the Workplace*, who has acquired a positive spin on this issue: "Some of our younger employees are an odd mixture of pseudo-sophisticated cynicism and high ideals. I try to find a way to break through the cynicism and capitalize on those ideals. I don't always succeed, but I try to let them know that it's their job to put meaning back into the workplace. Nobody else can do it for them."

There have always been generation gaps, but back when each segment was relatively homogenous, and change occurred at a snail's pace, the gaps were more easily bridgeable. Today, it takes a skilled leader — and one who is well aware of all the potential rifts just named — to pull more from teams than the sum of their individual parts. This is particularly true when each group has a radically different receptivity to the concept of hierarchy and the career as self-identity in the first place.

To better retain employees, tie rewards directly to performance, offer rewards closer to the time of the actions deserving them (immediately being ideal), create varying kinds of financial rewards, and consider pay-increase cycles. Also, increase employees' control over their physical work-space and address work/life balance and training needs.

In short, today's business leader, like today's marketer, is faced with a more fragmented "customer base," requiring more use of intuition and developing-technology to keep the ranks satisfied in precisely the manner to which each would like to become accustomed. Embrace the possibilities, lose workers, or let polarization and mayhem rule. In today's super-competitive market, is there really a choice? In the end, he or she with the best leadership skills for bringing together a diverse employee-base wins.

Let's contemplate the biggest differences between the generations:

Trend: Younger workers are more entrepreneurial.

Retention Strategy: It's wise to give younger workers more autonomy, and to reward top performance with the training for which they yearn (gradually, like slices of a carrot stick) — training they see as eventually allowing them to go out on their own. To those who think, "But if I do that, I'll lose them," we reply: "If you don't do that, you'll lose them anyway, and you just *might* keep them." Provide plenty of opportunities for them to ask questions, adapt information to the scenarios they present, and re-engineer titles to help them feel more entrepreneurial. (At one marketing agency, some of the more unusual titles include "Voice of Reason" and "What's Next Strategist.")

Noteworthy: One in five workers in the US work for themselves. Fifty-four percent of eighteen- to twenty-four-year-olds are highly interested in starting businesses, compared with thirty-six percent of thirty-five to sixty-four-year-olds. Eight of ten US adults trying to start a business are in the eighteen to thirty-four age group. In contrast, only two percent of the Harvard graduating class of 1942 showed any interest in self-employment. Also, one out of eight employees moonlights, and the fact that between thirty-five and fifty-seven percent of these own their own moonlighting business means it's likely that many are "incubating" an enterprise they hope will one day support them.

Trend: Older adults are feeling increasingly insecure, because for the first time in history, the tables are turning; layoffs are now more likely to hit boomers (people in their forties and fifties), whose fat salaries and — in some cases — lack of technological expertise appear to make them easy targets. And don't expect Gen Xers to feel like pulling out the violins for them. The shoe was on the other foot last round.

Retention Strategy: Wise leaders go out of their way to make boomers feel their positions are secure, and offer them training that keeps them up-to-date technologically. Incidentally, although seventy-four percent of US adults over eighteen are now online, according to a 2005 Harris Poll, fewer older than young adults are currently set up to go online (thirty-seven percent of the fifty-plus crowd).

Retention-savvy companies are inaugurating mentoring programs, which serve not only to ease the leadership transition, but also to make both older and younger workers feel more valued. Managers need to encourage oldsters to tell stories of "how it was done" to counteract their fear of looking stupid or outdated. Remember, too, to present change in a positive manner, explaining its benefits to overcome many older workers' risk-averse natures.

Noteworthy: Young adults suffered an unemployment rate twice the national average for most of the 1990s, but now age discrimination is catching up with boomers, counterbalanced only by a strong economy that asks some of them to stay beyond retirement age to ease the transition. By 2003, for the first time ever there were more workers over forty than under forty. When management firm Watson Wyatt Worldwide asked close to one thousand CEOs at what age they felt people's productivity peaked, the average response was forty-three.

Trend: Younger workers are less likely to wrap up their self-identity in work.

Retetion Strategy: Spend more time explaining the importance of a particular project or training session, discussing how it fits with the company's corporate culture and what it will do for one's career. Also, allow them to express skepticism without generating disapproval, and take pains to make work fun.

Noteworthy: Only forty-six percent of Gen Xers identify their jobs as an "expression of themselves," compared with fifty-six percent of boomers.

Trend: Younger workers process information fast, intuitively breaking down big chunks into smaller bites.

Retention Strategy: Switch them to new projects faster than has been done in the past, and when holding meetings or soliciting their input, keep in mind the following statistics: Television programs change scenery every twenty seconds. Trainers speaking to younger crowds have been advised to change their message or activity every eight, ten or fifteen minutes.

Trend: Since young people have a strong interest in "making a difference" in the world, companies inclined to help them with that goal will garner more loyalty. Boomers once felt that way too (remember Sixties idealism?), and in their later years, their material desires largely satiated, they're more than inclined to

rekindle some of that fire, especially if the company initiates a strategy.

Retention Strategy: See Chapter Five, which deals with expanding a company's activities to serve a noble cause.

Noteworthy: Three-quarters of college students say that making a difference in the lives of others is very important, and more than half say doing volunteer work is a worthy cause. Gen X volunteers more than any other generation in America. One expert has said of the Net generation, "They want spirituality incorporated into the company culture, more flexibility than even Generation X wants, and more information, more quickly."

Trend: Boomers enjoy competition and tend to be extroverted. Gen Xers are less inclined to stand out or speak up. The Net generation is particularly comfortable socializing and communicating via the Internet.

Retention Strategy: Instead of calling on people in a meeting, have people pick one another, perhaps via a talking stick. No one likes being put on the spot, and requests for a volunteer to "go first" may encourage the same few extroverts to set the tone every time. Generate other ideas for making participation feel safer. Involve younger workers right away and cater to older people's preference for interaction and discussion without frustrating younger people's desire to resolve an issue and get on with it. (Give workers the choice of participating in face-to-face or e-mail discussions, then link the two discussions to ensure a full flow of communication and input overall.)

Trend: Boomers have grown up with more structure and rules than younger generations.

Retention Strategy: Introduce plenty of ground rules and make expectations clear to prevent projects and meetings from turning into a party, while leaving room for enterprising behavior. Check regularly to ensure that everyone is helping to keep a project or session on track and relevant.

the gender gap

Which has more power to determine a pay gap, ethnicity or gender? The correct answer is gender. In fact, while seven out of ten human resources professionals believe minorities encounter barriers to career advancement, nine out of ten believe women do.

The five primary stumbling blocks for women are:

1. corporate cultures that favor men

2. stereotypes and preconceptions of women

3. a lack of women on boards of directors

4. exclusion from informal networks

5. management's perception that family responsibilities will interfere with work

The key to counteracting these obstacles is gaining high-level support for women in professional and senior roles, and putting more dedicated efforts into recruiting and retaining senior female managers.

Note that pay and advancement are not the top priority of working women. At a recent Los Angeles conference for women graduates in business, forty-eight percent of participants said balancing work and family represented the largest issue facing women today. Equal work for equal pay ranked a distant second, and the glass ceiling placed third. Ninety percent of attendees said they planned to start a family, and seventy-eight percent of those said they would keep working when they had children. Interestingly, too, 53.7 percent of mothers with children under one year participated in the labor force in 2003 compared with 57.0 percent in 1998. The number has decreased every year in between.

Women today can't fathom why employers continue to panic when they become pregnant. Unlike fifty years ago, the vast majority remain in their jobs and stop at one or two children. Most women return to work within six months after giving birth, according to Catalyst, a research organization specializing in women's careers (although in Canada mandated maternity leaves have been increased from six months to one year). Yet nearly one-fifth of all complaints received by the Canadian Human Rights Commission in 2004 involved allegations on the basis of sex, and a disproportionate number of those concerned women who suffered adverse consequences when their employers learned they were expecting.

Even as achieving a work/life balance moves up the priority list of male workers, there's no disputing that it's a hotter button with working women, whose numbers have grown exponentially. Fifty years ago, only a third of working-age women in the United States (and far fewer in Europe) worked outside the home. By 1990, the number had leapt to fifty-seven percent, and today, it stands at 59.2 percent. Meanwhile, two-thirds of unmarried mothers with a child under three are now in the labor force, compared with just over half in 1995. The presence of women at the senior-most levels, although still small, continues to grow. In 2004, almost sixteen percent of the most senior jobs in Fortune 500 companies were held by women (up from 8.7 percent in 1995), and they held 13.6 percent of the board seats in these companies, according to an article in *Fast Company* magazine.

Given the combination of a strong economy, growing labor shortage, and high number of educated women in the workforce, gender-based glass ceilings and walls may well shatter of their own accord. According to US Bureau of Labor statistics, the pool of talent that will supply the next generation of workers will soon be dominated by women and ethnic minorities. That will make their demands difficult to ignore.

As *Megatrends 2000* stated, *"There are not nearly enough people with college degrees or advanced vocational and technical training to fill the more than two million new managerial, administrative and technical jobs coming on-line annually. Without mass immigration from Western Europe (unlikely since it is entering its own boom years) or mass liberalization of immigration laws, there is no way the United States will have the optimum workforce needed in the information economy."*

While balance may be women's biggest issue (fifty-nine percent of working mothers would relinquish a day's pay for extra time off, while only forty-three percent of fathers would do so), savvy business leaders slip other insights into their toolboxes. For instance, "When it comes to praise in the workplace, women like it in writing, boomers like it more than they get it, and small companies are quickest to hand it out," quips *Inc.* magazine, explaining an *Inc.* / Gallup survey.

Research has also shown that women are more receptive to and appreciative of detailed feedback and assistance from others, and that female managers in organizations that offer flexible work hours experience a significantly higher level of organizational commitment and job satisfaction.

As mentioned previously, women also value relationships in different ways than men. According to a US Bureau of Labor study, the No. 1 predictor of job satisfaction for women is the relationships they form at work. Therefore, employers are wise to encourage social mixing by creating places for it, and to put as much effort into evaluating how employees work together as they do for what work employees are accomplishing. It's a subtle distinction, but so effective in keeping valued female employees.

diversity

The North American workforce is increasingly diverse in terms of ethnicity and national origin. Given this diversity, it is reasonable to wonder whether the shifts discussed in this book are a fair representation of the needs of that diverse workforce. Although a broad exploration of this issue is beyond the scope of this book, there are two key points to be made. First, John has made presentations on the shifts discussed in this book in Europe and throughout South America, afterwards asking audiences how relevant these shifts are locally. And most of the managers with whom he spoke suggested that these expectations hold true for their workforces, too.

AES, a global power company with offices from China to Central and South America, has conducted a worldwide values study for a number of years. According to Dennis Bakke, former CEO of AES, "There are no differences on [the results] of those values surveys from all over the world." That is, what an increasingly educated workforce wants from work appears to be reaching a point of convergence. Although our experience and that of AES is largely anecdotal, together they point in the direction of alignment. Having said that, we'd like to add that the key for your organization is to manage diversity in a way that both values and responds to the

EMPLOYEES at American Management Systems of Fairfax, Virginia, who go on long business trips can have their husbands or wives join them for the weekend at company expense.

differences that do exist, not only because it is the right thing to do but because it makes for a sensible human resources strategy.

"Effective management of a diverse workforce translates into bottom line results. That's different from saying just because you are diverse you are going to get the benefits of that diversity," David Thomas, a professor of organizational management at Harvard University, has said.

As much as North Americans boast of being a melting pot or mosaic of cultures, their cultural sensitivity has a long way to go. And yet, as a region with a long history of accepting immigrants, North America is well positioned to capitalize on global connections as the Internet and increased global trade all but melt international boundaries.

Theoretically, a skills-based economy abolishes class, gender, ethnic, and racial divides and judges people purely on merit.

"Many computer companies don't bother with affirmative action programs. The attitude is, 'Let's just get the best talent,'" says Phyllis Swersky, executive vice-president and chief financial officer at Artificial Intelligence Corporation, a software maker for IBM mainframes.

Certainly, young Asians who felt their career ladders blocked by Asia's more hierarchical system streamed into Silicon Valley, where almost a third of the region's scientists and engineers are now Asian-born. That's Asia's loss and North America's gain, proving that in today's economy, a work environment seen as democratic and supportive of diversity wins the talent pool.

As the current skilled-worker shortage grows more acute, educated immigrants and minorities — especially from such youth-filled countries as China and Mexico — will soon be sought after. They'll be catered to with all the intensity that North American information technology workers currently experience. Companies that get a head start on this process will be tomorrow's winners. A reputation for actively supporting minorities today is the ticket to success tomorrow.

For now, however, efforts to retain minority workers typically lack bite. As *Organizational Dynamics Magazine* has put it, "Current corporate attempts to address the specific needs of these new workers tend to consist merely of isolated programs...managed at relatively low organizational levels and rarely connected to larger strategic initiatives. Hence, the benefits of these programs to organizations go largely unrecognized, while the benefits to individuals may be overstated."

Moreover, as groups of new immigrants arrive, each culture brings its own age and gender issues, causing old battles to be fought all over again, and new views or solutions to be heard. Managers who tune into these team-dampening undercurrents are well advised to meet diversity challenges head-on, after securing plentiful resources and support.

Companies that have introduced initiatives for helping workers deal with the tension and conflict created by differences among them tend to include any or all of five approaches:

1. Multi-cultural and skill-building workshops that focus on group norms and behavioral do's and don'ts.

2. A program of "celebrating differences" that offers a calendar of cultural and educational events.

3. "Cross-cultural" or "inter-cultural" workshops that help participants learn the norms and practices of different countries.

4. Organizational development activities that focus on team building and values clarification.

5. Personal development through dialogues in small, ongoing groups.

Finally, there's a new trend afoot, often called the reversal of the melting pot syndrome, which fosters the sense that each interest group must be catered to on its own terms. If that sounds unreasonable, think again. As discussed in Chapter Two, technological developments have allowed us to "customize" marketing messages, an edge highly applicable to retention if human resources professionals want to reach different groups of employees with different messages. From an intranet bulletin board for Hispanic employees to custom-delivered holiday messages, the possibilities are endless.

Apply the following comment from an article in *Advertising Age* to employee retention, and you're on the right track: "Marketers must start from scratch in the language of each target market, work within the context of the original culture, and formulate copy and design rooted in the culture itself. And if you end up with ten different campaigns, so be it."

As with most of the shifts covered in this book, we're talking about a hope having become an expectation: "In education, minorities once thrilled to have their languages on schools' curricula at all, are now insisting that their children be taught the history, literature, myths, and music of their cultures of origin," says Regis McKenna in *Real Time*.

There has been a growing emphasis on cultural training as a customer service skill. Cultural training touches on geographical location, geopolitics, cultural values, roles and relationships, communication styles, and the effect of culture on business relationships. The bottom-line message: Diversity is appreciated.

Why spend all the money and effort to promote such a message? "Minority-friendly companies tend to be superior performers," states a *Fortune* article. "Diverse groups make better decisions. If everybody in the room is the same you'll have a lot fewer arguments and a lot worse answers.... Diversity is a competitive advantage."

When John first began speaking to business audiences about the generational differences in values at work, he received plenty of feedback confirming that the differences are real. That is why we've taken the time to identify how gender, age, and ethnicity affect perspectives. And yet, age, gender gap, and cultural factors are not as profound a force in today's work world as the seven shifts we describe next — shifts that largely transcend demographic influences in the long run.

The bottom line is that today's leader is faced with a new kind of worker, one whose fundamental values and desires about work is changing. We now move on to deal with these shifts, and to offer ideas for leaders who are anxious to respond to them in ways that promise significantly higher retention and engagement.

values

The bottom line is that a leader today is faced with a new kind of worker, one whose fundamental values and desires about work and life are changing. Before we look at what our research has told us about the shifting values in the workplace, it would be beneficial to explore what values are and how they impact an individual.

Values are deeply rooted and connect individuals to those things that give them energy and vitality. Values help to bring out our best and contribute to creating high performance and high fulfillment in our work and life. These values are created from imprints that are formed in our impressionable years. An individual's core values can change and adapt based on where they are and what they are going through in the course of their life.

Family and security might be placed at the top of your values list while you are raising a young family and still remain a value when your children leave home but chances are it will down the values list.

Values are important to recognize because they are key anchors and help individuals to make decisions on a daily basis, especially when placed in stressful circumstances or when having to make life-changing choices. What an individual values is most likely at the very center of what brings them joy and contentment.

In our consulting work with various organizations we suggest leaders take the time to find out what their employees value and believe in. Once leaders have a grasp on what motivates their team members personally it will go along way to understanding conflicts, communication and motivational issues. We suggest you use the values worksheet at the end of this section and share it with your employees as a way to get started.

The next chapters will deal with values on a larger scale, namely, what our research has shown us are the six shifting workplace values. We now move on to deal with these shifts, and to offer ideas for leaders who are anxious to respond to them in ways that promise significantly higher retention and engagement.

The bottom line is that today's leader is faced with a new kind of worker, one whose fundamental values and desires about work is changing. We now move on to deal with these shifts, and to offer ideas for leaders who are anxious to respond to them in ways that promise significantly higher retention and engagement.

Practical Applications for Your Organization

In Part one you were given an opportunity to see the changing landscape of work and how it directly and indirectly affects the business decisions you will make today and in the future.

Be proactive. Take a look at your own organization. View each of these landscape changes honestly and ask how they affect your organization today and will in the future if they continue?

The Changing Landscape of Work

1. Demographics: Do you know who works for you? Gender, cultural diversity and age differences?_____

_____

2. Early Retirements: What are the retirement numbers for the next few years?_____

_____

3. Voluntary Simplicity: What can you do differently to create more life/work balance for everyone who works for your organization? _____

_____

_____

4. Bold New Workforce: Do you need to adjust your recruitment and retention strategies. What about training and development? _____

_____

_____

Practical Applications for Your Organization

In Part One you learned about the demographic differences in work values. How workers see work, what they value and how these values shifts cut across age and gender lines. Our core values connect us to those inner energy sources that bring out our best, creating high performance and high fulfillment in our work.

Go through this list and pick all the values that are most important to you, then go back and narrow it down to your top 3 only. Once you have discovered what you value, ask your team to do the same. Spend time discussing as a team what each person values and why.

A Difference of Values

VALUES WORDS

Integrity	Clarity	Freedom
Meaningful Work	Flexibility	Mastery
Nature	Peace of Mind	Reflection
Intelligence	Accountability	Fitness
Learning	Choice	Competence
Spontaneity	Risk	Creativity
Simplicity	Acceptance	Self-Expression
Relationships	Adventure	Privacy
Faith	Leadership	Balance
Beauty	Change	Power
Security	Fast Pace	Self-Discipline

Wholeness	Wisdom	Community
Sharing	Humor	Independence
Productivity	Order	Process
Fulfillment	Excellence	Tradition
Commitment	Trust	Success
Growth	Challenge	Compassion
Achievement	Service to Others	Truth
Fun	Love	Partnership
Loyalty	Authenticity	Prosperity
Intimacy	Health, Well Being	Other
Ethics	Recognition	Inspiration

My top 3 core values I identified were:

1. _____

2. _____

3. _____

Practical Applications for Your Organization

Your business most likely will have a vision and mission but does it have values? Corporate values are principles, beliefs or standards of excellence you believe in and choose to represent to others. Values are considered 'most important' and essentially important statements of conduct. Values also give you a benchmark to start recruiting from.

Values Recruitment

Do you recruit with your business values in mind? _____

_____

_____

Do you ask questions specific to seeing if there is a values alignment between your business and the candidate? _____

_____

_____

Do you ask candidates what their values are? And what they expect from you?_____

_____

_____

Do you place a weight on the importance of each value? _____

_____

_____

PART TWO

The six expectations of the new workforce

CHAPTER FOUR

the expectation of
balance and synergy

*"The key to the good life lies in balance and integration
in all facets of our lives"*

– THE GOOD LIFE

At a large health organization in Western Canada, the corporate culture was so linked with overwork that all 18,000 employees regularly pushed the envelope of how much work and how little life could be fit into a day. Leaving the building late at night and carrying bulging briefcases home appeared to be *de rigueur* for managers of all levels. One day, however, the CEO stood before his entire management team and announced, "I don't want to lead an organization where no one feels they can have a life. We can't sustain it. I want each of you to push back on me, and on each other, when the demands are unreasonable."

Did the corporate culture change overnight? Of course not. But recognition by senior leadership of the tension building at this company was a critical first step.

The desire for greater balance and harmony between work and one's personal life comprises the first of the six shifts in what today's workers want from work. More than any of the other shifts, this one cuts across all demographic differences, even though its permutation varies. At first glance, this newfound desire appears to stem from longer work hours and demands. But a deeper look suggests that not only will workers today sacrifice a great deal to have more flexibility and personal time; they harbor an unmistakable desire for these two aspects of life to become more synergistic. By this, we mean that they want less compartmentalization of their lives, more flow across the boundaries, and a deeper trust that being their "full" selves at work won't be held against them. A boss who understands this desire and taps into it for boosting retention gives time off freely to allow employees to nurse a sick relative, comes through when asked unexpectedly for advice about a romantic entanglement, or organizes a surprise staff party to celebrate the recent tennis trophy they mentioned winning.

AT CREDIT CARD company Total Systems Services, every employee is made to feel an instant part of an extended family. To symbolize this, when the company built a new campus in Georgia, it designed a river walk of bricks, each inscribed with an employee's name.

As L.M. Baker, Jr., the chairman of Wachovia in Charlotte, North Caroline has said, "Most people think motivating people is about pushing others to do what you want them to, but I've found that the secret to motivating others has really been to adhere to simple values, things like honesty, fairness, and generosity."[7]

[7] *Harvard Business Review*, January 2003

extreme flextime

For one company, 9 to 5 is no way to make a living.[8]

Ricardo Semler, CEO of Semco (whose ventures include industrial equipment and environmental consulting), believes in allowing employees to work whenever they want, wherever they want. The result will be increased productivity, greater profitability, and longer-term loyalty, according to the Brazilian businessman and author of *The Seven-Day Weekend*. He even credits that strategy for increasing his firm's annual revenue from $35 million to $212 million in the last six years, with virtually no turnover among his 3,000 employees. Paula Lawlor, founder of Medi-Health Outsourcing (now Precyse Solutions) in King of Prussia, Pennsylvania. Her employees were allowed to bring their children to work and to arrange their schedules around their families' needs. Anyone could take a three-month leave of absence without risking job security. "There are companies that don't want people to talk about their personal lives, but I say, 'Bring it on.' If people can get something off their chests for an hour, then I've got them for the next ten," she says.

A wise company not only supports but proactively steers employees towards getting and maintaining a life outside of work. Old-style leaders are initially uncomfortable with this approach. We promise, however, that you'll be with the program and brimming with original ideas by the end of this chapter.

In Japan, divorced men lose work promotions on the assumption that if they can't manage home life, they are poor bets for managing work life. In contrast, our culture since the Industrial Age has been rather proud of

[8] *Inc. Magazine*, April 2004 | Page 91 By: Brad Wieners

the way it has partitioned work and the rest of life. Surely this church-and-state-style separation has led to more work efficiency and personal privacy, has it not?

Let's counter that question with three others. First, were the two ever successfully separated, even in the old economy? (Hint: Back in the 1950s, wives of executive candidates were sometimes interviewed along with their husbands, and the CEO's wife could tell lower-ranking corporate wives how to decorate their homes.) Second, since technology and the recent economy have blurred the lines between work and personal life, and societal changes have seriously wounded former after-work support systems, how valid remains the notion that the separation serves efficiency and privacy? And third, in whose interest were the two sides separated, and who's in the driver's seat now? (Hint: Answers to choose from are management and employees.)

Workers want more balance and synergy, and they want it now. Emerging signs of the "balance revolution" are everywhere. Workers say they'd be willing to give up a whopping twenty-one percent of their work hours *and salary* to achieve more balance — nearly double the amount they reported being willing to sacrifice just seven years ago. A lack of balance between work and personal life is one of the top six reasons new managers fail. But perhaps most telling of all, a poll of all employees on flexible schedules at one major company found that sixty-five percent of them would have left the firm without the flextime.

Even during the spike in layoffs in the early 2000s, the majority of Fortune 500 companies instigated a "no layoff" policy. Some, like Starbucks, gave their temporary employees full-timer benefits. These are the companies that enjoyed high retention problems as the economy picked up.

Companies that made the mistake of cutting employee perks during that period are paying for it now, as their employees flock to new jobs.

Richard Hadden, co-author of *Contented Cows Give Better Milk* (Saltillo Press), advises that during tough times: "If things have to be taken away, take them from the executives first."

Benefits to Remove:

1. Executive trips and toys
2. Non-job-related classes (i.e., yoga or craft classes)
3. Extensive travel
4. Gym memberships
5. Concierge/convenience services

Benefits to Keep:

1. Child-care services
2. Employee community-building activities (i.e., free-bagel Fridays)
3. Work/life balance programs (i.e., paid time off, flextime)
4. Job-related training
5. Hotels for business travel

Younger workers are especially inclined this way. Sixty percent of men and women under age twenty-five with children say they would make "a lot" of sacrifices in money and career advancement in order to spend more time with their families. Fifty-five percent of eighteen- to thirty-four-year-olds identify the freedom to take extended leaves or sabbaticals as a key workplace benefit. These values have not changed. Perhaps, because of recent job scarcity, they have been put on the back burner, but as the economy improves, worker demands will increase exponentially.

Having control over one's time ranks ahead of everything but making money and using one's brains. And the desire for flexibility is not generation-specific. Workers close to or past retirement age want flexibility to catch up on all the things that a lifetime of work has put off. In any case, when the boomers' mass retirement begins to wreak havoc with an already mushrooming employee shortage — spawning a need to increase the labor participation of those over fifty-fives by twenty-five percent — flexibility will be the key to wooing some of them to stay a little longer. The alternative is convincing younger workers to put in longer hours (good luck) and/or opening immigration floodgates, which is more expensive if immigrants lack the proper education and skills training, in any case.

There is a growing awareness in North America that home life and work life impact each other in significant ways. *In The Corporate Mystic*, Gay Hendricks and Kate Ludeman write, "Many people mess up by trying to get their home needs met at work, and vice versa. A person who is hurting because he does not know how to communicate with his kids becomes a blustery communication obstructer at work. Another person walks in the door at night so full of undigested work issues that no one in the family can get through to her. This problem, unless corrected, becomes a self-fulfilling spiral downward. He or she spends more time at work to get away from home problems, which creates more conflict at home, which causes them to withdraw into work more."

Leading-edge companies have begun to tackle the tricky business of creating a workplace that respects workers' personal lives. At the center of this shift is the need to see work through the lens of personal life. Work affects personal life in a myriad of ways, from the time away from home on business trips to childcare/eldercare issues. There is also a growing body of evidence that when employers demonstrate sensitivity toward these issues and move to help employees resolve conflicts, retention and productivity rise accordingly.[9]

[9] "Results of the most recent Work/Life survey conducted by global human resource outsourcing and consulting firm Hewitt Associates.

Many large companies have already seen the wisdom of providing family-friendly work environments. According to a 2003/2004 Hewitt Associates survey, fifty percent of employers provide some form of elder care assistance to employees, up from forty percent in 1980.[10]

The same survey found that ninety-five percent offer child care assistance, compared to 87 percent in 1998.

Who's trying it out?

- Ninety-eight percent of 100 Best Companies offer eldercare compared with only twenty percent nationwide.[11]

- One hundred percent of 100 Best Companies offer flextime, in contrast with fifty-five percent nationwide[12]

- The National Association of Insurance Commissioners reduced turnover by thirty percent in 1996 to below nine percent in 2003 by introducing a four-day workweek, flextime, telecommuting, casual dress, and a no-layoff policy — as well as allowing employees to bring their infants up to the age of six months to work with them.[13]

- Aflac (No. 74 on the Fortune magazine's 2006 list of 100 Best Companies to Work For) pays 100 percent of tuition (up to $20,000 per year) for employees' college-age children or grandchildren (if they receive a GPA of 2.5 or higher).

- At Goldman Sachs (No. 36) employees get up to twenty days of free

[10] Hewitt's 2003-2004 Work/Life Benefits Survey, in 1998, a survey of 1,020 employers

[11] Society for Human Resource Management's 2003 Benefits Survey

[12] Society for Human Resource Management's 2003 Benefits Survey

[13] Workforce, March 2003, pp. 45-47

backup care for three- to six-month-olds at the on-site children's center, in addition to twenty free days available for all kids.

- Referral bonuses at PricewaterhouseCoopers (No. 58) average $8,000 for new hires.

- Credit-card issuer MBNA (No. 89) offers eight child-care centers, generous reimbursement for tuition, up to $20,000 per child for adoption, and even a paid week off for new grandparents.

- JM Family Enterprises, the largest independent Toyota distributor, (No. 25) provides unusual perks such as free prescriptions delivered by a "pharmacy concierge," professionally made take-home dinners and cruises on the company's 172-foot yacht.

- Timberland (No. 78) offers a six-month fully-paid sabbatical for those who want "to pursue a personal dream that benefits the community in a meaningful way."

- At Capital One Financial, vacation days are available on half an hour's notice.

- Seventy-four percent of respondents to Hewitt's 2003-2004 work/life survey offer such programs, the most common arrangements including flextime (offered by sixty percent), and part-time employment (offered by forty-six percent). Other scheduling arrangements offered: job sharing, compressed workweeks, and telecommuting.

Clearly, each of these companies believes such policies will pay off in the form of retention and engagement. Or maybe they feel they have no choice but to try *something*. For employers, the critical question is, when people say they want balance and synergy, what does that mean? How do employees view these issues, and what do they really want from leaders? What are the components in life in need of balancing, and what constitutes synergy between work and the rest of one's life, anyway?

According to a MORI survey, the four major factors that contribute to happiness are health, family life, employment, and financial considerations. Yesterday's employers felt they could influence or support only one of these — employment — but today's forward-thinking companies are expanding that frame of reference.[14]

Annette Winkelman, a Chicago technology leader for information technology services at professional services firm Deloitte & Touche, has been able to arrange her own schedule for more than five years. "It's taken some creativity, and now I successfully can do my job, take care of my children, and have some personal time, amazingly enough," she recently told ABC News.

These days, forty-three percent of U.S. employees have access to traditional flextime, up from twenty-nine percent in 1992. Another twenty-three percent — compared with eighteen percent in 1992 — can select their start and quit times within a range of hours on a daily basis.

a balanced "diet"

Above all, today's worker wants a balanced "diet." If the four "food" groups have always been work, family, leisure, and health, society has been bingeing with growing intensity on work at the expense of the other three since the 1950s. Of course, if work and the material goods it buys weren't

[14] Source: Adrienne Mand, ABC News, Sponsoring Organization: Families and Work Institute, Date: May 10, 2004

rewarding, society would never have reached this point. But it has to stop somewhere.

Time spent on the job in a given year has increased by 164 hours in the last twenty years, translating into about an extra month of work time, while leisure has declined by one-third. All this at a time when a stable family life and community involvement (still our best stress-busters) appear to be unraveling right along with job security. Like bodybuilders who get muscle-bound from overdeveloping one set of muscles in relation to another, we need to back off, reflect, and build a new program. Workers are way ahead of management on this, and as the power dynamic between them shifts, only the companies that understand and respond will succeed.

It's time to rebalance for overall long-term health and happiness. If this means taking a few days off, joining a volleyball team, or doing a bit of volunteer work, employees who can do so guilt-free and on work time — maybe even at their manager's suggestion — will reward their company with a loyalty that no money can buy. If workers also get positive reinforcement for it from a boss who appears to genuinely care, just watch their dedication soar.

At one large accounting firm, employees have permission not to answer their voice mail and e-mail over weekends and while on vacation, and committees monitor employee overtime and redistribute work when the total workload consistently registers more than fifty to fifty-five hours per week.

Workers need company brass to take the lead on the balance issue. Forty-one percent of British managers say they are disappointed with the work/life balance they find in their current job and eighty-five percent believe vacation should be compulsory. Yet forty-eight percent of people say they feel guilty when they leave on time. The culprit here is the outdated "face time" tradition, in which work is measured by presence rather than output.

Employees are obviously hungering for more balance. Information gathered by Catalyst over the past five years indicates that eighty-seven percent of women and eighty-two percent of men in dual-earner families would seek out flexible work hours in a new employer. Home office telecommuting options appealed to women and men almost equally (sixty-seven and sixty-five percent).

Employers that respond to these desires appear to be getting payback. In the UK, a 2005 Department of Trade and Industry Work-Life Balance Survey at 1,200 workplaces and among 2,000 employees turned in the following results:

- Ninety-four percent of employers agreed that people work best when they can strike a healthy work/life balance;

- Eighty-one percent of employers that have work/life balance practices in place report a positive effect on employee relations;

- Seventy-five percent of employers said they had a more motivated and committed workforce as a result of these practices; and

- Sixty percent report reduced turnover.

At the workplace of one of John's clients, an international real estate investment firm, employees told us that they felt it was more beneficial to play solitaire for an hour on their computers around leaving-time, than actually to exit at five o'clock. This company's entire corporate culture is built around the belief that putting in long hours signals commitment. The first step for this client was to recognize the company's dysfunctional focus on long hours over productivity. Such a focus is often based on the misguided notion that working more hours leads to greater productivity.

In contrast to Japan which exercises a three-week minimum annual paid leave (other industrial countries mandate a four-week minimum). The US has no minimum paid leave. In fact twenty-six percent of working Americans get no paid vacation.[15]

Benjamin Hunnicutt, a historian at the University of Iowa, has spent a lifetime advocating the six-hour workday as optimal for human performance. Whether or not he is correct, today's leaders are well advised to seriously question whether long hours devoid of personal time can truly lead to better performance.

Here are a few findings that suggest this is not the case:

Almost half of junior managers say they value their home life more than work time, while only twenty percent of chairpeople, chief executives, and managing directors say the same. And yet, fifty-five percent of *all* managers admit that long hours actually make them *less productive*.

Half of middle managers believe that working long hours has more to do with inefficiency than workload. And only one-third agree that companies do enough to help staff maintain a healthy work/life balance. Current policies are shrugged off as mere window dressing.

Dr. James Mass, author of *Power Sleep*, advocates allowing workers to take power naps during their breaks as a healthier alternative to caffeine-laden drinks. He also believes that employers who ensure that shift workers receive sufficient sleep reduce accident rates by forty percent.

"You must sleep sometime between lunch and dinner, and no halfway measures," Winston Churchill once said. "Take off your clothes and get into bed. That's what I always do. Don't think you will be doing less work

[15] Take Back Your Time Fighting Overwork and Time Poverty in America by John De Graaf

because you sleep during the day. That's a foolish notion held by people who have no imaginations. You will be able to accomplish more. You get two days in one — well, at least one and a half."

As a thirty-six-year-old employee told us, "It's normal in my company to hear negative jabs about people who leave at five, or who take lunch, even if they have incredible output. If your boss works until ten, you feel coerced to do the same. I want the flexibility to spend time with my family, and I get frustrated that face-time is valued over accountability or actual quality of work."

The solution, of course, lies in senior managers sending an important message to employees by focusing on results rather than hours worked — and role modeling some balance themselves.

There are indications that company leaders are rising to the challenge of workers' need for balance:

- A 2004 survey by AT&T and the Economist Intelligence Unit found that two-thirds of executives surveyed had some staff working from home regularly, with eighty-one percent identifying the support from such work as a "critical" or "important' network goal." John Chambers, CEO of Cisco, predicted that by 2010, sixty million Americans would be telecommuting.

- At IBM, forty percent of employees telecommute and administrative workers accomplish tasks online. Is it coincidental that the firm's voluntary turnover rate rests at three percent?

- At Hewlett Packard, customer engineers were on call 24/7, leading to rising overtime costs, disgruntled employees, and soaring turnover. Today HP employees choose their own workweek. That has decreased overtime costs by thirty-six percent, increased employee moral, and lowered turnover.[16]

- Retailers, law firms, and management consulting firms in the UK are using sabbaticals for retention with increasing popularity. Angela Brown, policy advisor for the Institute for Personnel and Development, said, "Rather than lose them completely, you eventually get them back, hopefully happier and more skilled."

- Catalyst reports that in 2003-2004, seventy-four percent of U.S. employers offered flexible work arrangements, up from sixty-seven percent in 1995. The arrangements offered include: flextime (60 percent), part-time options (forty-six percent), job sharing (twenty-seven percent), compressed work weeks (twenty-two percent), telecommuting (thirty percent), and summer hours (eleven percent).

An International Telework Association survey confirms that Americans are spending more of their work time at home. Here are some highlights of the 2004 survey, conducted by the Dieringer Research Group:

- The number of employed Americans who work from home (from as little as one day a year to full time), grew from 41.3 million in 2003 to 44.4 million in 2004, a 7.5 percent growth rate.

- 16.5 million are self employed, a 4.4 percent increase over 2003.

- This represents 18.3 percent of employed adult Americans, nearly one-fifth of the workforce.

- The greatest increase in the number of teleworkers (fifty-seven percent) occurred in medium-sized businesses (100 to 999 employees).

[16] HP Technology at Work e-newsletter

• When employers convert employees to teleworkers, they save $5,000 per employee per year.

Undoubtedly, telecommuting also helps reduce job stress, to cost US industry an estimated $300 billion annually in absenteeism, diminished productivity, employee turnover, accidents, workers' compensation, and direct medical, legal, and insurance fees.

responding to the shift towards balance

Gemcom Software International in Vancouver, a mining software producer that employs primarily Gen Xers and Yers, views employee retention as a life-or-death matter. Former supervisor Mark Metin attributes the firm's low turnover to its relaxed management structure, flextime, social atmosphere, and emphasis on honest communication and positive feedback. Above all, managers stay vigilant for burnout, actively discouraging sixty-hour weeks.

"This industry tends to burn people out extraordinarily quickly," Metin says. Programmers are a different breed, more artists than scientists. Sometimes the inspiration strikes at three in the morning. We have core working hours here, but many special arrangements for people not good at getting up at seven in the morning, myself among them."

A Gen Xer himself, Metin has found that mentoring younger employees with personal problems also goes with the territory. "We make an extra effort to feed people's souls as well as pocketbooks," he explains. "They could get as much money working somewhere else, but we have a family relationship with most people in the company."

Dangerous? Perhaps, although mentoring training should make it less so. Necessary for retention? Absolutely. Untraditional? Who cares? Times have changed, and Metin is a savvy manager with his finger on the pulse of the new workforce's needs.

There are employers who scoff at the notion of letting personal matters creep across the office doorstep. But companies mindful that it can cost upwards of 100 percent of a worker's salary to replace her understand that boundaries between work and home began fading with the introduction of the cellular phone, laptop computer, and fax. These are the companies that will attract, keep, and maximize the performance of the best workers today. The rest will maintain the necessary number of warm bodies in their ranks while failing to tune in to high turnover and the "B-grade" aspect of their workers.

In an age where there is a shortage of educated and self-reliant workers, responding to workers' desire for balance and synergy is a surefire way to win loyalty. A *Fortune* magazine poll of headhunters determined that the employees most likely to turn down job offers have flextime. Other studies show that flextime isn't enough on its own; employees are often hesitant to use it if they feel it may sideline their careers. Leaders who are serious about using flextime to increase retention must ensure that no ambivalent messages seep into the process. When a low percentage of workers appears to be taking advantage of such policies, it's time to broadcast a "no strings attached" message and live by it.

John once worked with a company in which a senior manager was denied a promotion because during her interview, she expressed the opinion that taking one's allotted vacation time is key to staying sharp enough to excel. So ingrained was the culture of imbalance at the company interviewing her that no senior person openly challenged the thinking behind rejecting her. When word got out as to why she wasn't hired, lower-ranked employees were reluctant to take vacation time. While we have no statistics on how this affected retention in the long term, we're willing to bet it wasn't positive.

One of the best predictors of retention for women is whether they sense that they can attend to personal life and still develop in the company. That is, flextime and parental leaves mean little to ambitious women who find that exercising these policies puts them on a "mommy track" against their will. Again, double messages and hidden agendas are the usual reasons that expensive perks sometimes have little impact on retention or employee commitment.

When Dawson Personnel Systems conducted an in-house survey, the firm found that its employees rated two items — making a contribution toward the good of the company and spending time with their families — above earning more. Based on this, executives formulated a daring new policy. First, they met with the sales team and assigned it productivity goals twenty percent higher than the previous year. Then they informed these salespeople that as soon as they hit their target, they could go home each day at two o'clock for the rest of the month. Also, the first salesperson to sell more than $50,000 would have the last two days of the month off. The result? The team broke every record in the company's fifty-two-year history as members focused like never before and worked well together.

Next, senior management allowed other departments to set their own goals and hours, and promised that for particularly productive weeks, everyone could go home early on Friday. They also mandated a noon closing on holiday weekends. Sales for the year increased by twenty percent, and profits shot up forty percent.

roots of the balance revolution

Today's search for balance and synergy has deep roots in North American society. Poet and social commentator Robert Bly has a theory as to how we've reached a point of gross imbalance. As mentioned in Chapter Two, he wrote a book called *The Sibling Society*, named for the way in which the parent-child relationship has become a sibling dynamic. Bly says that when the Industrial Age removed men from the home (where, in the Agrarian Age, they mixed work with family and enjoyed more intimate relationships with their children), it eroded their "soft" side and led them to overvalue work and devalue family life. Eventually, they learned to stake their identity, sense of contribution, and self-esteem on the job, which led to increasing hours at work and fewer at leisure and home.

As the Modern Age dawned, women flocked to the world of work, where a "higher" status — compared with the devalued work of parenting — seemed to be waiting. Birth control, liberalized divorce laws, the siren of consumerism, and a sense of "pioneering" a new role for womankind all encouraged this. But women became ensconced in the work world just as the global market accelerated business demands to an astounding degree. This, combined with a lack of flexibility for childcare, gave them pause for thought. They applied pressure on male partners to shoulder more house-hold responsibility, only to learn that males (both boomers and Gen Xers) were also growing weary of an overemphasis on achievement and were hankering for intimacy.

In fact, according to a 2004 Ipsos-Reid survey, the top two contributors to absenteeism and/or health costs in the workplace are depression or anxiety (sixty percent) and stress (sixty percent). These are followed by supervisor/manager relationships (forty-four percent), childcare issues (thirty-five percent), co-worker conflict in the workplace (twenty-eight percent), parenting issues (twenty-one percent), and eldercare issues (nineteen percent).[17]

Fast-forward to 1993, when Joe Dominguez and Vicki Robin first published a book entitled *Your Money or Your Life* that instructed readers on how to live well for less and better align their financial priorities with their values. It became a national bestseller. In it, the authors said that in the previous five years, twenty-eight percent of workers had voluntarily made changes in their life that resulted in making less money, primarily in pursuit of a more balanced life. We can only assume that number has increased since then. Employers who equate salary with retention need to bone up on this text because it represents where things are headed.

Recent years have seen an expansion of books, articles, and websites on how to recapture leisure time and simplify your life in this age of overwork. But the bestseller *Your Money or Your Life* remains one of the most popular for charting relationship between spending and fulfillment. It depicts a graph in which the fulfillment line moves steeply upward, hand-in-hand with money spent, until it reaches a point called "survival." Here, it slows but continues to journey upward in relation to spending until it reaches "comforts." Now its climb tapers significantly, as it wanders toward the peak labeled "luxuries." Here, things get interesting: Fulfillment is now inclined to free-fall unless its owner begins giving *away* time or money. Yes, volunteerism and charity are all that can exert upward lift on fulfillment once it has drunk its fill — even though, curiously enough, individuals continue to believe otherwise for quite some time, according to surveys.

While not everyone in North America has arrived at the post-luxuries dot on the graph flagged "enough," plenty of evidence points to star per-

---

[17] WarrenShepell, Human Resources Professionals Association of Ontario (HRPAO)

formers shrugging off raises and gravitating to companies that seem to represent a higher cause. We believe this is occurring with more regularity than in the past, and across generational lines. We'll get into "boosting retention through noble corporate causes" in Chapter Five, but for now, remember that individuals don't always know when they're satiated, or what will re-ignite their fervor. Workers who have been racing blindly for years toward that illusive spending peak often get felled by burnout before they see the light. Leaders who've made note of the graph just described have a canny new insight for retaining and engaging those workers.

Not only do today's workers want synergy between work and non-work hours; they are launching a deep-rooted, unstoppable rebellion against statistics like these:

- In 1935, the average working man had forty hours a week free. In 2002, the Families and Work Institute says working mothers report 0.9 hours/day of personal time, while working fathers report 1.3 hours/day personal time.

- Twenty-six percent of males under age forty-five feel that they cannot have a good family life and get ahead in their current job.

- Full-time employees under age thirty-six rate the work/life balance issue above the challenge of their job, the quality of their immediate manager, and the opportunity for promotion.

- The number of managers working forty-nine hours or more a week has risen by thirty-seven percent since 1985.

- Seventy-two percent of British managers surveyed said that long working hours affect their relationship with their partner and eat into

[12] America's Children in Brief: Key National Indicators of Well-Being

the time they spend with their children. Seventy-seven percent said long hours had an adverse impact on their leisure activities, and fifty-nine percent said long hours are damaging their health.

- Nearly one in five employed parents is single, twenty-seven percent of single parents are men, and two-thirds of employed parents with pre-kindergarten children rely on partners and relatives as the primary childcare source. (In other words, childcare is one of the most pressing issues.)

- Twenty-three percent of children live with only their mothers, five percent with their fathers, four percent with neither[12]

- One out of six primary-age children and two out of five grade-school children arrive home after school to an empty house.

- The majority of babies born in the United States are placed in full-time daycare within a year, commonly within two or three months, so that both their parents can work.

- Nearly a quarter of the population over 18 suffers from a definable psychological problem; depression in particular appears to be growing, and according to the National Institute of Mental Health, it may be appearing earlier in life in people born in recent decades. Many mental health professionals attribute this growth to a lack of deep friendships and personal time for reflection, compounded by a lack of time for healthy eating and de-stressing techniques such as exercise.

- Twenty-one percent (one in five) employees say depression either "completely" or "occasionally" interferes with their work performance.[13]

[13] Public Opinion Strategies, February 2004

more than time

As the economy continues to speed up, the desire to add balance by devoting more time to pursuits outside of work grows accordingly. Balance is becoming increasingly critical to workers' mental and physical health. A company of 1,000 employees loses $1 million per year in stress-induced absenteeism alone. If so much of workers' waking life must be spent at work, they yearn for work to take on some of the qualities of fun and community that they used to enjoy after hours. And if work no longer lays primary claim to their sense of identity, contribution, and self-esteem, commitment to it is easier to shrug off — unless the workplace deliberately offers synergy in this regard.

It's also true that an increasing number of men and women are finding themselves alternating between periods of underemployment and overly demanding employment — that is, they are either trying to find work or drowning in it. One of our clients, a senior vice-president at a large bank conglomerate, is fond of answering the question, "How are you?" with the quip, "Like drinking water from a fire hose." When companies respond to the worker's profound sense of frustration by offering tangible solutions, they impact engagement and retention in a powerful way.

Younger workers are particularly likely to speak of balance as a matter of harmony, not simply time. Again, workers define synergy as feeling free to be themselves, a sense that they need not pretend that the company is their life's work.

The other day John met a twenty-five-year-old woman at a large marketing agency in Washington, DC. Although she enjoys her job, she is quick to admit that singing and acting are her first loves. What she appreciates most about her job, she told us, is that the owner understands this and allows her — indeed, encourages her — to talk about her aspirations. She likes the fact that her "real" job supports her outside-work passions. This is synergy.

Workers want the company to take an interest in their personal lives. Gallup found that managers who were perceived to care about their staff enjoyed the highest employee engagement. Royal Bank of Canada found a similar rise in productivity when supervisors took an interest in employees' personal lives.

Fairmont Hotels & Resorts' annual performance planning process encourages employees to set goals for their lives outside of work and to share those goals with their bosses as part of the performance appraisal process. Why? Because the company realizes that younger workers appreciate companies that take an interest in the intersection between these two aspects of life. Contrast this with the senior executive of a bank who asked us in all seriousness, "Isn't it illegal to talk to people about their personal lives at work?" Clearly, he doesn't get it, and odds are, neither does his company.

What is it he and his company are supposed to "get"? They are supposed to get the fact that a powerful phenomenon is reshaping how workers see work and the rest of their lives.

what does the desire for balance mean for your business?

What, you may ask, has all this got to do with the work world? Can't society simply get on with sorting out the balance issues and childcare debate on someone else's time? Isn't how much one indulges in leisure or family time up to the individual in the long run? Work is work, social and family life are private, and it's illegal, impractical, and unprofitable to get involved in workers' private lives, right? Besides, hasn't the business world already responded admirably to the so-called work-family tug by introducing personal days, flextime, corporate daycare, job-sharing, and counseling services?

On the contrary, the bottom line is that workers' efforts to balance the work/life ratio is now part of the corporate landscape, whether we like it or not. Flextime may get great workers to turn their heads your way, but it won't entice them through the door or keep them in your company. And family problems are one of the top five reasons that relocations fail.

According to a 2004 Mellon Financial Corporation' survey, employers that are responding to employees' work/life balance so to enhance recruitment efforts (seventy-three percent); raise morale (seventy-four percent); and remain competitive (seventy-two percent). The results compare 1996 and 2004 responses:

Companies who offer:	2004	1996
Flextime	71%	32%
Telecommuting, work-at-home arrangements	50%	9%
Compressed work weeks	44%	16%
Part-time (fewer than 1000 hours per year)	86%	50%
Family sick days	54%	42%
Domestic partner benefits	35%	6%
Work-related tuition reimbursement	88%	
General resource and referral services	55%	
Unpaid family leave beyond legislated requirements	47%	

Today's stars — highly sought-after, self-reliant, workers — have come to *expect* flexibility as a *starting point*. They want much more. Where technology initially seemed to offer the freedom and flexibility for which many workers yearned, no one argues that it has also invaded the privacy of their homes. It has inflicted longer, less predictable hours on many. In collusion with fading international boundaries, work across time zones, and speeded-up product cycles, work has evolved from a nine-to-five proposition to an "everywhere/anytime" scenario. Fanatical amounts of time spent on the computer now ranks No. 3 on the list of reasons for divorce.

The Wall Street Journal reported on an Internet search firm executive whose two children, ages nine and fourteen, presented him with a "Family Miles" program — a system of rewards for staying home more, resisting a ringing phone, and "getting home on holidays and breaks without being days late." He responded to the wake-up call by learning to let the phone ring during meals without breaking out in a cold sweat, and by working fewer weekends. Today's offices are filled with workers who feel they were robbed of intimacy with their parents by unreasonable corporate demands and by their parents' misguided expectation that loyalty was a two-way street. Determined not to fall into the same mold, today's workers want to be "true to themselves" in each and every chosen role. The point that *employers* often miss is that this is no idle whimsy; it is a goal for which employees will leave a good job. As Claire Raines writes in *Beyond Generation X*, "Members of the X generation … have witnessed firsthand a work ethic that eats peo-

DELOITTE & TOUCHE, the accounting firm, took steps to add flexible schedules and control business travel, thereby helping to launch itself into Fortune magazine's Top 10 list of best companies to work for in America.

ple up and spits them out — and they want something different…. They believe that work should not be more important than their friends, families, and hobbies."

We're talking about at least two generations' worth of workers aware at *some level* that an all-new balance is required to begin healing hidden wounds and to prevent the next generation from a similar fate. And just as they know that tossing a few tin cans in a recycling box is not going to save an environment in distress, they know — at some level — that flextime in the workplace is less than a finger in the dike of family distress.

Their quiet revolution may even be reaping results already. In 2002, the Families and Work Institute reported that working parents with children spend 6.2 hours/day caring for those children, up an hour a day from 1977. The result is that children are receiving somewhat more attention from their employed parents than they did almost thirty years ago. However, seventy percent of all parents still feel they do not spend enough time with their children and that they have less time for personal activities.

Time is one issue. But as we can't overstate, today's workers want something else they can't quite define, and something many managers are far from willing to accept: balance on a very deep level. Synergy between work and what some euphemistically call their "real life." Acknowledgment, if you will, that their work and personal selves need not be chopped up and displayed selectively to different audiences. Support — physically and psychologically — of their goals and activities outside of work. Confirmation that if work can invade the rest of their lives, then the rest of their lives can do "field trips" to work.

Classic Packaging, a packaging manufacturer based in Vancouver, Canada, pays for employees' music lessons because they believe that if people are learning, they will come to work happier and more willing to contribute and do their best for the firm. Their employees never hesitate to tell customers it's a great place to work.

A recent survey by Workforce.com found that recent college graduates from the US, UK, Spain, Germany, and France, want the following from employers:

Training programs:	71%
Fair compensation:	61%
Flexible schedules:	59%
Approachable managers:	55%
Ethical management:	48%
Mentoring programs:	45%
Social events:	30%
Discounts at local shops:	23%
Telecommuting:	16%[20]

responding

How does a company respond to this search for balance and synergy? As with so many of the shifts we have identified in this book, each organization must find its own best answer, but we have identified some of the trends and supplied examples of companies that have forged creative solu-

[20] Workforce.com, (September 9, 2004, Volume 2, No. 17

tions. It all begins with helping people juggle work and personal life more effectively. For example, companies are taking increasing responsibility for helping their people with the day-to-day challenges of parenting. In 1984, when *Fortune* magazine first started publishing its list of the 100 Best Companies to work for in America, only two of the hundred had on-site daycare. In 2006, one-third of the top 100 had such facilities.

Alston & Bird in Atlanta, No. 2 on Fortune's 2004 list, offers three-month, fully-salaried maternity/paternity leaves, as well as an onsite day-care that costs employees an average of $500 per month.

The same is true for things like flexible work schedules. In the early 1980s, only two of the top one hundred offered flextime. By the late 1990s, eighty-seven percent of the top one hundred offered telecommuting, seventy-two percent offered job sharing, eighty-nine percent boasted the option of a compressed work week, and seventy percent included flexible work schedules. Times have changed, big time. These figures demonstrate how

Balance has come to be identified with great places to work.

As mentioned earlier, fifty-nine of the companies on the 2004 best employers list added staff despite the massive layoffs witnessed from 2001 onwards. The high-tech industry, most vulnerable to the economic downturn, contributed only sixteen companies to the list, compared to twenty-two five years earlier.[21]

One of the greatest challenges facing company leaders today is ensuring that the desire to support balance and synergy runs deeper than a slogan of the month. That's why managers at the brokerage house Edward Jones (ranked No. 1 in *Fortune* magazine's Best 100 Companies to Work For

[21] 2004 Special Report, 100 Best Companies to Work For

in America for the second consecutive year in January 2003), are encouraged to handle flextime requests with the following guidance: "Do what is right and human."

Offering flextime and support for people's lives inside and outside of work is not just a retention technique. It is a philosophy. Either a company accepts the need for this synergy or people will leave, even though the company's childcare center is full.

What happens when a company creates balance and synergy? At one manufacturing company, the simple act of changing a work shift to coincide with the end of the school day, cut turnover in half and created a buzz in the community that working women should try to get a job at this particular plant. This company is now the employer of choice in its community.

As a young American entrepreneur has said, "The biggest challenge for our generation is providing our own children with what we didn't have: fathers, time, attention, and security."

Work today is filled with ironies. Here is one of the more profound and important ones: On the one hand, work is becoming less important to people. Work has eaten up so much of people's lives that many are saying, "Wait a minute. The rest of my life deserves attention, too." On the other hand — thanks to a lack of job security, more invasive technology, and the new empowerment of front-line workers — work is by necessity a greater obsession than ever. Younger workers, especially, must constantly groom new skills and networks in order to "make a living." Older workers must live with increasing age discrimination and a sense that they had better stay on guard lest they become expendable at work. All of this means that companies must deal with their employees' growing desire for balance and their obsessive compulsion about staying employed. Perhaps it is this paradox — the desire to work less and the need to focus on it obsessively — that drives today's workers to demand more synergy.

A mid-level manager in a large technology company said it best: "In this company, you get the feeling that they really care about your personal life. Whether it's a sick kid, a death in the family, volunteer work you believe in, or a course you want to take, there seems to be a core philosophy that these things are central to productivity. How do I know that? I think it's the little things they do and say every day, not the daycare center. If I can, I'll stay here forever!"

Profile:
Tazeem Nathoo, former Senior Vice President
Vancity
Vancouver, BC

When talking about VanCity, Tazeem Nathoo, former VP of Operations, is quick to remind listeners of its modest beginnings as a small credit union in an underprivileged area of the city of Vancouver, Canada. Indeed, she credits those beginnings for a corporate culture that has never strayed from its determination to serve and respect people from all walks of life.

Since its early days, VanCity has grown into Canada's largest credit union, renowned for its leadership in corporate social responsibility. With 1,500 employees, it has been voted one of the top thirty-five companies to work for in Canada and one of the top ten companies for women. In 1998, it received the Distinguished Service to Families Award from the B.C. Council for Families.

In an industry where employee turnover averages 18.4 percent, VanCity currently maintains an eleven percent average — all the more astonishing when one considers that its employees are relatively young (the average age is thirty-seven) and seventy-two percent are women.

Typically, organizations heavily staffed by women suffer high turnover due to women's greater tendency to move for husbands' relocations and their more frequent entries into and exits from the workforce for child-rearing. And yet the measures addressing these concerns that many firms consider progressive, Nathoo shrugs off as "the usual ones." VanCity has had flexible hours, four-day work-weeks, an ability to work from home, and excellent maternity and paternity benefits for years. It's not always easy to grant these, given the demands of the customer base, but VanCity has never flinched in supplying whatever is needed to attract and keep good employees.

"We have a culture that is renowned for putting people first, and if you want to keep your members happy, you have to make sure your staff are looked after," Nathoo says, adding that retention is becoming ever more challenging in the age of the knowledge worker. Among VanCity's more generous policies is twelve "care days" per year that staff can put aside for their own relaxation needs or for family emergencies. Among the more unusual policies is free provision of a pager to pregnant staff and their partners.

VanCity also takes a strong position on contributing to the community. Not only does the credit union make funds available for community programs, but it encourages staff to get involved as volunteers. It leaves it up to the discretion of managers as to whether employees can do volunteer stints on company time.

One initiative grants points that lead to prizes for employees who are physically active, nutritionally conscientious, and environmentally sensitive. This Living Well program, which evolved from one that rewarded those who took part in physical fitness programs, was overhauled for a more strategic, preventative-health outlook and a more holistic definition of "living well." Whereas in the past, this program operated on an honor system and supplied participants with gifts like sweatshirts and running shoes, it now focuses on prevention and detection and encourages behavioral change.

As for diversity issues, Nathoo says that originally, the company brought in speakers to stimulate thought and conversation, had a diversity council check out the company for any inadvertent barriers, and ensured that all branches were accessible to the disabled. Eventually, however, the firm found that diversity was a non-issue. After all, this is a credit union that was one of the first to offer loans to women without requiring their father's or husband's signature, and worked from the start to ensure employees of many different backgrounds excelled within the company. As Nathoo points out, VanCity draws staff from the highly multicultural city of Vancouver, which has inevitably resulted in "a myriad of people" throughout its branches.

"We reflect the diversity, and our staff feel comfortable in their backgrounds. The culture for this was already there."

She looks instead to tomorrow's diversity issues: ensuring that policies and programs for members reflect the reality that women have acquired tremendous purchasing and financial power. "Women are estimated to control more than eighty percent of consumer and household spending, and comprise 40 percent of all Internet users. The number and size of women-owned firms is also increasing.

Women's more collaborative and consensus-building leadership style is needed in the current economy, alongside men's generally more controlling style. When you look at corporate senior management and corporate boardrooms, they're still so dominated by white males. The number of women on corporate boards, the number of women CEOs, is pitiful. Don't women make up fifty percent of the population? Where does it say that only one segment of our population should make up corporate boards? How can they claim to reflect the views of a diverse population? Due to globalization and the greater complexity of the world, we need all kinds of minds to come together, people with different perspectives. Those companies that understand and value diversity have the competitive edge."

assessing your company for balance

Using the statements below, assess how your organization, division, and/or department is doing at responding to employees' search for balance and synergy. The assessment is meant to guide your thinking, not to provide a definitive quantitative assessment of your progress. For each question below, answer how true the statement is of your work environment using the scale provided:

_____ Our company encourages workers to discuss conflicts between personal and work commitments with the supervisor (if yes in general, give yourself one point; if managers have been given guidelines for how or why to do so, tally three points).

_____ Managers in our company take an interest in the personal, outside-of-work goals of employees (one point if generally true; two points if they're actively encouraged or trained to do so; three points if a formal program addressing this is in place).

_____ Our company offers and/or pays for education and training even when it has no immediate, direct work application (one point if company offers flextime to specifically accommodate this; two points if the company subsidizes it; three points if company pays in full).

_____ Our company offers flexible hours and/or job sharing (one point if these are offered, three points if people don't lose status or opportunities by taking advantage of them).

_____ Our company offers services to ease the burden of personal chores or stress (on-site concierge or dry cleaning, free massages, subscription to e-mail services such as medical advice) (one point if available to all permanent, full-time employees; total of two if also available to part-time and temporary workers).

_____ Our company offers flexible hours to all workers, not just managers (one point if available to all permanent, full-time employees; total of two if also available to part-time and temporary workers).

_____ Workers who have personal commitments that make it difficult to work overtime are not penalized in terms of status and promotions (two points).

_____ Both males and females at all levels discuss balance and family openly in our company as a legitimate concern (two points).

_____ Workers in our organization are encouraged to take their vacation time (one point).

_____ Our organization supports sabbaticals, where employees take a period of time off to achieve a personal goal (two points).

_____ Our company actively monitors and attempts to prevent work burnout (one point if applies to permanent, full-time employees; total of two if also applies to part-time and temporary workers).

_____ Our company has managerial guidelines in place to ensure that parents returning from maternity or paternity leave need not feel they have to "re-prove" their dedication. At the same time, we allow all employees the option of designing a less demanding schedule for a chosen period of time that need not lead to a loss in status or promotion (two points).

_____ We sponsor many events to which workers' families are invited (one point).

_____ We encourage/underwrite partner accompaniment on some business travel (one point for encouragement, two for encouragement plus underwriting).

_____ We actively address childcare concerns by providing a referral service or on-site or subsidized childcare (two points for referral; total of three if on-site facilities or subsidies are involved).

_____ Our company offers confidential counseling services and/or trains managers to proactively identify and supportively handle employees' "personal" situations (one point).

_____ Managers in our company actively reward deserving employees with positive reinforcement delivered in creative ways (days off, surprise lunch, personal thank-you notes) (one point).

_____ Our company organizes social, leisure, or sport clubs/teams (one point if true for permanent, full-time employees; total of two if also open to workers' families and part-time and temporary employees).

_____ TOTAL SCORE:

20 or under: Take a full week's management retreat for brainstorming policies that address these concerns.

21-25: You're beginning to look responsive.

26-30: You are above average in meeting today's workers' needs, but there is still room for improvement.

31-37: You are an inspiring example, and probably have the best workers and a strong bottom line to show for it. E-mail us: info@theizzogroup.com

CHAPTER FIVE

the expectation of work as a noble cause

"The experience of making a difference and the pleasure of giving something back to the local community pays huge dividends to the company in psychological, cultural, and therefore financial ways."
– CORPORATE CELEBRATION

At the Park Hotel in Charlotte, North Carolina, general manager Wayne Shusko runs a tight ship with a very clear mission: "To exceed the highest expectations of every customer and every colleague in every inter-action." From the very first day of orientation, Shusko talks to staff about what these words mean and how to live them out. The first time John stayed at the hotel, he arrived late on a Thursday night for a Friday morning keynote speech. At midnight, he realized he had forgotten his contact lens solution and called down to the front desk in the faint hope that the gift shop might still be open. The front desk clerk said the store would not open until 8:30 a.m., half an hour after John's talk would begin.

"What is it you need, sir?" she pressed. After John explained, she placed him on hold long enough to get security to open up the shop and bring two brands of solution to her. Minutes after asking John if either of these would work, she had the correct one delivered to his room by an attendant who wished John a cheery good night and disappeared before John could even offer him a tip. Clearly, here was staff that felt they were working for a cause greater than tips or filling rooms; they were inspired by the rewards of *truly* making people feel at home.

Workers today want their work to be about something deeper than the bottom line. They want a sense of sweating for more than a profit: making a meaningful difference in customers' lives or, if their work itself can have no such connection, a strong belief that their company takes its community and global citizenship seriously. If they're going to work longer hours at more complex jobs than previous generations, with less community-oriented time, they need more than a money motive to ignite their enthusiasm and loyalty. Sure, they know their company must make a profit to survive. But those lucky enough to work for companies that give them something else to latch onto — a more noble reason to pour their energies into daily tasks — offer so much more of themselves. This third shift in worker attitudes is about workers wanting to "do good" and make a living all at the same time. Call it multi-tasking in its most noble form, or the "ennobling" of the workforce!

Companies are increasingly aware of this trend. Mary Kay Cosmetics says it exists to give "enrich women's lives" and "to provide an open-ended opportunity for women." Merck aims "to preserve and improve human life." Sony plugs "creating products that enrich people's lives." 3M exists "to deliver innovative solutions to life's everyday puzzles." Hewlett-Packard is about "inventing technologies and services that drive business value, create social benefit and improve the lives of customers — with a focus on affecting the greatest number of people possible."

Then there are the actions beyond the words. The British food and drinks conglomerate, Diageo, allocates one percent of pre-tax profits — currently, eighteen million pounds — to community involvement through its foundation, which provides kick-start funding and expertise to worthy projects around the world. Fannie Mae of Washington, DC, gives employees ten paid hours every month to do community work, and provides grants to nonprofit organizations where employees volunteer their time.

Workers flock to such companies and, all else being equal, stay longer. For companies, that means being "seen to do good" is no longer enough. Donating a hamper of food to the needy at Christmas is not sufficient. Most significantly, options about "doing good" have moved from "warm, fuzzy, and optional" to being key for attracting and keeping talent. Perhaps that is why Oxfam, the charity, receives a constant stream of résumés from high powered executives looking for a change.

Although people have always appreciated working at companies with a deeper purpose beyond profits and money, we are arguing that a definable shift is occurring; employees now *expect* companies to state and live up to higher aspirations. When Gallup studied employee engagement, it found that a key predictor of engagement was poll respondents' agreement with the sentence, "The mission statement of the company makes me feel my job is important." This shift is most pronounced among younger workers. Three-quarters of college students say that making a difference in the lives of others is very important. More than half say that doing volunteer work is a worthy cause. And Gen X volunteers more than any other generation in America. Another driver of this shift is the aging of the workforce. Erich Fromm and other psychologists have clearly documented that as human beings age, they move from a focus on self, or what they will take from the world, to what they can leave behind. The combination of the aging baby boomers' focus on what they can contribute and the quiet activism of younger workers is having a marked impact on worker attitudes.

Seventy-two percent of corporate and human resources executives polled said their companies' values motivate them personally. Back in the days of tall hierarchies, that's where the influence may have ended: in the executive suite. Today, however, employees of all ranks are watching and waiting to translate corporate values into meaningful actions. As an employee of Bright Horizons, a worksite childcare center provider in Watertown, Massachusetts, explained, "I love knowing children walk away from here better people."

A worldwide Millennium Poll on Social Responsibility by Environics International asked more than 25,000 people in twenty-three countries to name the factors that most influence their impressions of individual companies. The majority named labor practices, business ethics, responsibility to society at large, and environmental impact. Only one in three mentioned factors associated with the traditional role of business: financial issues, company size, business strategy, and management. The irony of this finding is that most corporate events and documents focus on the growth and size of the company as a major motivator for employees. Those polled — and in particular those in older Western economies — said they expect companies to become more active in social responsibilities, although those from countries just coming out of communism were less likely to say so. How both consumers and workers evaluate companies is changing. What we're saying is that individuals are becoming more assertive in their demands that corporations become good corporate citizens. Nearly half of the poll's respondents said they have recently "punished" a company they saw as not socially responsible!

And increasingly, corporations are striving to respond to that call — not always willingly, evenly, or for entirely altruistic reasons, but the operative word is "increasingly." Two things are driving this: One factor is a growing recognition on the part of forward-looking CEOs *and* workers that greater social responsibility is required, and that governments and individuals cannot achieve sufficient change alone. The other driving factor is the volatile new mix of democracy and demographics, in which highly educated workers employed in less-authoritarian work environments have the power and gumption to demand that corporate and individual values align. (The same can be said for more demanding consumers, of course.)

Although ours is a book about winning employee commitment, we can't help but remind the reader that the case for corporate citizenship has never been stronger:

- Every one hundred pounds of product manufactured in the US creates at least 3,200 pounds of waste.

- The US produces 1,637 pounds of garbage per person per year, France only 572 pounds per person.

- We are now producing almost five times per person what our ancestors produced in 1900.

- The world's population nearly quadrupled between 1900 and 2000.

- The world's income is now less evenly distributed than it was one hundred years ago.

When 1,000 working adults were asked whether they would rather earn high salaries or earn "enough" doing work that makes the world a better place, eighty-six percent chose the latter. This is in sharp contrast to a decade or two ago, as confirmed by the results of a survey (previously mentioned in Chapter Two) of graduating MBAs taken ten years apart. The Class of 1989 defined their primary measures of success as power, prestige, and money. The Class of 1991 cited successful relationships, a balanced life, and leisure time. Even more recently, respondents responded marriage, health, and ethics! That's our point: Values are shifting in significant ways.

Reflecting these values, more than one hundred college campuses operate what are called "pledge programs," through which graduates pledge to investigate the social and environmental responsibility of any employment they consider. These campaigns (an example is http://www.graduationpledge.org/) help job applicants define the issues and stick with their goals).

The corporate manifestation of a noble cause can take many forms: a mission statement that reveals the deeper meaning of the work, a firm that trumpets its socially responsible policies, a policy that encourages workers to do volunteer work on company time, or a company that matches employees' charitable donations. Recognition for service above and beyond the call of duty is another staple of companies determined to show their noble side.

Although workers' desire to contribute is more intense today (thanks to less after-work time and organizational involvement), corporations making contributions to their communities is a longstanding tradition. When a devastating flood hit Dayton, Ohio, in the early 1900s, John Patterson, owner of a multimillion-dollar cash register industry, set his assembly line to work turning out rowboats and engaged his cafeteria in baking bread for refugees. Despised as a tyrant before this, he was feted with a massive parade afterwards. Of course, that was a one-off.

What is new and significant is this: Only recently have large numbers of employees come to work with the heady notion that they should be able to fulfill their desire to serve others meaningfully *at work, on an ongoing basis*. Workplaces that find a way to meet that desire sprint far ahead of their competitors, as was driven home to John when he paid two closely spaced visits to two very different firms in the same industry.

The first was a world-renowned life insurance company holding its annual company-wide employee meeting. After providing the keynote speech, John took his seat and watched quietly as fifty PowerPoint slides were used to walk the audience through the financial results of the company's year. Although the figures themselves were impressive, at no point during the show did the presenters refer to how the insurance policies behind the numbers had benefited real people, the customers, in significant ways. The meeting ended with polite but subdued applause. Follow-up conversations with employees revealed to John a workforce barely committed to the enterprise.

The following week, John attended the annual sales meeting of another financial services company. Here, the requisite slide show of financial performance was kept short to make time for a viewing of custom-prepared videos. The first video featured widows and widowers talking about how much the company's products meant to them when their loved ones died. In the second video, recent retirees expressed thanks to company employees for helping them manage their lifetime savings for the exciting and daunting moment of retiring. Now the CEO rose to tell stories that drove home how various departments' work came together to positively impact people's lives. He ended his inspiring, "big picture" speech with the words, "When you serve people this way, people buy your stuff. Thanks for our best year ever."

The meeting ended in a five-minute standing ovation, and from subsequent conversations with employees, John could only marvel at how passionate they were about working for this company, how "on fire" they were about their jobs.

Take a moment and reflect on the last "big" meeting in your organization. Was the focus on "making the numbers" or on the service you provided that made for that success?

what business are you in?
mission statements that inspire loyalty

The search for a noble cause is fed or starved by the way a company celebrates its achievements and by how it presents its mission. And yet, a read through 301 corporate mission statements from America's top companies (*The Mission Statement Book* by Jeffrey Abrahams) revealed to us that only ten percent of them put a noble cause *front and center*. Another four percent came close. The vast majority had no hesitation in telling it like it is — through chest-beating, shareholder-fawning, and self-promoting language. Reading through excruciatingly repetitive phrases such as "to enhance shareholder value," "to become world class" and "to be the most successful," one begins to yearn for anything with more noble content or a more original turn of phrase. Even the company that identified its mission as "to be the most efficient competitor" seemed a relief. Do sycophantic mission-statement writers envision only shareholders reading their statements? If so, why not provide a second set for workers — mission statements that will light a fire beneath them to deliver what shareholders want? Yes, work-ers read mission statements, as do prospective employees shopping around for the best corporate culture with which to align their souls. Potential applicants may eye the noble words with a healthy dose of skepticism but during the early winnowing process, they assume that mission statements, like the design of a front door, offer some clues as to what's inside.

Here's a peek at some of the more crass mission statements in the past:

Ford Motor Company (early 1900's)
"Ford will democratize the automobile."

Sony (early 1950's)
"Become the company most known for changing the worldwide poor-quality image of Japanese products"

Boeing (1950)
"Become the dominant player in commercial aircraft and bring the world into the jet age"

Wal-Mart (1990)
"Become a $125 billion company by the year 2000"

PEPSI
"Beat Coke"

HONDA
"We will crush, squash, and slaughter Yamaha"

NIKE
"Crush Reebok"

To state the most crass goals of business up-front borders on insulting workers' intelligence and surely misses an opportunity to strike a chord with their values. Let's look at a few examples of companies with a more clever spin on their mission statements, if not a genuine commitment to noble goals:

At Marriott, founder J. Willard Marriott coined the mantra, "Take care of our associates, and our associates will take care of our guests, and our guests will return."

Medtronic's mission is "to alleviate pain, restore health, and extend life." IKEA's driving purpose is "to provide a better everyday life for the majority of people." The aim of pharmaceutical/biotechnology firm ICN Pharmaceuticals Inc. is "to make health care products that improve the quality of life for mankind." (Note: Although the second and third lines promise to "provide a fair return to our investors" and "become one of the largest and most successful," at least the writers sensed what needed to come *first*.)

Here are some out-takes from the credo of Johnson Wax, one of the world's leading manufacturers of chemical specialty products for home, personal care, and insect control: "We must be mindful of ways to help our employees fulfill their family responsibilities. We are responsible to the communities in which we live and work and to the world community as well. We must be good citizens-support good works and charities and bear our fair share of taxes. We must encourage civic improvements and better health and education. We must maintain in good order the property we are privileged to use, protecting the environment and natural resources." (Note: The credo goes on to add, "The stockholders should realize a fair return," but how subtle to hold this off until near the end!)

The nation's largest security company writes, "[The] freedom to pursue economic goals is constrained by law and channelled by the forces of a free market... For some companies, that is enough. It is not enough for

Borg-Warner. We impose upon ourselves an obligation to reach beyond the minimal. We do so convinced that by making a larger contribution to the society that sustains us, we best assure not only its future vitality, but our own." The statement goes on to endorse "the dignity of the individual, our responsibility to the common good, the endless quest for excellence, continuous renewal and the commonwealth of Borg-Warner and its people."

Just a few more for good measure: Global pharmaceutical company Pfizer is "dedicated to helping humanity." AES, a world leader in power generation, exists to "meet the world's need for electricity in a socially responsible manner." Jostens Inc., the graduation-products company, desires to "help people celebrate achievement, reward performance, recognize service, and commemorate experiences." Shaklee US (consumer goods and services) "enables all people to own their own lives, make a positive difference in the world, and earn the respect of customers and communities." And finally, Tandy Corporation, known for its Radio Shack stores, "demystifies technology for the mass market" — surely a notion more likely to get a worker out of bed in the morning than enhancing shareholder value.

Semantics and spin, some will sniff. So what? A noble phrase doesn't prove these corporations will follow through with noble measures, nor does it prevent the companies with blunter, less eloquent mission statements from doing more for local communities than those who claim that's their orientation. True, but it's a start, a savvy recognition of this all-important shift in worker attitudes, a chance to make employees sit up, take notice, and grasp at the notion that they're doing more than serving their nine-to-five and paying off a mortgage. Of course, companies with a noble mission statement still have to prove that they're made of more than words. Our experience is that most are, and that far more than ten percent of companies will soon "ennoble" their mission statements *and* their missions.

A 2002 MORI Survey for a major financial company found that seventy percent of staff who considered themselves committed to the values of the company had increased their productivity that past year. In contrast, uncommitted staff had improved their productivity only one percent.[22]

As Steve Robertson at Catholic Healthcare West says, "Retention is as much about alignment of values as it is about having values. In our hiring process, we try to highlight our values — dignity, stewardship, excellence, collaboration, and justice — and use selection processes that are tied to the values." If an organization hires people whose values align, those people are more likely to stay.

Whatever business you are in, there is a noble cause at its root, and today's employees want you to talk about it.

demonstrating the connection

Mission statements, videos of grateful customers, and carefully crafted awards programs are all effective tools for helping workers see a connection between their work and a higher cause. Yet even leaders who are intent on creating an engaged workforce may miss the importance of connecting words with a noble purpose.

A client of John's in the software consulting business designs systems to help government agencies manage finances. When the firm hired John to help increase employee retention, they were surprised at his finding that the software consultants — mostly under thirty and highly marketable — felt under-fulfilled in their service role. These consultants expressed the

[22] Staff Happiness and the Bottom Line 30 August 2002

feeling that the product they provided made little real difference in people's lives. The leaders of the division were surprised because to them, the deeper impact of the work was evident.

Over the next year, through customer forums, the company's leadership team worked hard to illustrate the connection between the services the company provided and the positive experience of the end user. They talked about the importance of government agencies being more aware of where hard-earned tax dollars went, so that they could be held accountable. They even went out of their way to bid and win a contract to consult with a United Nations relief agency. By the time this project was complete, employees were telling us that they intended to stay at this particular firm because the company has a genuine commitment to their clients' success, not just to "selling products and services." Turnover dropped an impressive thirty-five percent in one year.

In *The Hungry Spirit*, Charles Handy describes how a high-tech company in Silicon Valley, California, was growing so fast that it had no time for training new employees and could afford to fire any who made mistakes. The result was an increasingly tense atmosphere that choked initiative. As company leaders pondered how to turn this around, they focused on how the equipment they made saved lives, how it had helped to revolutionize education in poor countries, and the potential it had for bringing government closer to people everywhere. They decided this was the real purpose of their company, and that "the money bit was the scorecard." They decided to invest in the people who would be their future and put a stronger value on creating a trusting atmosphere. Employees were now encouraged to learn from (instead of fearing or hiding) their mistakes. In other words, the company decided to shift its focus from maximizing profit at all costs to longer-term thinking, while still ensuring a decent return on capital.

Why emphasize to workers the noble aspects of the company's endeavors? Because, says Handy, "a match of corporate and individual souls releases energy, enthusiasm, effort, excitement and excellence... Without that match, work and life are dull." Words can facilitate or trip up companies that are endeavoring to respond to workers' desire for a noble cause. Empty platitudes served up to cynical employees will backfire on the leaders who parrot them. On the other hand, lofty words sincerely intended, if not perfectly practiced, will stimulate high levels of employee engagement.

Companies can begin to work with this shift when leaders reflect on the deeper ways in which their products and services make an impact on people. Perhaps, instead of managing money, they are "creating wealth." Surely "making people feel at home" is a better goal than selling hotel rooms. Are they selling insurance or "creating security"? Are they selling theme park tickets or "making memories"?

Of course, some corporate leaders look at others' efforts to insert noble cause into their agenda and say, "Well, that's a good idea, but the widgets we make can't be touted as saving the world or adding critical value to someone's life." Perhaps this was the line of thinking at the dog-food company that handed over the task of rewriting their mission statement to employees. The previous mission statement had read something like, "To kill the cornmeal competition!" The workers astonished management by kicking off the statement with the phrase, "Dogs contribute to human fulfillment..."The moral of this story? Even those who package dog food want to feel they are laboring for something deeper. Toss them a milk bone to gnaw on, or better yet, let *them* come up with something they can truly get their teeth into — then reorganize to help support them in more than words. Put bite into the bark.

The noble cause in a business does not always have to ring of Mother Teresa. Paul Hollands, CEO of A&W Canada, when reflecting on people who serve hamburgers, told us, "Higher purpose on the front line is quick service, great food, and friendly, caring staff who take pride in their work and have the power to make choices." In other words, even the act of feeding people has appeal when people feel appreciated for doing so with care and dignity.

At a real estate investment firm in Calgary, employees work very hard in a busy, fast-paced environment. Ask them what they like about the company and they comment on how much they believe in the products they provide and how their services are creating wealth for their clients. We found the same scenario at a software-consulting firm in Virginia, where employees describe what a difference it makes working for a company that really cares about their clients' success, and not just about selling software.

Beneath all this lies a simple paradox. Companies spend millions of dollars on public relations aimed at *consumers*: They promote the fact that they're in the business of caring, of flying friendly skies, and so on. Yet how many extend this campaign to portray their best side to *workers* (or prospective employees, who are becoming ever more discerning "shoppers"), remembering that additional follow-through is required to drive home the communication and render the noble words into noble deeds?

A general manager for Placer Dome reports that university students come with tough questions about the company's business practices both nationally and abroad. "They want to know what our values, policies, and vision are."

At Southwest Airlines, known for its loyal and engaged employees, corporate values are supported by regular meetings at every level of the company. During these meetings, workers and managers are expected to identify ways they are currently not living these values, and ways they can take steps towards greater alignment. This illustrates that putting values on paper or a lobby plaque is not the sole ticket to the game. The allocation of time and resources to underscore commitment to values is what ensures employee participation, engagement, retention, and loyalty.

Perhaps the rise of ethics or compliance officers in major companies is proof that companies recognize a need for special measures to ensure mission statements' validity and vitality. Ethics officers act as in-house moral arbitrators, mediators, watchdogs, and receptive listeners to whistleblowers. Companies such as the CIBC, Canada Post, Magna International, the Royal Bank of Canada, and McDonald's Restaurants all retain ethics officers. Nearly ninety-three percent of US companies with more than 500 employees have formalized ethics codes, and many have ethics officers or specialists to support their ethics programs. The number of corporate ethics officer positions has increased dramatically in the last several years. Launched in 1992 by a dozen ethics officers, the US-based Ethics Officers Association now boasts more than 860 members — mainly from North America, but also from around the world. The group gained more than 100 new members in 2002. The Ethics Practitioners Forum, a similar European-based network, was launched in 2002.

AES, one of the world's largest power companies, says it is "committed to meeting the world's needs for electricity in a socially responsible way." The company has backed up that statement in hundreds of ways, from planting a million trees in Latin America to pledging five percent of after-tax profits to socially responsible projects. (By 1999, the company had reached three percent.) Like every business, AES has faced daunting challenges made even tougher by its mission statement's promise. For example, when the company took over a power plant in Panama that employed 300 people, and knew 100 could operate it just as efficiently, it offered laid-off workers not only a generous severance package, but loans to help them start up new businesses. To date, this program has inspired sixty-seven entrepreneurial start-ups.

More importantly, every year AES issues a "principles survey," in which it asks employees to state how they are doing on their four goals — which are "to act with integrity, to be fair, to have fun, and to be socially responsible." In 1999, the survey elicited 28,000 responses, and CEO Dennis Bakke promised he would read each and every one personally.

When a *Fortune* magazine reporter worked for a week at a Container Store outlet to determine how the company managed to hit No. 1 on the *Fortune* 100 list in January 2000, and to stay on the list for six consecutive years, he was told by a manager that when a customer comes in for one item, "You're cheating the customer if you're not offering them the opportunity to buy more."

"Hmmm," reflected the reporter in his follow-up article: "In other words, selling is good for the customer." Or, the company's six esoteric principles have been driven home so well, that they "allow you to be a pushy salesperson but feel as if you're a public servant — a useful sensation for a company that doesn't offer sales commissions." Argue that this organization's principles are strange and the employees suckers if you like, but remember, this was a relatively small company that hit No. 1 on the Fortune 100. Nor would customers return if they felt ill-served. This outfit is an example of a company that has learned to help employees make the connection between company principles and daily work, and "ennobled" them as a proud team.

Our favorite story of how a company gets its noble message across involves the Body Shop, which used to broadcast inspirational messages such as the following to its delivery trucks as they went about their business: "If you think you're too small to make a difference, you've never been in bed with a mosquito," and "You think education's expensive? Try ignorance."

the new corporate citizen

"Until recently, the idea that a company should take on the additional responsibility of social and environmental degradation was anathema," acknowledges Paul Hawken, visionary businessman and author of *The Natural Step for Business*, which outlines a program that helps corporations adopt measures for sustainable development. And yet, not only is payback possible, it can also be twofold: financial and in the form of a fired-up workforce.

The four companies profiled in *The Natural Step for Business* all over-hauled operations to be more environmentally sensitive and reported significant cost savings as a result of their initiatives. One company realized $75 million in savings in the first four years; another saved an estimated $500,000 to $750,000 in replacement costs for just one technical change, and $525,000 per year in raw material costs. IKEA North America expected annual savings of more than $500,000 from just one program. But as the author points out, "These cost savings are only part of the story. As employees become engaged in sustainability efforts, they become more conscientious, creative, aware and interested in how they use resources and thereby contribute to reducing the aggregate impact of the company on the environment. This creates leaner production and operations and often leads to innovations that improve both operational and environmental performance."

Another organization promoting sustainable development on the part of businesses is the Coalition for Environmentally Responsible Economies (www.ceres.org), representing more than eighty businesses, nonprofits, and public agencies. Mission Statement: "Our mission is to move businesses, capital, and markets to advance lasting prosperity by valuing the health of the planet and its people."

Two hundred years ago in Great Britain, George III's chancellor, Baron Turlow, asked, "How can you expect a corporation to have a conscience, when it has no soul to be damned and no body to be kicked?" But today, corporations without a soul and conscience risk being damned by the press and kicked by talent that has moved on to the competition.

David Packard, co-founder and inspiration of Hewlett-Packard, said, "I think people assume, wrongly, that a company exists solely to make money. Money is an important part of a company's existence, if the company is any good. But a result is not a cause. We have to go deeper and find the real reason for our being. As we investigate this, we inevitably come to the conclusion that a group of people get together and exist as an institution that we call a company, so that they are able to accomplish something collectively that they could not accomplish separately — they make a contribution to society, a phrase which sounds trite but is fundamental."

When Anita Roddick was CEO of the Body Shop, she was renowned for advocating business as a powerful force for positive social change. In *Spirituality and Service*, she says corporations were invented to serve people and society, and business managers therefore have a moral obligation to designate a higher purpose and demonstrate good corporate citizenship.

The list of leaders who understand this is growing — and those leaders are at the head of the pack. Take Michael Dell, chairman of Dell Computer Corp. in Round Rock, Texas, who has said, "The best advice I have about giving back is this: Do it. If you're leading a company, or if you're in a management position of some stature or power, it's just as important to serve as a role model as it is for you to help a specific cause."

The impact of a noble cause on employee loyalty is often subtle but nonetheless profound. Fairmont Hotels & Resorts, formerly Canadian Pacific Hotels, has had an extensive recycling program on its premises for some time. We vividly recall a maid in one of their hotels telling us how much extra time it took her to sort the recycling property. "But," she added proudly, "doing the recycling is the most important part of my job and makes me feel like I did something important in my day." Winning over today's workforce — or, better put, serving them — can happen in any of thousands of ways, many all too invisible to executives.

Corporations that attempt to be good corporate citizens may win better and more engaged employees, but they'll never be free of the trail of cynics who accuse them of making fraudulent, contradictory, or self-serving claims. When John's first book, *Awakening Corporate Soul*, was published, he received a scathing e-mail from one critic who said, "Now even the spiritual traditions have been called upon to support the corporations' lies."

While detractors inevitably help keep the game honest, we think many of them are missing a few points. First, why remove the incentive to try? Second, if noble initiatives make a company a more fulfilling place to work, and if the movement toward corporate citizenship is often inspired by and for the rank and file, who's hurting whom by joining an anti-corporate crusade? The reality is that we have experienced firsthand an awakening amongst the rank and file, one increasingly shared by executives. We celebrate this cause.

altruism on company time

If mission statements set the stage, communication rallies the crowd, and organizational acts of corporate citizenship counter skepticism, then offering employees the chance to practice altruism during work time is the most powerful medium for driving home the message that a company cares about more than profits. The effect can be surprisingly powerful.

Employees who were previously focused entirely on work discover new emotions, an unexpected release of tension, a flood of warmth or joy that spills over to co-workers and managers. Work-sponsored volunteerism can be especially beneficial to young, self-absorbed workers, helping to mature their outlook on the world. Business-culture psychotherapist Francis Hope writes, "People's maturity and happiness ultimately depends on their concern for others and a living sense of connection to their environment." As discussed in Chapter Four, the simple act of volunteering can begin to redistribute an individual's energy more holistically, which makes for a healthier, more alert and focused worker.

A *USA Today* survey found that eight out of ten workers would be more likely to volunteer if their companies recognized their volunteer work by providing time off to do it, and yet only fourteen percent have that time off.

While it's difficult to measure the payback on this increasingly popular form of noble cause, the fact that many of the Fortune 100 companies have installed such programs, and that employees flock to those companies and their charitable programs, implies much. At TDIndustries, employees are encouraged to volunteer and their work schedules are adjusted accordingly.

IBM put a new corporate initiative called "on demand community" in place in 2004. Employees are encouraged to volunteer their technological expertise in their communities while IBM supports their efforts with cash and equipment donations. The reasoning is that employees are skilled, talented people who have a lot to offer schools and not-for-profit agencies in their communities.[23]

---

[23] Source: Friday February 27, 2004 Roderick Benns, Axiom News Source. http://www.axiomnews.ca/2004/February/feb27.htm

Toronto management consultants Bain & Co., concerned by the fierce competition for hiring newly minted MBAs, recently brainstormed a way to grab students' attention, distinguish the company as supporting noble causes, *and* get a close-up view of participants' leadership skills all at once. The company invites new recruits to volunteer anywhere in the world with Habitat for Humanity (the organization dedicated to building affordable housing for poor people worldwide) for two weeks before they start their full-time posts, and covers expenses. Students reportedly get excited about it.

General Mills also likes to demonstrate its social conscience in a way that directly involves employees by encouraging them to get involved. "We believe we have a responsibility to reach out to others, to take what we know, and do what we can to make a difference," says Stephen W. Sanger, chairman and CEO of the Minneapolis-based company. In 2004 alone, the company and its General Mills Foundation contributed more than $86 million in cash and in-kind donations to fight hunger, strengthen youth nutrition and fitness, and support schools and social services. It also strives to make the neighborhoods in which it operates safer. For example, the Foundation initiated a monthly meeting of local residents, businesspeople, and public officials in a troubled north Minneapolis neighborhood and committed $3 million to new housing. This initiative has led to a thirty percent reduction in crime in the area. Seventy percent of General Mills' employees and a large number of its retirees are involved in volunteer activities, but is that a contributing factor to the company placing on *Industry Week*'s best managed companies list?

Industry Week itself responds with a definitive *yes*. "All of the 100 Best-Managed Companies… have qualities beyond just financial performance that put them among the elite. Some work to curb child abuse or domestic violence. Others go the extra mile to provide the best benefits packages for employees or to provide an environment conducive to balancing work and family issues. Some have a strong orientation to recycling materials and waste and keeping the environment clean… They understand that their success is tied to their people and their willingness to be responsible corporate citizens."

It's important to remember that workers respond best to hands-on efforts. Giving to the United Way is nice, but employee loyalty grows from the touch and feel of work-associated volunteering. When a friend of ours took over the management of a retail outlet in Vancouver, Canada, she identified her first challenges as low morale and poor sales. She could have kicked off with a motivational talk about increasing sales. Instead, she involved her young staff in sponsoring a local AIDS march; they raised money from customers and helped promote the walk. Within a month, the employees were super-motivated, and guess what? Sales started going up and absenteeism went down. It wasn't the donations that had built team spirit and commitment, but the warm

THE SERVICE PROVIDER DDC Inc. has teamed up with Medela, a supplier of breast pumps and breast-feeding accessories, to offer a new lactation program called M@W (Mothers at Work). M@W offers prenatal training, twenty-four hour counselling services of a certified lactation consultant, and equipment and support for employers who are introducing the lactation program. The program also provides a guide for managers that explains the benefits of workplace lactation programs and the manager's critical role in the mother's return to work. The program has proven positive for both employee retention and productivity.

feelings the employees had gained and had come to associate with their workplace.

Need a few more examples? How about Whole Goods Market in Austin, Texas, which offers up to twenty hours' annual paid time off for community service? Or Timberland, the boot maker, whose employees get forty hours of paid time each year to do volunteer work and after three years' service are eligible to apply for up to a six-month sabbatical at a non-profit of their choice. Timberland also contributes nearly $1 million annually in cash and product to City Year, an urban Peace Corps active in fourteen US cities.

why people are drawn to value-driven companies

Employees are attracted to businesses where corporate values are strong and respected. Put another way, highly sought-after workers wither within — or won't even join — a company without a noble cause. But why, skeptics wonder, do employees suddenly want work to have a higher meaning? What makes them think they should be able to practice altruism on work time? Why should companies suddenly have to "go noble" to retain prized workers?

Like so many of the shifts we outline, this one has historic roots, and there are observers who have seen it coming for some time. Essentially, the search for a noble cause at work is a belated and bottled-up reaction to what the Industrial Age did to workers. The re-engineering of the 1980s uncorked that resentment, and more recent worker empowerment has given full-throated volume to its whisper.

Michael Hammer, author of *Beyond Reengineering*, explains: "The Industrial Age forced us to strike a Faustian bargain. In return for higher wages and an improved standard of living, we largely sacrificed the benefits to the spirit that pre-industrial work provided. How could it be otherwise? By focusing on isolated and atomistic tasks, by disconnecting people from the end products and customers of their labours, modern work squeezed all sense of transcendent value out of people's lives. It is difficult to take spiritual nourishment from processing a piece of paper or tightening bolts day in and day out. Without a sense of where your product goes or why you are making it, it is hard for your work to mean anything. It is empty, a mechanical ritual performed for transitory reasons."

If modern-day video clips of gushing customers, carefully crafted corporate party speeches, smoothly polished mission statements, and newly triggered avalanches of corporate altruism provide workers with a sense of where the product goes and why they are making it, of course retention and engagement will soar. Certainly, companies looking to build a world-class employee base are beginning to "buy in" to this theory. If workers lost pieces of their soul during the Industrial Age and have only just decided that material plenty was not a sufficient trade — if they are trying to recoup their loss just as work has all but bumped off family and "soul time," make way. It's yield or get run over. Or, as the saying goes, never wound a tiger.

Are workers seeking to grow back some of their soul on work time (either because they blame work time for taking it away, or because there isn't a lot of other time)? If so, understand that the three parts of one's soul, according to Charles Handy, are a sense of making a difference, a feeling of responsibility for others, and the satisfaction of living a life that is true to one's real values. Not at all an impossible slate for employers to fill, as this book demonstrates.

During a visit to the offices of Synovus Financial, the bank and credit card processor in Columbus, Georgia (No. 50 on Fortune's Best list in 2005), fiercely loyal front-line employees told John they hope their children will work there. Indeed, lifetime, multi-generational family employment is alive and well at this firm, as is in-house talk about "doing the right thing." This phrase may be part of the company directive, but unlike other organizations with noble-sounding mantras, Synovus and its subsidiaries demand a daily focus on making those words real. One employee told John how she turned down a project that a client requested, explaining to the customer that it was more than he needed. Following the company directive to "do the right thing," this employee knew she would not suffer negative repercussions for turning away the work. Undoubtedly, the sense that her company walks its talk is a cornerstone of her loyalty and motivation, while her honesty significantly raised the client's long-term loyalty to the company.

As the Synovus story attests, the three factors common to *Fortune* magazine's 100 Best Companies, which may contribute to good morale of employees, are these: visionary leadership, a positive work environment, and a desirable mission or purpose. These are values that a company must build slowly and consistently from the roots up, not assets that can be custom-ordered from a consultant and plugged in tomorrow.

Profile
Stephen Smith, Former CEO
WESTJET
Calgary, AB

"Anyone can go out and buy a 747, charge the same fares, serve pretzels, and fly," quipped Stephen Smith when he was CEO at Westjet, the western Canadian upstart with a reputation as a great place to work. "What's going to differentiate us from any other airline? The only thing is people: customer service."

And how does WestJet ensure leading-edge customer service? Not through complicated training, because all staff have flown somewhere before, explains Smith with his trademark sense of humor: "They can look in a mirror and ask what guests want, and get straight answers."

No, WestJet's edge is having neither employees nor management-only partners. "We don't believe in the word 'management.' We don't supervise or manage people here; we lead. And we don't have employees; we have people. We don't have human resources; we have a people department. Our emotional contract with people is to treat them with respect, allow them to have input into the company, and allow them to self-actualize within their jobs."

WestJet conducts an annual salary survey and pays its people ninety-five percent of the industry's median wage. In lieu of the other five percent, it offers a profit-sharing program paid out every six to seven months, which amounted to roughly thirty percent of workers' total salaries — or $7.4 million — in 1999. Why a profit-sharing program?

"This allows us not to have supervisors, because we know the decisions people are making are coming from the same place where [our CEO] would make them," says Smith. "They're motivated to make the right decisions. We want employees to make the decisions that owners would make, and the best way to do that is to make them owners. They think like shareholders — completely differently than people coming for a paycheck."

Of course, when a company is growing at WestJet's current pace — hiring hundreds of people per year — getting the right people to start with is critical. Smith says he ensured this by showing applicants the company's mission statement: "To enrich the lives of everyone in WestJet's world, by providing safe, friendly, and affordable air travel."

"I say, 'We have a mission statement. If its words match what you feel, stay with us. If they don't, don't feel badly; it's not a matter of right or wrong.' Unlike at other companies I've worked at, our mission statement's words actually mean a lot. We refer to them all the time. And we try to work with our people so that they believe there is something beyond what they're contributing, that they're part of the team, that the company needs them — the team, the community, our guests need them. We're not trying to say that by working at WestJet, you're going to solve the hunger problems of the world, but there's a whole other gestalt of reasons that your expertise is needed at our company: not letting people down. There are people who need us to get them to children's events, weddings, and so on."

Smith smiles. "In a customer service business — and to me every company is a customer service business — if you don't support people to make their job easier, you're never going to succeed in the long-term."

assessing your company for noble cause

The statements below allow for an initial assessment of how your organization, division, and/or department is doing at responding to the employee search for work as noble cause. The assessment is meant to guide your thinking, not to provide a definitive quantitative assessment of your progress. For each question below, answer how true the statement is of your work environment using the scale provided:

_____ Our company has a statement that describes the deeper meaning of our product or service — for instance, making people happy, making people feel at home, preserving and improving human life (If your answer is "Yes, but it rarely gets talked about," assign one point; if your company's statement is alive, talked about and considered "real," tally three points).

_____ Employees are involved in community service or volunteerism on behalf of the company (one point if the company provides opportunities; two if they're actively encouraged or trained to do so; three if they can do so on company time with pay).

_____ Our company has a set of values that are meant to inspire people to higher ethics and doing the right thing (one point if you have it but it rarely gets talked about; three points if you have methods for ensuring that employees stay focused on those values; lose two points if you have such a statement but employees joke about how much you don't live them).

_____ Our company has a reputation in the community for its commitment to the larger community (one point).

_____ At large company meetings, results are often presented in terms of how our services have made an impact on people, not just profits (one point if done at all, three points if there is a stronger focus on service than profits).

_____ TOTAL SCORE:

5 or under: Take a full week's management retreat for brainstorming policies that address these concerns.

6-9: You're beginning to look responsive.

10-11: You are above average in meeting today's workers' needs, but there is still room for improvement.

12-13: You are an inspiring example, and probably have the best workers and a strong bottom line to show for it. E-mail us:info@theizzogroup.com.

CHAPTER SIX

the expectation of growth and development

"Learning organizations are able to respond to a rapidly changing environment because they embrace change as the norm."
– THE NATURAL STEP FOR BUSINESS

Short of any sense of job security, restless by nature, and living in the era of personal growth, today's workers seek both personal and professional nourishment. Career-building skills are the new security, and companies that fail to provide them lose out, especially given that the desire to leave the corporate hearth for an entrepreneurial venture has never been so strong. But as any observer can attest, the line between "personal" and "professional" development is fading in acknowledgement that skills such as leadership draw from a well so deep that more than one source feeds it.

In Japan, companies have traditionally recognized the need for ongoing education and have underwritten it. Until recently, fewer employers in the West have wanted to risk training and re-training employees who might disappear tomorrow. And yet, more and more leaders are looking beyond the risk that their investment may "walk," and realizing that not investing in workers will influence them to walk faster.

How important is it to support career development? In a recent survey, new MBAs put "developing a career" first on their list of nine priorities. Meanwhile, a Gallup study on employee engagement found that opportunities to learn and grow are tightly linked with commitment, in sharp contrast with a 1968 study, which indicated that few employees associated these two.

More and more companies are advertising their learning labs in recruitment materials, mentoring has come back into favor, it's trendy to build corporate campuses for "continual learning," and human resources staff are finding themselves charged with helping employees of all ranks in career planning.

It is not that the desire to learn and grow is new, but rather that employees are now expecting employers to make their learning and growth a top priority, and employers are willing to go along with this in hopes of keeping turnover low. Three unrelated but powerful phenomena are fuelling employees' expectation of constant growth and development. First, job insecurity has made it necessary for them to become mercenary about their own skill development. Employability rather than employment is now the contract between worker and employer. That is, although companies can no longer guarantee jobs, they can guarantee skill development that will keep workers employable.

Second, younger workers — born and bred in the sound-byte era, joystick in one hand and channel surfer in the other — get bored more easily than their older counterparts. They grew up in a rapidly changing technological world where new games and toys were a constant, and they learned to press a button whenever they felt jaded. In fact, members of the Net generation get itchy feet and frequently scout around for new job opportunities. It's hardly surprising, then, that the two most successful retention strategies are offering exciting work and ensuring the chance to work on leading-edge technology. When it comes to attracting, engaging, and keeping talent, perhaps the new take on the decades-old bumper sticker is, "He who offers the most toys and training, wins."

The third fuel for this shift is the personal growth movement, which has now adopted the workplace as a new forum. This movement, exemplified by rows and rows of bookstore self-help bestsellers, has accelerated exponentially, especially among baby boomers, who buy more self-help books per person than any other generation.

If job insecurity, boredom, and the personal growth movement are driving this fourth shift in worker attitudes, successful employers are meeting the challenge with three offers: the opportunity to learn new skills, assistance with career management, and opportunities for discovering oneself at work.

learning new skills

Back in 1996, in *Boom, Bust & Echo*, David K. Foot described four kinds of career paths and predicted that the two fastest-growing of these would require a serious investment in employee training:

1. **Linear career path:** characterized by upward mobility, associated with tall corporate pyramids, and offering a reward system based on steady promotion up a career ladder.

2. **Steady-state career path**: characterized by one occupation for a lifetime (say, professor or doctor); the reward system based on autonomy, fringe benefits, and tenure.

3. **Spiral career path:** characterized by lateral moves mixed with promotions (each lateral move involving a change of occupation), some within the same organization and some between different organizations. Associated with a squat pyramid and involving a reward system based less on promotions than on the satisfaction employees get from mastering new challenges through re-education and lifelong learning.

4. **Transitory career path:** in which the worker adopts whatever occupation is necessary to get a job — from management consultant to bicycle courier.

Have you guessed yet which two were tipped as the career paths of the future? They are spiral and transitory, both a comfortable fit with flattened hierarchies — and both requiring such constant states of learning that the company might as well hook up an intravenous tube between employees and local institutions that offer continuing education.

"A lateral organization needs to know people's job preferences, help them plan their career paths, and give them the training they need.... Companies that invest in worker training are more profitable than those that don't," declares Foot.

Many argue that employability is the new deal in employer-employee relations. John Rayson, the CEO and Executive Vice-Chairman of MDS

Metro in Vancouver, Canada, told us, "I may not be able to offer people a guarantee of employment anymore, but I can guarantee that while they are here, they will always be learning new skills that will help them stay employed here or elsewhere."

Training accomplishes several things, all of which add up to higher retention:

- It broadcasts confidence in the employee ("We're willing to invest in you because you're worth it, and we hope you'll stay for a while).

- It raises the value of that worker to the organization (hopefully translating directly to profits).

- It acknowledges employees' need to keep skills marketable and to continually challenge themselves.

- It counters boredom.

Creating opportunities for people to try new skills and tasks also protects against young workers' nightmare: Boredom is death! If performing repetitive tasks dehumanized workers in the Industrial Age, imagine how well mindless work goes down today, given a highly educated workforce raised to prize personal freedom. Responding to the desire for constant professional growth means creating opportunities for people to learn and contribute outside the confines of their present jobs. AES is a global power company that aims to be socially responsible and the employer of choice. Its mission to be a place where "people can maximize their gifts and skills" is exemplified in one of its coal mine operations, where miners serve on a rotating basis as members of a task group that manages the portfolio of their pension fund investments.

A diversity of job assignments may keep employees in place, but this retention strategy must be matched with training that offers skills prized on the current job market, as well. Even in the warmth of a hot economy, one in five employees worries about losing his or her job. As we mentioned in Chapter Two, two in five say their résumé is always up-to-date, and six in ten have taken a course in the past year to upgrade their skills or develop new ones. Four out of five are confident that they have the skills to find a comparable position if they are laid off. The studies behind these statistics underscore the fact that employees today are competitive to an almost mercenary degree.

Need some evidence?

- A recent national survey on job training concluded that employer-sponsored training attracts recruits and contributes significantly to retention. It also indicated that employees particularly want high-quality training in technology, communications, and management skills.

- A *ComputerWorld* survey found that seventy-nine percent of respondents remained with their employers because of training opportunities.

- A Gallup poll named the lack of opportunities to learn and grow as one of the top three reasons for employee *dissatisfaction*.

- The authors of *Chips & Pop: Decoding the Nexus Generation* say that at least every three months, Netters reflect on their satisfaction with their current position according to five key factors: compensation and benefits; opportunities for mobility, learning, and skills development; regularity of feedback; peer and management support; and the meaningfulness of work. The same authors quote Canada Information Office research showing that one in four members of this generation strongly agrees with the statement, "My skills and knowledge could grow obsolete in five years."

- A survey of workplace benefits valued by Netters placed paid training as No. 3 on the most desirable list, after basic dental/medical benefits and extended leaves, and above flexible work hours, up to date technology, and casual dress.

"Train to retain" has become a common mantra for good reason, and that training must be available right from the start. A common question from job candidates these days is what kind of ongoing training the employer will offer, and the younger the candidate, the more influential the response will be on job selection.

As a twenty-eight-year-old bank employee told us, "Things have changed in the corporate world; there simply aren't as many promotion opportunities as there once were. So, growing and learning is the replacement. I want to be learning new things constantly and becoming more valuable."

If great training serves as an inducement to young talent, it's increasingly essential for retaining boomers who may be wavering between early retirement and staying on. Seventy percent of companies believe that phased retirement may be the solution to the growing labor shortage, and three out of four

> **THE 2004** Fortune "Special Report on 100 Best Comanies to Work for" noted that: "Overall, today's lesson is that perks are nice, but employees are looking for something more basic. They want to be told the truth, for one thing, especially if the news is bad. They also want, as corny as it sounds, to feel they make a difference and to be given a chance to grow."

older workers prefer to reduce hours gradually. But how many boomers slipping away early are feeling unnecessarily insecure due to a lack of training in the latest technology? It's been suggested that workers over 55 receive, on average, less than half the amount of training than their younger employees. While this may once have seemed reasonable, perhaps it is time to reconsider such policies in light of the coming labor shortage.

In 2002, fourteen percent of the workforce was age fifty-five and over. By 2012, nineteen percent will be at least fifty-five — an increase of more than ten million.[24]

According to the American Association of Retired Persons fourth annual survey of best employers for workers over fifty, thirty-five U.S. employers made the grade in 2004, up from twenty-five in 2003. AARP judged applicants based on four major criteria: recruitment of older workers, continued opportunities and training, benefits, and retiree relations.[25]

It is difficult to overemphasize how effective training is as a retention tool for all age groups. A Watson Wyatt survey of employers revealed that training was their No. 1 tool of choice for employee attraction and retention. Ninety percent of employers responding said they used training and development to encourage applicants, and ninety-four percent used training to retain workers (flextime and compensation were the second and third choices for successful recruiting and retention). And yet, in another Watson Wyatt survey, respondents stressed that the critical factor was not training itself, but "the degree to which training is integrated into company culture and strategy." Companies that performed best had adopted a

[24] Labor force projections to 2012: The Graying of the US Workforce," Monthly Labor Review, February 2004

[25] Source: Kristen Gerencher, CBS MarketWatch, Indianapolis Star
Sponsoring Organization: American Association of Retired Persons
Date: September 2, 2004

continuous learning culture using informal methods such as mentoring and job sharing. In fact, seventy-five percent of higher-performing companies had linked training programs with strategic goals, compared with only sixty-seven percent of other organizations. This point is essential to comprehend: Meeting the development expectation is not simply about classes, but involves a philosophy that providing opportunities for learning is paramount.

Globalization has upped the ante for systems to embrace change, and has made constant training a requirement for organizational success.

Fortunately, training existing workers is getting cheaper and less disruptive by the minute, thanks to technological advances and the potential of distance education. In fact, job-related training really took off when technology made it more cost-effective. Technology-delivered training — which can be integrated into a workday, thus both reducing costs and making the training more relevant — is being adopted extensively.

Getting a head start on this trend, Days Inn of America has introduced Web based training via the corporate intranet to help stem an industry-standard 120 percent annual turnover. It's the company's way of coping with the limitations of eleven trainers serving 18,000 workers at 1,800 sites around the world. Compared with traditional classroom training, this technique has produced a fifty percent savings in time and cost, although it's difficult to factor in up-front costs of computer upgrades and content design.

Still, distance education will never entirely replace classroom settings. Critics note that intranets are not suitable for teaching "soft skills" such as listening and coaching, and programs always need modification to maximize effectiveness. Recognizing these issues, Days Inn has arranged for instructor-led components to constitute eighty percent of their Web training program.

Other companies have acknowledged the need for continual training by establishing on-site centers, which utilize current employees and managers as teachers. Still others are partnering with suppliers, customers, and institutions of higher learning. What some of these programs miss are courses in languages other than English, or in a manner that acknowledges attendees' lack of fluency. Where once it was relatively easy to train non-English-speaking employees to operate a machine or provide a service, today the tools they need to cope in the workplace are more complex — for instance, identifying safety procedures or supporting cross-functional teams. To quickly bring a diverse workforce up to world-class levels of productivity, it's vital to design the training around the task, not the language, keeping in mind that the desired outcome is productivity, not fluency.

training is a philosophy, not a class

To meet employees' expectation for learning, employers must focus not simply on providing opportunities, but on communicating that company's commitment and intention to develop people. New employees often come to the workplace with unrealistic expectations. A software client of John's found that promises of exciting projects and the chance to work on leading-edge technology right away had wooed many of its new recruits. Once on the job, the new hires discovered that initial projects used old technology. After noting these new employees' frustration, the company initiated conversations that helped the recruits modify their expectations and put a more realistic time frame on moving to the kind of work that they coveted. These conversations alone — all of which emphasized the company's intention of providing opportunities for growth — helped cut turnover by thirty percent.

A learning philosophy involves putting employees at the center of their own learning, thus meeting two expectations at once: partnership and growth. One mid-sized insurance company gives every employee a career development account amounting to 2.5 percent of their annual salary. Employees are allowed to accumulate funds in this account for up to three years and can use it at their own discretion for career-related courses, conferences (including travel), association dues, and PC hardware for home use. The clear message: "You're responsible for your own career development, but we support you in your endeavors."

Responding to this shift may require your organization to rethink its philosophy at a very deep level. For example, Mercer Human Resources Consulting of Vancouver, Canada, a leading consulting firm, realized that many of its consultants are ambitious people with a need to try new things. So the company instituted an "externship" program, whereby employees could take a full-time job at another company for up to one year, with no obligation to return. Since implementing this program in November 1999, Mercer has enjoyed a soaring number of applicants. Why would Mercer Management try such a counterintuitive idea-losing people to keep them? Because, like many consulting firms, the company was losing people to start-ups and this was a way to give them a chance to try new things, spread the word about "Mercer flexibility," and feel welcomed back to the fold if they rejoined. Presumably, those who return are that much more experienced and committed.

This is the kind of radical focus on employee growth and development that will ultimately win today's worker. As the vice-president of human resources at Mercer Management says, "We are learning how to hold on with open arms. You have to hope you have built something attractive enough that your people will want to return and stay. If they don't, you were going to lose them anyway!"

- At TDIndustries in Texas, entry-level employees are given unlimited training and development. Former CEO Jack Lowe says, "Five years ago, we had a plumber who wanted to get his bachelor's degree. We paid for it. Then he wanted his Masters, and now he has his Ph.D., all paid for by TD. Mind you, there are not too many of those, but we support them. We expect a minimum of thirty-two hours per year of classroom time." Ranked No. 7 on Fortune's Best Places to Work in 2004, the firm also offers 100 percent tuition and all textbooks.

- Benefits at Johnson & Johnson of New Brunswick, New Jersey, include 100 percent tuition reimbursement for employees who pursue college course to advance their careers.

- Alston & Bird, one of the few law firms to appear on Fortune's "100 Best Companies to Work for in America," offers CollegeBound*fund*, a tax-advantaged college savings program.

helping people manage their careers

Flatten a pyramid, shrink a ladder, bust up a hierarchy, and what are you left with? A nimble system based on merit, perhaps, but one with fewer opportunities for advancement. Many a young worker will say that's okay because they don't buy into "advancement" so much as constant challenge and stimulation, anyway. Today's workers may understand the shrinking vertical ladder, but they want and expect plentiful opportunities for lateral moves that come with raises and a never-ending stream of stimulating projects.

Meeting this need for lateral career moves requires organizations to be very intentional about how people make moves within the organization. In conducting employee-retention assessments for companies, John frequently hears about the difficulty of changing assignments within companies. A software consultant at one large firm told him, "It's easier to quit around here and apply to another division as an unemployed person than to get transferred." Companies that want to retain talent must make it easier for employees to change projects or roles, like Electronic Arts, which holds internal job fairs every year. Wiser still are the companies that proactively help people manage their careers, like American Express, which created workshops for its call-center staff to help them identify what they like to do, how that matched their present job, and how to plan for their future growth.

Now that the crumpled career ladder makes an employee's next step unclear, career management becomes critically important. Career moves — especially lateral ones — tend to be highly personal and stressful decisions. Some individuals have strong navigational instincts, but most workers appreciate direction. Hence, the term "career sculpting," and the rising tide of in-house or on-retainer career counselors and corporate mentoring programs.

SAS, the largest privately held software company in the world, has a turnover rate of less than five percent (compared with the industry average of twenty-five percent). This is surely in part because the company has told employees that they can expect to have three or four careers in their lifetime, and it hopes these will all be at SAS.

Once the bastion of job security and long-term employment, utilities are also being forced to acknowledge the need for more lateral career moves. In the old days, technicians would learn a trade (for example, high-wire splicing) and stay in it for a lifetime. Now, when young employees master a trade, they ask their supervisor what the next step is. That is, as soon as they experience a level of mastery, they want more challenge. Part of this trend is a desire to expand skills, but much of it is that generational tendency to get bored quickly. Either way, older supervisors with an eye on retention are well-advised to respond to this new and growing reality in ways that help the company — as in proactively implementing opportunities for change, challenge, and career mentoring.

The benefits of such an action plan go three ways: Employees motivated by new challenges are more productive, the company benefits from longer-term and cross-trained employees, and workers tapped to act as mentors develop their leadership skills and experience new energy and commitment as a result of making a difference in someone else's life.

"People who move laterally to another department seldom carry any occupational burdens or past obligations with them. All of a sudden, new ideas come rushing to the surface," says David K. Foot in *Boom, Bust & Echo*.

Because professional development keeps them marketable, employees don't want things left to chance when it comes to learning. And because constantly acquired new skills and challenges have replaced promotions as a carrot stick, workers need feedback and guidance more than at any other point in history. A Royal Bank of Canada study of worker attitudes commissioned in 2000 concluded that "Canadian employees rate their workplace high in terms of fairness, flexibility, and vacation allowance, but are significantly less pleased with communication, feedback, rewards, and opportunity for advancement." Sadly, fewer than four in ten were satisfied with the degree of recognition they receive at work.

When surveyed about factors that negatively affect the workplace mood, fifty-two percent of executives and thirty percent of employees said a lack of open, honest communication takes a heavy toll on morale.[26]

---

[26] Source: Urvaksh Karkaria, Journal Gazette [Indiana], OfficeTeam, July 27, 2004

A Gallup study found that two of the top twelve predictors for employee engagement relate to learning and development: "Highly engaged" employees reported that someone in the company had spoken to them about their progress within the past six months, and they felt they'd had the opportunity to learn and grow within the past year. How would your employees answer those questions? How often do you sit down with people and talk about their progress, where they desire to go next, and what your plans are for them? If the answer is once per year or less, consider yourself vulnerable to unnecessarily high turnover.

A well-worn maxim in business is, "What gets measured gets done." In many organizations, managers and supervisors are not held accountable for developing their people. To improve in this area, organizations might begin measuring the extent to which employees feel their careers and development are being managed by supervisors and to make high scores on those measures a key part of managers' evaluations.

One facet of professional growth we've only touched upon so far is *job sculpting*, the art of matching people to jobs that embrace their life interests and values, of forging a customized career path. Once fitting person to job was seen as the responsibility of the employee, but today it stands as one of the newest and most effective methods for drawing and retaining skilled workers. During a recruiting session, one employer — a Wall Street firm — snatched numerous recruits from competitors simply by emphasizing its commitment to their career development. Students confirmed this in a follow-up session, citing the firm's promises to help them manage their careers as key in their decision to join up.

"Make no mistake: job sculpting is challenging; it requires managers to play both detective and psychologist," notes The Harvard Business Review.[27]

---

[27] The Harvard Business Review September/October 1999 issue.

Of course, managers in a position to help employees with career decisions could use some specialized training for the job. But the real skill is caring enough to listen to the employee's aspirations. And as we've mentioned, managers most inclined to take on this role have been encouraged to do so by forward-thinking organizations. Unfortunately, many managers and project leaders fail to consider career development as one of their responsibilities.

One fast-growing trend is peer mentoring, which involves like-minded individuals exchanging ideas, perspectives, and experiences through a deep level of exchange to gain new insight and clarity into the business, personal issues, and opportunities they face. Peer mentoring was developed around 1975, and many business people find it works better than other models because of the definitive shift in society away from authoritarianism. The concept of an older know-it-all matched with a sponge-like protégé doesn't apply in peer mentoring. Participants believe they can learn much from their peers, especially because it is likely these peers have battled the issues in question more recently than a semi-retired sage.

"We don't have a need to impress each other. We can be open and honest about what it is we're going through," explains one new convert.

Joan Mara, a Vancouver-based consultant who trains businesses around North America in this concept, helps entrepreneurs move from what they do best — help people solve problems — to what they do less well: come together in a peer context to discuss the most important issues they face, business or personal, with a high level of vulnerability.

"We create a non-judgmental, confidential, non-advice-giving environment that supports people to talk about what's keeping them up at night. These are often topics not easy to discuss even in a group of peers. The model moves away from trying to fix it, to one of storytelling and sharing from experience."

Mentoring is more personal and, perhaps in the end, more effective, than access to formal career counselors. And since up to seventy percent of employee knowledge is obtained informally on the job, it makes sense to assign workers problems that will expand their repertoire of skills and contacts (with or without the help of mentoring) than to over-rely on formal learning programs.

Beyond mentoring, formal training, and problem-solving opportunities lies the overseas assignment. When *Fortune* asked employees who had resisted headhunters' offers why they stayed put, one of the most-cited reasons was the opportunity for an interesting overseas assignment. Global-minded workers want the opportunity to explore new places on company time. Perhaps that is why HSBC Bank of Canada, known for its overseas assignments, is one of the favored employers in Western Canada.

discovering oneself at work

Until the twentieth century, work was secondary to other parts of life, and certainly not a celebrated portion. The Spanish word for work—*trabajo*—comes from a Latin root for "torture." The Irish word for job has its roots in the words for "a temporary assignment" and "excrement"! Yet, since World War II, the status of work has risen steadily to the point where some have called it the "new religion," the place where people look for growth and development. This is in sharp contrast to a 1960s study in Great Britain, which found that even among the most affluent workers, work was seen purely as a means to an end, and "job satisfaction" translated as plenty of salary to spend on after-work social opportunities, the primary focus of life.

Today, fifty-six percent say work is more a "sense of identity" than a way to "make a living" — a major about-face that has taken *less than a generation* to occur. In evident agreement with this, a 2002 survey by the National Opinion Research Center, Center for Survey Research and Analysis, University of Connecticut, found that sixty-eight percent of Americans would continue to work even if they didn't have to. Why? They wish to contribute, connect with others, and grow. In other words, work offers personal fulfillment.

Since a growing number of workers are *rebelling* against the work-as-self-identity trend, today's employers need to walk a fine line between catering to that need for personal fulfillment on work time, and respecting those who wish to deny or back away from it. Remember Mark Metin, the former manager of a mining software company described in Chapter Four? He promoted flextime, a social atmosphere, and in-house mentoring, while staying vigilant for burnout. He was known to send over-dedicated workers home to get some rest, knowing that burnout only triggers employee turnover. Metin clearly understands the contemporary employee's often-conflicting needs.

What *is* personal fulfillment on work time? Countless studies boil it down to three variables: ability (the skills, experience, and knowledge that make a worker feel competent); values or preferred rewards (money, challenge, prestige, power, or influence); and life interests. The first, ability, is the weakest predictor of job satisfaction; one can be good at a job and not enjoy it. Matching personal and corporate values is much more important for keeping retention high. But matching life and work interests is the most important of the three for long-term career satisfaction, according to *The Harvard Business Review*. An employer can impact such a match best through a mentoring or career-sculpting program.

There are other, subtler ways of linking work and personal fulfillment, however. Skillful trainers can help workers make the connection between workplace communication skills and communication in the family. The six hundred people who went through a "spirit-at-work" program John designed for a client in Calgary told the trainers that an unexpected and valuable benefit of the program was how it applied to their lives outside of work.

Among the most popular life-management skills are leadership, financial planning, retirement planning, stress management, creating a work/family balance, and time management. Leading-edge companies are beginning to offer personal coaching in these areas, especially for high-level executives. Clearly, the next step would be to roll that out to the rank and file. Offering personal growth opportunities to employees has had some surprising effects. Employers who thought that employee loyalty was dead have learned that this is the hot button for reviving it.

In 1997, Arlie Hochschild wrote a controversial book entitled *The Time Bind: When Work Becomes Home and Home Becomes Work*, in which she suggested that dual-income couples were working long hours to escape their hectic home lives. If we extend her hypothesis, it implies that the complexity of modern family life — dual incomes, unclear roles, blended families — have produced less satisfaction outside of work and put even more pressure on the workplace to produce personal development.

Along those lines, *Fast Company* once ran a cover story with the headline, "Betrayed by Work," which focused on people whose lives were being ruined by negative work situations. Expert after expert talked about how people were letting work become too central to their lives, and how their stories of missed promotions and abusive bosses were symbols of a work-addicted culture.

This trend has even extended into attitudes about retirement. Although once work was a way to pay the bills and retirement was something for which people longed-with dreams of cruises, golf courses, recreational vehicles, and gold watches — in 2004, the American Association of Retired Persons shed light on a major change in attitude. A staggering seventy-nine percent of boomers plan to work in their retirement years. Instead of retirement, they anticipate flexibility — the opportunity to work part-time or pursue a new career. The magnitude of this shift should not be underestimated. Today's workers see work in a whole new light, as a place where they find themselves and contribute. Although work often disappoints in this regard, the fact that people are coming to work today expecting to grow is beyond question.[28]

The impetus for personal development on work time is the assumption that it goes hand-in-hand with one's development as an employee, and promotes company loyalty. Does it work? Just look at the phenomenal popularity of Stephen Covey's *Seven Habits of Highly Effective People* to answer that. All over North America, employees are going through Covey courses on company time, and associating their growth as a person with the company for which they work.

promote growth or pay the price

Whether today's employee is a workaholic or is simply taking work too seriously, the point for today's employer is that work has become a part of who we are, not just what we do. We may say that family and personal life is our real lifeblood, and it may well be, but the first question hurled at strangers in North American social gatherings is, "What do you do?" Work has become more than a means to make ends meet; it has become an end in itself.

[28] Source: AARP 2004 Baby Boomers' Expectations for Retirement Survey).

Profile
Brian Scudamore, CEO
1-800-GOT-JUNK?

When he recently surmised that an employee was having personal problems, Brian Scudamore — CEO of North America's largest junk-collection firm, 1-800-GOT-JUNK — told her where to go: "Take the rest of the week off, and next week too if you need to. Nothing in this business can't wait."

He meant it kindly and sincerely, and she knew to take him up on it, because the 105-employee firm is known for recognizing and supporting its employees' lives, both personal and professional.

Founded in 1989, 1-800-GOT-JUNK? supports more than 100 franchisees around North America, and boasts annual sales of more than $7 million. 1-800-GOT-JUNK? is in its eighth straight year of 100 per cent revenue growth, and turnover is 1.4 percent despite the fact that hardly any employees are over the age of thirty-five. It also recently placed No. 1 on the 2004 list of Best Companies to Work For in British Columbia. What's it doing right?

"I've always believed it's all about people," says Scudamore, who founded the business at the ripe age of nineteen. "It starts with the personal side; the business side comes later."

To that end, he not only ploughs twenty-five percent of profits back to employees (typically lifting their paycheques by fifteen percent), but several months after each employee is hired, they're given twenty minutes to jot down their top 101 personal goals.

"If they don't have goals and passions, then we as a business don't thrive," Scudamore says.

Scudamore himself regularly emails employees to ask to see their list of personal goals. Then he spends time trying to help them achieve one. Once he noticed that an employee hoped to locate the back issue of a favorite comic book. After cruising eBay and finding it, he bought and presented it to that employee.

"His reaction was, 'Wow, you actually looked at my goals and made it happen!'" Scudamore recalls.

"I ask myself how we as a company can help people hit their goals. Some require money, some require time, and some require connections. I've seen everything from wanting a month's sabbatical, to wanting to fly a fighter jet, to wanting to grow a lemon tree and make lemonade from it. My own goal is meeting Oprah and giving her a hug."

Every once in a while, he'll stroll over to a high-performing, stressed-out employee and say, "Take a day off and go check something off on your goals list."

Peers and supervisors also pitch in to help someone achieve a goal. Once, after learning that an employee dreamed of playing golf on a prestigious course near his community, a supplier arranged it all.

"We become cheerleaders of sorts by looking through each others' lists," Scudamore says. "It reminds us that the personal side of our relationships is important. When one item is marked off, they're required to replace it with another."

The company's culture also involves coming up with surprise rewards. Last year, pleased with a new male employee's performance and knowing that his wife was expecting their second child,

Scudamore celebrated the employee's six-month tenure by handing him a gift certificate for taking his wife out to dinner.

Asked to describe 1-800-GOT-JUNK?'s culture, that employee, Jerry Gratton, says, "energetic, compassionate, and fun." He describes Scudamore as charismatic and inspirational, and notes that the CEO eschews a corner office and fancy cars, instead working at a nondescript workstation outside the boardroom.

Although Scudamore encourages employees to share their personal goals at work, the youthful CEO also remains alert for workaholics who fail to draw a sufficient line between work and personal lives. When he noticed an eleven p.m. tag on an email his second-in-command had sent to a manager, he called him to his desk the next day. "We don't have anything so important that it requires late-night emails. Others think they have to keep up with that," he lectured his righthand man.

Hand-in-hand with celebrating personal goals and relationships at work, Scudamore has formalized the notion of setting professional goals. Every day, the leadership team participates in an "adrenalin meeting," rising from their desks to summarize what they're working on, and relating their week's goals and concerns. As often as not, fellow leaders resolve their concerns on the spot.

Everyone in head office also gathers for a daily seven-minute "huddle," during which they share good news, metrics, and hurdles. And by afternoon, they're indulging in a third daily tradition: meeting with their immediate supervisor to check their progress on work goals. In fact, every employee and franchisee at 1-800-GOT-JUNK?, in league with their supervisor, is required to name their top five work goals each week, their top three goals for the quarter, and an ultimate annual goal.

"Goals create energy and passion," Scudamore says. Clearly, both CEO and employees at this successful firm have both in abundance.

Profile:
Brenda Reed, Director of Employment Services
Total System Services, a division of Synovus Financial
Columbus, Georgia

A recent employee survey made Total System Services (TSYS) sit up and take more notice of employee development. "We already had a great place to work, but we thought we could do a better job on career-pathing," says Brenda Reed, Director of Employment Services, who has watched turnover at the 5,000-employee company drop from 15.5 percent in 1998 to 11.4 percent in 2000. (It was at 9.4 percent last check.)

By career-pathing she means improving the company's performance evaluation system through a new process called "Right Steps," listening better to the career aspirations of "team members" (the TSYS word for employees) and offering them more feedback to help with career development and growth. Central to this aim was the parent company Synovus' implementation of three new initiatives: Foundations of Leadership, The Leadership Institute at Synovus and Right Steps, all administered through a restructured Center for People Development. And these are separate from two newer facilities, one for on-site day-care, and the other a new campus complete with library, fitness centre, dry cleaner, cafeteria, bank, travel agency, store, and rental car service — accommodating 2,500 employees.

Where once team members received feedback annually, they now sit down with their managers three times a year through the Right Steps process and review where they want to go, in addition to a year-end session. "That's a lot of constant feedback from the manager, which helps with career development and growth," says Reed.

All managers and team leaders are required to complete Foundations of Leadership, which teaches the company's "Leadership Expectations:" live the values, share the vision, make others successful and manage the business. Foundations of Leadership is a prerequisite for managers who might be chosen to attend the Leadership Institute, which "cultivates leaders who are going to take us into the next millennium," Reed says. Acceptance is competitive and selective, and applicants must be recommended. First there's a one-year "emerging leader" course for experienced, high-potential managers that includes two week-long retreats offsite focusing on individual development An eighteen-month course for more senior "executive leaders" includes three week-long offsite retreats for coaching on performance, and a two-year course for presidents, CEOs and other "organizational leaders" who attend four week-long offsite retreats with guest speakers and special attention on strategic planning and direction.

Besides these more formal programs, TSYS has introduced a "lunch and learn" program, allowing employees to attend free workshops during their lunch hours, on financial planning, purchasing a home, writing a will, and so on.

Why such emphasis on employee development and growth? "In my father's generation, people believed in taking a job and staying with that company until they died — forty years without missing a day's work," Reed says. "This generation sees that they have to grow in order to be successful and happy with what they're doing. And they have to feel they're growing personally as well as professionally. They're able to do a better job if they feel they're growing."

Employee surveys have also led TSYS to do away with traditional titles in a process the company calls "leadership titling," and introduce a "family education leave" program, which allows employees twenty hours' paid leave per year to participate in their children's school programs (to attend a play, help with a field trip or eat lunch with them). They're also entitled to leave for volunteer work, "because they want to be in a place through which they can contribute; they want to feel like they're giving back to the community, making a difference," Reed says.

"We're more like a family than co-workers," says Reed. "A lot of what we're doing is listening."

assessing your company for development

The statements below allow for an initial assessment of how your organization, division, and/or department is doing at responding to the employee search for personal growth and development. The assessment is meant to guide your thinking, not to provide a definitive quantitative assessment of your progress. For each question below, answer how true the statement is of your work environment using the scale provided:

_____ Managers in our company sit down with employees and discuss their development and the organization's plans for their growth at least every six months (If the answer is yes, informally, one point; if managers have been given guidelines for how or why to do so and are held accountable for doing it, tally three points).

_____ Employees are often given the opportunity to be part of task groups and assignments outside their core job responsibilities (one point if it happens informally; three if a formal program addressing this is in place).

_____ Our company has a career development program that helps people become more aware and responsible around their own career development (one point if the company offers such a program to most people; two points if it is considered a priority and the program is a success).

_____ Employees in our company have learning plans that identify what skills they want to learn and they have input into those plans (one point).

_____ The training programs in our company and the trainers who lead them focus on the application of the learning to personal as well as to professional life (one point).

_____ Transferring to a new project, assignment, or division in our company is an open process with few barriers (one point if generally true, two if this has been formalized so that "people" movement is a priority for leaders).

_____ During their first year, new recruits are often disappointed by the lack of opportunities for growth and/or opportunities to do interesting work. (lose two points).

_____ The annual performance appraisal is the primary if not the only opportunity to discuss development needs (lose one point).

_____ Our organization supports sabbaticals, when employees take a period of time off to achieve a personal goal (two points).

_____ TOTAL SCORE:

4 or under: Take a full week's management retreat for brainstorming policies that address employee development concerns.

5-7: You're beginning to look responsive.

8-10: You are above average in meeting today's workers' needs, but there is still room for improvement.

11-14: You are an inspiring example, and probably have the best workers and a strong bottom line to show for it. E-mail us: info@theizzogroup.com

CHAPTER SEVEN

the expectation of partnership

*"I sometimes miss the old days, when offices operated on the feudal system. There
was the boss, or liege lord, who occasionally dispensed favors (raises, that is) but
more often withheld them. For his gaze to fall upon you was supposed to be reward
enough. There were the knights, in their three piece armor of worsted and shark
skin, and beneath them were the courtiers — the toadies and rumor-mongers who
pored over the entrails of the wastebasket, in hopes of clues to the lord's disposi-
tion...The whole system depended on everyone's knowing his or her place... [but] if
you were patient and kept your nose clean, you could slowly, almost effortlessly, rise
from serf to squire and maybe even all the way to knight, in which case you, too,
would be entitled to quaff bowl-size martinis at midday."*

– CHARLES MCGRATH, NEW YORK TIMES MAGAZINE

Time-traveling knights would have a hard time identifying "place" or
status in today's work world. They'd be rattled by participants' total disre-
gard for knowing it. And depending on which establishment they dropped

by, they might even have a devil of a time identifying the boss. That's because everything from dress code to office architecture, paycheck to training, has been turned inside-out to accommodate today's demand for speed and efficiency — which has resulted in an ongoing collapse of hierarchical structures.

By now, everyone knows that to survive in today's marketplace, work teams must be able to make key decisions at lightning speed. It's old news that the environment that best nurtures these qualities is short on rules and middle managers, and long on a solid understanding of core values that allow for greater freedom, flexibility, and experimentation. Intellectually, we accept the result: a squashed hierarchy and empowered workers. But "empowerment" was only a transitional stop on the new-economy express ride — and one through which many a passenger slept. We've long since moved on. The destination for which business-class travelers must now prepare is partnering with the employees they've only just backed off micromanaging.

The desire of today's workers to work on more equal terms with their bosses defines the fourth of the seven shifts we've identified in workplace attitude. Although this desire is more prominent among younger workers, in the end it cuts across demographic categories. Never confuse partnership with empowerment. Partners command more "say," respect, and stake. Empowerment is passé, at best a half-measure that was hopelessly open to meaningless mantras. In fact, if your company is just beginning to work on empowerment, we suggest that you skip it and proceed directly to a partnering strategy. It won't be easy and it won't be comfortable. But done right, it might help increase employee retention and send profits soaring.

Among other things, the retreat of hierarchies means age is no longer equated with wisdom, nor youth with a need for deference. Boomers who can't handle reporting to supervisors who are half their age will find their own success at risk.

The signs of this desire for partnership can be found in a variety of places. In a study of employee engagement, Gallup discovered that workers who felt their opinion counted at work were most likely to contribute with full energy and dedication. While many executives believe that corporate hierarchies have already been busted, employees beg to differ. A 1999 Watson Wyatt Canada survey indicated that sixty-one percent of senior managers feel they treat employees as valued business partners, while only twenty-seven percent of employees share that opinion. The reality is that flattening a hierarchy is easier than creating a new system in which people feel they are truly a part of a decision-making process. This is the real shift we see happening: People are no longer satisfied with involvement; they want ownership. Toppled hierarchies are only the halfway point toward partnership, and most corporate hierarchies that think they have collapsed are still just swaying dangerously.[29]

Earlier, we discussed demographic and sociological trends that have accelerated this shift toward boss/worker egalitarianism. Smaller families and a more permissive parenting style have produced young workers who feel that the right to debate is inherent. What's more, the very independence for which employees have longed — embodied in contract work and flextime — has given them a taste for freedom that leaves them wanting more. Add to this the democratizing effects of technology and the Internet, and the roots of this shift become apparent. What may be less apparent to business leaders is that we are not talking here about a minor shift in expectations. When we say people expect to be partners, we mean it in the most

---

[29] in 2002, (Source: Gallup's US Employee Engagement Index, 2002)

literal sense. What does that mean for a business? It means leaders who fail to take this expectation seriously will lose talent to others who do, or to the workers' own entrepreneurial pursuits.

To embrace the concept, companies need to understand that partnering entails five distinct traits:

1. **Communication above rank:** workers don't just want more say; they fully expect it.

2. **Open books:** workers desire a true stake in the game, which means employers must take a deep breath and provide them with a free flow of previously heavily guarded information.

3. **Performance-based pay:** a true stake also means devising profit-sharing plans of the generous variety. Options are getting more creative by the day as they shimmy down a melting ladder.

4. **Partnering leaders:** training more leaders in a less authoritarian style is emerging as the make-or-break factor in retention, engagement, and long-term survival.

5. **Vigilance and attention to symbolism:** younger workers in particular have no time or respect for false hierarchies, and they're as ready to read signs of them into day-to-day work processes as road-rage perpetrators are to imagine driving slights on the road. Here's where leaders must come squeaky clean, which is no simple task. Symbols such as titles and office layout become important clues to job applicants and employees who are looking for a collapsed versus structurally intact hierarchy.

Vanquishing centuries of hierarchical rule is difficult to accomplish in a day, especially when the alternatives are only vaguely understood. The truth is, we had a better grasp on the alternatives *before* the science of management appeared.

Prior to the twentieth century, the only giant organizations in existence were religions and armies. Both glued their ranks together with a combination of authoritarian rule and shared values. Today, companies are striving to banish heavy-handed authority, which is incapable of responding to rapid-paced change and dehumanizing to a highly educated, democratic workforce.

As a twenty-six-year-old employee with a boomer supervisor remarked to us, "I am a competent professional. What drives me nuts is that so many managers make changes for change's sake. If the changes matter, fine, but don't micro-manage me."

Salaries and benefits still count for something, and flexibility — which almost everyone is offering by now — is critical. But values represent the most powerful tool for engaging and retaining workers, assuming leaders know how to articulate those values that are common to the corporate culture. If being treated like a partner is one of the most universal and coveted values on workers' minds, a company need only meet that desire to achieve a high level of commitment.

communication above rank

Ever heard the urban work legend about the office workers who continuously complained that their office was either too hot or too cold? A wisecrack executive arranged for a thermostat to be installed on the wall, after which employees stopped complaining, content instead to trot over to the device and alter it from time to time. The kicker, of course, was that the thermostat wasn't wired into heating controls. The workers were calmed by a mere *sense* of control.

We know a general manager of a small firm who, faced with requests for a bottled-water stand, purchased a model and refilled it with tap water each evening after hours. No one knew, so no one complained, and he smirked at the savings.

While neither of these stories speaks much for office integrity, both back up the Gallup finding mentioned earlier, that "having your own opinion count" is an important predictor of how engaged employees are. Most managers are afraid to ask workers what keeps them at the firm and what would entice them to leave. "They're afraid they will be asked for something they can't give," says Sharon Jordan-Evans, a Los Angeles leadership consultant and co-author of *Love 'Em or Lose 'Em: Getting Good People to Stay*. Just the act of asking them can make them feel valued.

Yet clearly, asking employees for their opinions isn't enough. Employees must feel safe to respond and they must believe that their opinions may bring about change. Authors of a report on worker engagement found that while one-third of US organizations have employee involvement programs, only ten percent of workers say they are part of a participatory environment. A cartoon of several years ago, depicting an employee suggestion box connected to a paper shredder on the other side of the wall, may have expressed it best. That is, sleight of hand and the pretence of wanting to hear from people enhance cynicism.

Another survey revealed that employees in the United States rate two-way communication and individual recognition as highly important to job satisfaction, second only to salaries and benefits. And yet fewer than thirty-five percent frequently share opinions with top management. This discrepancy points to shortcomings in corporate commitment to communication over rank and/or to a need for more and better leadership training.

Companies that wish to respond to this shift must make listening a form of religion. Getting out there and hearing what people have to say must be a priority for leaders. As often as not, the biggest obstacle to communication over rank is not so much poor communication as a lack of time set aside specifically for communication and the lack of an agenda for breaking down the remnants of deference by rank.

BC Hydro in Vancouver, Canada, has countered this problem by urging its executives to spend fifteen percent of their time talking to employees. Without this kind of commitment, busy schedules and commitments fence out the very face-to-face communication that helps employees feel a sense of ownership.

At TD Industries, a large employee-owned mechanical engineering firm in Texas that has been on *Fortune's* "Best Companies to Work For list" numerous times (No. 22 on the 2005 list), active listening is a corporate value described on the company website: "Servant Leaders are active listeners…they elicit trust…and share power." Chairman Jack Lowe attributes the success of the company to conversation. "Our company was really influenced by the work of Robert Greenleaf on the concept of servant leadership," he said. "One of the ingredients of trust is listening. Recently I asked a young man in our company what he liked most about working here. He said, 'I came here and you asked me what I think. It's the first place they have ever asked me that.'"

Employees at TDI — called TDPartners — are lucky; fewer than half of workers in other firms report regular communication with their supervisor regarding their work performance. Free and open communication has always been a staple ingredient of true partnership. Employees who regard themselves as partners never hesitate to offer an opinion, on the assumption it might influence the course of things. Unfortunately, too many are inclined to agree with the young employee who confided, "We're not here to decide anything — just to create the illusion of support for what top management wants." Such employees see their role as guessing what the boss wants. They brainstorm to play along or they say nothing, convinced that their participation is token. Knowing their place in the hierarchy all too well, they also fail to take surveys seriously, so management is blind to its naked-emperor status. The best way to engage workers who have felt shut out for so long that they've grown a cynical shell is to ask them questions that cannot be answered with one word. Ask specifically what might go wrong with a project, what challenges they anticipate. Frame questions with an explanation of why you want the worker to respond and what you'll do with the information. Concentrate on questions of fact rather than fishing for opinions and attitudes — then act on the feedback. Effective leaders learn how to accept criticism because not doing so discourages employees from contributing.

Cruise through any popular website or blog and you'll see that the opportunity to comment, complain, or "soapbox" has grown exponentially. The result is that younger workers in particular have come to feel that having a say is *their right* and *management's privilege*. They seek out work environments in which they need not have any qualms about speaking up, no old-world sense of "knowing their place." Wise leaders indulge or harness rather than quash this state of mind.

Hundreds of thousands of blogs created by dissatisfied employees bemoan their companies for all to see.

"People who are difficult to supervise and free to leave, people who think for themselves, who question authority, are a leader's best source of information and only hope for achieving organizational goals," wrote the authors of *Megatrends 2000*.

It was Irshad Manji's outspokenness, lack of deference, and assumption that she had a contribution to make that got the Ugandan-born, twenty-three-year-old journalist the boot from the *Ottawa Citizen* in 1992. In her book, *Risking Utopia*, Manji recalls, "During one board meeting, I locked horns with the *Citizen*'s publisher, who advocated axing the country's deficit — and fast. Not at the expense of the unemployed, I piped up. His eyes fixed on mine, the veteran journalist snapped, 'Look, young lady. I'm saying this so people like you will have a future.'

"'People like me need a present before we can have a future,' I retorted."

Manji also relates "periodic comments from superiors that I should dress more delicately, and instructions…not to dispute the biases of older journalists."

Claire Raines, in *Beyond Generation X*, tells of a franchise company founder who, while visiting one of his outlets, asked a young employee how she was doing. "Well, a little hung-over this morning, but okay," she responded, clearly unaffected by his title. Generation X's "comfort with authority allows them to speak up with fresh ideas since they're not seeking approval from those in charge," Raines says. "This outspokenness is important to companies striving to stay on the cutting edge."

Noel Tichy, a professor at the University of Michigan Business School and author of *The Leadership Engine: How Winning Companies Build Leaders at Every Level*, masterminded the Business Leadership Initiative, by which leadership training and previously guarded company information filters quickly throughout an enterprise. Ford's former CEO, Jacques Nasser, had realized that few of his executives, never mind employees in the lower ranks, understood the fundamentals of Ford's business. So, guided by Tichy, Nasser educated the first 300 people who reported directly to him, and they were instructed to pass on what they had learned to another 2,000 employees, who in turn were told to update subsequent layers. Within nine months, 55,000 Ford employees had learned about Ford's price-earnings ratio and why it mattered. Within another year, all 100,000 salaried workers worldwide had taken the message to heart. The next task was to extend the principles of this leadership method deep into the organization.

At Imagination Ltd. in London, England, employees are expected to come up with ideas outside of their own area. "People have roles, but rather than jealously guard those roles and say, 'You can't question me! I'm the subject matter expert,' they are willing to really listen," explains an account manager.

When communication crosses lines of rank and titles fade into the background, profound things can happen in a company, as demonstrated by Teknion Corporation in Toronto. After adopting a decentralized and non-hierarchical innovation process, the company found that it could identify a need and respond with a product within twelve months. The weekly steering meetings, which involve representatives from sales, marketing, and manufacturing, have been described as "messy, turbulent, and noisy," but with increased sales figures that outperform industry growth, who cares? Karen Anne Zien, author of *Innovation Explosion*, calls this approach "the fuzzy front end that, combined with strong senior leadership and support, creates the ideal microclimate of sustainable innovation."

> **IN 2006,** 61.5 percent of American households had computers, more than half of those accessing the intranet.

We call it partnering, or dancing on the grave of hierarchy.

AES Corporation of Arlington, Virginia set a goal of eliminating hierarchy in its operation to build "an engaged and accountable workforce." The company aimed for bottom-up, employee-led strategic, operational, and capital allocation planning processes. During a radical overhaul, the chairman of the board and CEO eliminated the majority of staff titles, including human resources, in favor of "employee generalists." The company reassigned decision-making to the team level, reduced the number of management "approvals" necessary for team decisions, and implemented team-based performance management that focuses on achieving results. As of 1999, the share value of AES has performed better than average by between 200 and 600 percent. But AES isn't finished yet. Its goals include eliminating all approval processes, integrating operations and maintenance, eliminating hourly work in favor of salaried positions, and handing over responsibility for setting compensation rates to the individual employee level.

"Sooner or later, executive leadership becomes crucial, especially in sustaining change that can have organization-wide impact. The real role of executive leadership is not in 'driving people to change,' but in creating organizational environments that inspire, support and leverage the imagination and initiative that exists at all levels," says Peter Senge, author of *Dance of Change*.

Need still more inspiring examples? Southwest Airlines turns its planes around in less than half the time of its competitors because employees' training emphasizes both individual and group discipline. Marriott's housekeepers and bellhops endeavor to accomplish their tasks with no delays or complaints because they're driven by a desire to make themselves and their organization proud. Instead of an executive-imposed, top-down system telling them what to do, there are only a strong commitment within a flattened hierarchy and conspicuous rewards for those who demonstrate self-discipline and teamwork.

"Working here is truly an unbelievable experience," one enthusiastic employee of Southwest Airlines in Dallas wrote in a *Fortune* survey. "They use your ideas to solve problems. They encourage you to be yourself. I love going to work!"

Let's examine the Harley-Davidson Inc. saga. Shortly after Richard Teerlink joined as CFO in 1981, the company's market share dropped precipitously, and thanks to a forty percent downsizing exercise, its workforce plummeted. Teerlink decided to invest in the people through massive training, an employee-driven performance-evaluation and effectiveness system, and workgroups made up of both blue- and white-collar employees. In other words, he collapsed the hierarchy, emphasized a lifelong learning environment, and "partnered" with workers. The result? By 1999, Harley-Davidson's market share had more than tripled, unit sales had more than quadrupled, and the employee count had nearly tripled.

"Managers can't manage by fear anymore. Long-term rewards, twelve-month reviews, and annual raises and bonuses are obsolete. So stop managing time and place, and start managing people and performance," says Bruce Tulgan, founder of New Haven, Connecticut-based consulting firm, Rainmaker Thinking.

Citrus Valley Health Partners, a multi-hospital organization in Los Angeles, opened communication by initiating what they called "what's-in-the-way meetings." Departmental leaders conducted monthly meetings for more than a year in which they asked employees the simple question, "What's in the way of you doing your job the way you want to?" All over the organization, the fire of commitment burned brightly because employees were given a say. They were made to feel their opinion counted.

One of John's first supervisors had a great way of welcoming new employees. At their first meeting, this manager said, "Look, you are new around here and will see lots of things we old-timers have let become habit. Many of these things make no sense, so in about six weeks, I want to sit down with you and hear all your ideas on what we need to re-think." He did have those follow-up meetings with new people and implemented some of their advice. The message from the start was simple: no false hierarchy around here. Everyone's ideas are welcome.

At Sun Microsystems, here's an early tradition that has stayed intact: No matter where you sit in the organization's pecking order, you can send an idea to anyone else in the company with a question or idea. Of course, many companies *say* this is allowed, but without regular evidence that there will be no negative repercussions and that the ideas submitted could change the way things are done, employees are usually loathe to go over the head of their immediate supervisor. In addition, information is shared openly by the president and COO, and executive vice-president and CTO, among other executives, who all have blogs, as do many employees, who are encouraged by the company to contribute.

Dallas-based Texas Instruments is clearly a company determined to give the rank and file more say: Employees are actively encouraged to speak their minds, a quality that helped the company clinch the No. 197 spot on the Fortune 100 in 2004.

"You can't build loyalty with just a paycheck," says Adrian Woodridge, a Washington-based correspondent for *The Economist*. "Building long-term commitment depends on four things: the nature of the work itself, the opportunity to grow, the chance to speak up and be listened to, and the feeling of making a difference."

Partnership means eradicating many of the traditional barriers to communication. Today's employees, children of permissive parenting and the Internet, have little time for any other kind of system. What's more, baby boomers have had to pucker up for such a large portion of their careers, that they, too, are flocking to companies where partnership-style communication exists.

open books

Responding to the desire for partnership also entails opening the books and sharing more strategic and financial information than many old-economy executives can fathom. Is it safe to share such details with the ranks? they wonder. What about confidentiality, potential leaks? And yet partners rarely worry about sharing these types of information with one another. Is not trust and confidence the basis of a high level of commitment? How can a partner see the big picture, execute his or her duties, or sustain all-out commitment if large chunks of information are withheld, signaling that the other partners do not trust his or her intelligence or integrity?

Dance of Change describes open-book management as training all employees in financial literacy, or de-mystifying the numbers. Every team tracks and interprets the numbers that reflect how their unit makes a profit and occasionally compares their results with those of teams with which they must interact, to make "mutual decisions."

"In an open book management system, people assume ownership for their actions — and are paid accordingly...not through bonuses or incentive pay, but through a genuine stake in the action...As workers become increasingly proficient at playing the game of business, they change the game. They set their aspirations higher."

A group of International Harvester managers once engineered a leveraged buyout of a truck engine remanufacturing plant, put every employee into an Employee Stock Ownership Plan, and taught them about the business. Three years later a janitor in the company (who happened to be a burned-out former Wall Street broker) stopped a manager and suggested that although the company's industry was currently doing well, since it tended to experience a recession every six years, why not diversify to avoid layoffs? The astonished manager researched this plan and ended up doing precisely that, profiting richly from the move within five years.

"A funny thing happens when you take the time to educate your employees, pay them well, and treat them as equals. You end up with extremely motivated and enthusiastic people," says Kip Tindell, president and co-founder of the Container Store, which placed No. 3 on *Fortune* magazine's list of the "100 Best Companies to Work for in America" in 2004. Every first-year full-time salesperson receives more than 235 hours of training — in a retail industry in which the average is about seven hours. Employee turnover at the Container Store registers between fifteen and twenty-five percent, compared with an industry average of 100 percent. The company is also big on partnering. Everything from daily sales and company goals to expansion plans are shared with everyone. Corporate leaders believe this approach adds up to a sense of ownership.

At AES Corporation, mentioned earlier, information is shared so freely that the US Securities and Exchange Commission considers all employees to be insiders for stock trading purposes.

The real point here is that employees today respond to the partnering model. Information is the lifeblood of partnerships, and when employees are aware of what the company is doing, they want to help. Examples abound at TDIndustries, where all stock is in the hands of employees and a monthly meeting fills them in on financial matters.

Open books lead workers to see and understand the big picture, contribute in a bigger sense, take more initiative, and improve things in their own area of responsibility, particularly if they are recognized for it.

We recommend the following four books on open-book management:

- *Open-Book Management: The Coming Business Revolution* by John Case (New York: HarperBusiness, 1995)

- *The Open-Book Experience: Lessons from Over 100 Companies Who Successfully Transformed Themselves* by John Case (Reading, Mass.: Addison-Wesley, 1997)

- *Open-Book Management Bulletin:* Resources for Companies of Businesspeople, edited by John Case (Somerville, Mass. 02144)

- *Open-Book Management: Creating an Ownership Culture* by Thomas L. Barton, William G. Shenkir and Thomas N. Tyson (Morristown, New Jersey: Financial Executives Research Foundation, 1998, 800-680-FERF).

performance-based pay

The old contract between employer and employee was simple: A worker traded time for a defined amount of income. Hourly wages and defined benefits were the norm. But today's increasingly entrepreneurial employee wants a greater stake in the game. Workers are interested in being paid based on the value they add rather than the time they put in. This represents a major shift in thinking, and according to a recent Royal Bank of Canada study, companies are not responding well to it. Forty percent of workers said that the average employee doesn't benefit from profitable periods, and forty-six percent said they are finding it hard to make ends meet. Still, companies are beginning to change their tune.

Partners have always received a bigger slice of the pie than run-of-the-mill employees, and as today's workforce becomes mass-deputized as partners, profit-sharing is being extended far beyond its original boundaries.

These days, the economy is "about unlimited opportunity, democracy in the workplace and a commitment to link financial rewards to individual contribution and effort," *Fast Company* has declared.

For almost as long as there have been CEOs and senior executives, their compensation pies have been sliced into four portions: salary (sixty percent), short-term incentives or an annual bonus (fifteen percent), long-term incentives or stock options (fifteen percent) and benefits (fifteen percent). Pies for executives on lower rungs differed only in having smaller long-term incentive slices and proportionately larger base-salary portions. Workers, of course, received a sliver of benefits within their salary tarts. All that changed in the early 1990s, when global competition made shareholders more demanding and "pay for performance" entered the business lexicon. Suddenly, executives were pressured to put their money where their mouths were and, to a lesser extent, apply this formula right down the ladder. The result: Salary growth has slowed while incentives have grown. In other words, where salary once "defined the man," it now means relatively little. Instead, short-term (one-year) incentives like the annual bonus are shriveling relative to the fast-expanding, longer-term (three- to ten-year) incentives, which no longer consist solely of stock options.

During its first decade, pay for performance attracted controversy, but now that early loopholes that gave some poorly performing executives a windfall have been detected and clamped shut, trackers are more confident of the correlation they've found between an increase in bonuses and company profitability.

Wall Street kicked off the pay-for-performance trend in the late 1980s, according to the *New York Times*. Leveraged buyouts meant that companies ended up, via stock, in senior employees' hands. The theory was that with a greater stake in the business, they'd work harder and smarter (now a widely accepted maxim). But remember, these were senior executives, and after watching the risks they took for personal gain, lower-ranked employees were soon demanding their own stock packages. By the mid-1990s, the profit-sharing model had trickled down to the rank and file. In 1999, ten million held company stock. Today, in new-economy firms, even janitors and secretaries have become wealthy through stock options. Now *that's* partnership.

Somewhere along this journey, employees have become far more informed about their personal market value, their companies' performance and potential, how competitors are operating, and what benefits they offer. Since the Internet makes such research easy, profit-sharing programs that contribute to employee retention and boost profits are mimicked in a flash. Let's explore a few examples of innovative pay programs.

- A growing number of companies have traded in the traditional pension plan for a cash-balance plan that pays employees for their current performance, not past performance or longevity of employment. They grant everyone the same annual credit (between four and eight percent of salary) plus interest on eventual pension. Employees generally take their cash balance with them when they leave.

- One pharmaceutical manufacturer offers annual bonuses to information technology staff who have skills that are in particular demand.

Staffers nominated at the beginning of the year get a bonus of up to fifteen percent of their salary if they stay through year-end. The company also offers bonuses based on projects or for staying with the company for a predetermined amount of time.

- One company came up with "elder grants," whereby for every 6,000 hours (about three years full-time) an employee has been with the company, he or she is given 200 stock options, which vest twenty-five percent every year.

- At one financial institution, all employees find a share of stock waiting for them on their first day on the job, a powerful symbol that they are partners, not just employees.

Leaders need to catch up with workers' preferences on this issue, especially when addressing the best and brightest — the employees most challenging to keep. Pay for the value they add, even if this requires dealing with the headaches of developing variable pay based on individual and corporate performance. If paying for value means ripping out the roots of the old compensation system in favor of a system more tuned to the partnering desires of your people, hesitate no longer. To be sure, there are those in your ranks who still prefer the old fixed system, but their numbers are shrinking.

the practices of partnering leaders

Management guru Mary Parker Follett wrote that, "the person who influences me most is not he who does great deeds, but he who makes me feel I can do great deeds." Although she preached this philosophy in the 1920s, only recently have corporations begun to tune into this line of thinking.

Leadership, having shed its authoritarian image to cope with the new worker, has never been more challenging or more in demand. Today's leaders face highly self-reliant workers whose primary motivation often is garnering enough experience to leave and start their own businesses. Until they reach that goal, today's workers can and will change jobs at the drop of a hat. Managing them and coping with the pace of change demands more, not fewer leaders.

"We are long past the time when leaders can do it all alone, or even by the dozen. It takes hundreds to lead," Harvard Business School professor John Kotter has said.

Leaders, defined as people who are willing to stick their necks out and grant others the rope to do the same, are "in." Managers, defined as people who enforce orders from above, are "out."

Blaine Lee, author of The Power Principle, says that true leaders inspire loyalty, trust, admiration, and honor, and they possess principle-centered power. Coercion and compromise have no place in the new leadership. Lee presents ten principles of power:

1. Persuasion
2. Patience
3. Gentleness
4. Teachability
5. Acceptance
6. Kindness
7. Knowledge
8. Discipline
9. Consistency
10. Integrity

"In our business, it used to be clear who had the financial muscle to be on top. Now we're facing a wide range of well-financed competitors. So it's more important than ever for us to draw upon our entire organization," explains Andrall E. Pearson, founding chairman and Yum! Brands in Louisville, Kentucky.

Today's most successful leaders are cut from a different cloth than last generation's, yet they must operate within the toppling confines of yesterday's corporate structure. Not surprisingly, all this has fueled phenomenal growth in the leadership industry: It generates $15 billion US annually across North America. Although Follett has long since passed away, her advice has never been so current. True business leaders, she said, lead from within a group, listening to different points of view and integrating different ideas into a workable solution. Follett saw this method as distinct from both domination and compromise. She called it "the third way." We call it partnering. Since partnering is precisely what today's workers are cut out for *and* what they hotly desire, it's a concept that — applied with commitment — works like no other.

Let's face it. Today's workers are the best-educated in history, extremely entrepreneurial, technologically savvy, and global-minded. This makes them "unmanageable" in the traditional sense, but ideal candidates for partners. Can a company "let go" its entire workforce and "rehire" them all as partners? Wouldn't such a move break the bank and cause mayhem? As we've pointed out, partnership doesn't promise employees a bigger pie, just one cut in a different fashion (although in fact, experience has shown that the pie does tend to expand). We'll say it again: Leadership has become the make-or-break factor in retention, engagement, and simply staying in business. Where once leadership was one of several tools in the toolbox — along-

GENENTECH EMPLOYEES in South San Francisco can indulge in six-week sabaticals every six years, as well as unlimited paid sick days that can also be used to care for an ill child.

side salary, promotions, and a buyer's market (more qualified applicants than job openings) — now leadership must do the job almost single-handedly. Salary and benefits will still sway workers, but nine times out of ten it's a respected boss for whom employees get out of bed in the morning, and a despised one for whom they quit. Yes, this was always true. No, it was never as sharply true. The currency of leadership has skyrocketed in value, along with a demand for more leaders.

So what, precisely, is the task of today's leaders? Identifying, articulating, and sustaining the organization's values. Treating employees more like partners, paying heed to shifting values, and coming up with inspiring solutions to meet these desires. Leadership no longer has any connection with rank — security guards can nurture and practice it as easily as CEOs, in the right business climate — and while some appear to be natural-born leaders, others, with training and mentoring, can learn to fill the role.

Nokia, a Finnish company that is the world's leading maker of cellular phones, has been called the least hierarchical large company in the world. Divisions are encouraged to make as many decisions as they can for themselves without corporate permission. Nokia has always taken the time for deep listening through something the company calls the "Nokia Way." The process begins with groups of employees meeting worldwide to brainstorm what the priorities of the company should be. These discussions move up the ranks to the top managers, who use the information as the roots from which to grow strategy, which is then rolled back out to employees. Such a mechanism for listening is what creates an aura of partnership within even the largest of companies. Nokia lives up to its mission statement, "connecting people," both internally and externally.

Steve Robertson, vice-president of human resources at Catholic Healthcare West, says, "Today's employees want to have an experience of partnership, which means being listened to, but also means a culture based on values rather than rules. Our values guide people's thinking and become internalized. When the values are internalized, the need for rules diminishes."

According to *Harvard Business Review*, the four qualities that characterize effective leadership are morality, courage, initiative, and respect for others. Initiative and respect amount to giving others recognition. Of course, recognition, or full appreciation for work done, is the No. 1 factor in retaining staff. It builds self-esteem, which inspires workers to do their best work. Unfortunately, compliments, recognition, and praise are not a natural part of our day-to-day culture. We could all learn a lot from Toastmasters International's technique of always sandwiching constructive criticism between two compliments.

Or we could learn from James Champy, co-author of *Reengineering the Corporation*: "Keep a sharp eye for bureaucracy disguised as discipline!" Indeed, the very popularity of the cartoon strip "Dilbert" is witness to the negative experiences most employees have with rules that seem irrelevant, if not demeaning.

When business consultants studied the US Marines to determine how to build a committed team, they returned with five recommendations: First, ensure that new recruits comprehend the organization's core values. Second, prepare every person to lead, including frontline supervisors. The traditional method of feeding an elite minority into management training keeps the hierarchical model alive and wreaks havoc with team loyalty. "The Marines believe every member of the Corps must be able to lead.... In a flash of gunfire, any Marine may find that he's the person responsible for giving orders. The policy of training every frontline person to lead has a powerful impact on morale. The organization's belief that everyone can and must be a leader creates enormous collective pride and builds mutual trust."

Third, distinguish between teams and a gathering of individuals. As we've said in an earlier discussion, there is danger in using meetings to legitimize preconceived plans, or in assuming that the most vocal member of a team speaks for all.

Fourth, take the time to bolster anyone who is floundering. Such support reinforces the individual's sense of belonging and promotes an intense loyalty from everyone. "Loyalty and a sense of belonging are components of the mutual trust that is critical," the researchers concluded. This advice is particularly apt because, unlike in past decades, when it comes to knowledge workers there is no crush of applicants waiting to replace the unsalvaged underperformer.

Finally, the Marines use discipline to build pride, and their secret to applying discipline without seeming authoritative lies in the way they place equal emphasis on self- and group-discipline. The Marines also demand that everyone act with honor, courage, and commitment; when followers find themselves living up to these expectations, they experience a great surge of energy.

vigilance and attention to symbolism

Although everyone from president to janitor can be a leader, in a business climate still stumbling out from under a top-down culture, it is the "top" that must begin the process and protect it until it has taken firm root.

One way to do that is to initiate changes that on the surface may seem purely symbolic. For example, at many tech companies, the CEO sits in an egalitarian-style cubicle along with the other employees. In others, office space may be allotted based on the particular job, rather than on a person's rank. And on the human resources side, new hires in one company are voted in by a team of fellow employees to become permanent.

Maybe by now you've got it. Symbols matter, especially when they are rooted in a deeper commitment to treat people like partners. When it comes to vigilance and symbolism, the temptation to do a surface renovation is strong. Unfortunately, it's as tough to camouflage an iron-clad hierarchy as it is to disassemble it. Flattening an entrenched hierarchy is a Herculean task. Keeping it flat after centuries of conditioning is an ongoing challenge that requires constant vigilance and effort. But taking on these challenges pays more than dividends; it ensures survival in the current environment.

Vigilance requires exerting a sense of caring, as in having no executive parking areas, special executive benefits packages, separate executive eating facilities, or more expensively decorated executive offices. In one British manufacturing company, there are no reserved parking spots or separate entrances for management, everyone eats healthy meals at modest prices in the same cafeteria, and an open space floor plan encourages interaction.

Similarly, a corporation that located the company cafeteria in an area with a "prime view" that the architects had originally assumed would accommodate the executive suite, is just one of many organizations leading the charge for a more democratized office.

A joke about automation is currently making the rounds: The factory of the future will have only two employees — a person and a dog. The person will be there to press a button that activates the factory in the morning, and the dog will be there to make sure that his master doesn't touch anything else until the end of the day. Although work has become more automated, and top-down companies can make today's highly educated employees feel useless, the truth is that companies are becoming more dependent than ever on the innovation and creativity of their people. What is the ideal company in terms of the shift toward partnership? One where the CEO goes by his or her first name, where titles are employee-chosen (if titles exist at all), where pay is based on success rather than seniority, where listening is a religion, and where truth is spoken in the scheduled meetings, not just in the bathrooms. It will all seem natural once you've turned the tide.

Profile
Dennis Bakke, Former CEO
AES
Arlington, Virginia

Dennis Bakke doesn't believe in responding to shifting employee values to boost retention, for two good reasons. First, he doesn't believe in employees. At AES, all workers are called "AES people." Second, he believes we've got it the wrong way around: Rather than respecting employees' values in order to boost retention, company leaders should respect employees because it's the right thing to do. If retention follows, so be it, but stop going about it the wrong way around, he urges.

"I want these [values] to be lived with in good times or bad. That linkage is very dangerous, filled with hypocrisy. The most radical thing about AES is its purpose, not its values. Why does business exist? It's not to make profits or [serve] shareholders. It's to serve the world. That's why business is allowed to exist as a public entity and that's what we should be focused on."

We applaud his point but live in the real world, where most CEOs crave a bottom-line incentive for doing the right thing, and most companies are not as super-successful as AES, whether due to that craving or not.

What does impress many a corporate observer is the stage of Bakke's hierarchical crash. At AES, acres of rubble lie where most companies have intact or slightly flattened pyramids. And "AES people" appear to move about the ruins unconcernedly, if not downright contentedly. After setting a goal of replacing hierarchy with accountability, the company eliminated most titles, moved decision-making to teams, and began replacing management approval processes with team-based performance management.

"Every person is a thinking, creative person capable of making decisions," Bakke declares. He also believes that AES is one of the few companies that lives its declared intention of serving the world before shareholders. People, he says, "want to serve the world, deep down...Overwhelmingly at AES, you can go to a higher calling, make a difference in the world, do something useful, and be somebody — not with a title, but making a contribution to the world. To have a whole company like that, it has awakened what was already in people. We don't motivate. We make it possible for people to live out their dreams."

As for people development, Bakke proudly declares, "We don't do any training, none whatsoever. We started off back when it was popular, when everyone had their own university and all that garbage. We realized that was a throwback to the 'we take care of you' [philosophy]. We don't want to have anyone dependent. Everyone wants to grow and learn, but the best way to do it is to actually make decisions and be responsible for stuff. When you're put in a decision-making role, something magic happens. What we do here is put people in decision-making roles day one. All decisions are made by people on the front line. The learning process is unbelievable. The only rule we have is that before you make a decision, you have to get advice. The first thing that happens when someone asks advice, is they inform a community about what they're doing and they draw that community to them. But we don't have communities making decisions. The individual, by humbling himself or herself before the group and asking advice, ties themselves into the community, and it's very difficult to find a person Lone-Rangering then. They get the best education on the history of the world from people who love them and the world. The role of educating and training in this company is all at the instigation of the individual. Groups can get together and hire a teacher, can go to courses. You're not in training, ever. You're always working. Our people learn faster than any school I've ever seen. All of us, every one of us, all the time, are in an educational process. The whole company is an educational institute."

Nor does AES believe in sick leave, vacation days, or career counseling. "It's all unlimited. It's whatever you decide in conjunction with your colleagues. When you need a vacation, you take a vacation. You're a responsible adult. If you need to see your kids play lacrosse at four o'clock in the afternoon, you make arrangements with your colleagues, not with your manager... Since we don't have a human resources department to tell you where to go, everyone chooses where they want to move to. There are no rules. There are no constraints."

And is the AES philosophy catching on elsewhere? Bakke has an opinion on that, too: "Everyone says, 'That's really interesting, but it won't work here. People here really want...'" He scoffs. "It's always the leaders that say that. You don't hear it very often from the persons themselves... You have to be really suspicious that people want to be treated like babies or children and be told what to do and taken care of. I know, or at least I think I know, that that is not how we were made. Henry Ford once said, 'All I want is a pair of hands, and every time I get a brain it messes things up.' You don't have to force managers to go to work, because they're having a great time, being responsible. I reject the hypothesis that a lot of people just want to be told what to do." Bakke goes right to the point of partnership when he adds, "Being treated like an adult and making choices is the core of making a workplace fun.

"I'm not at all an anarchist or someone who says there is no such thing as authority. We have leaders, and they have authority. What holds us together is integrity, purpose, fairness, justice, and fun. Those things are in fact very much the province of leadership."

assessing your company for partnership

The statements below allow for an initial assessment of how your organization, division, and/or department is doing at responding to the employee search for partnership. The assessment is meant to guide your thinking, not provide a definitive quantitative assessment of your progress. For each question below, answer how true the statement is of your work environment using the scale provided:

_____ Managers and leaders in our company spend a good deal of time listening to employees' ideas, formally and informally (in general, 1 point; structured, consistent and pervasive, tally three points).

_____ Pay is variable and rewards both team and corporate performance (one point if you are moving in this direction; two if your pay system has been re-vamped based on the core principle of pay for performance).

_____ Our company is governed more by principles and values than by policies (1 point if you have values that often let one break the formal rules; three points if the policy manual is thin to nonexistent and the values strong; lose two points if you have a policy manual thicker than the Bible).

_____ Hierarchy is not important in your company. For example, anyone can e-mail anyone, people are called by their first names, and challenging those in formal leadership is common (three points).

_____ The books are pretty open, and strategic information on company and team performance is shared regularly (one point).

_____ Workers have a "stake" in the game via profit-sharing or stock ownership (one point if limited to a few people, three points if pervasive, open to all, and financially meaningful as a percentage of salary).

_____ Leaders and managers have a style that encourages people to take responsibility and authority with little micromanaging (three points; micromanaging is common and pervasive, lose five points!).

_____ TOTAL SCORE:

5 or under: Take a full week's management retreat for brainstorming policies that address these concerns.

6 - 10: You're beginning to look responsive.

11 - 14: You are above average in meeting today's workers' needs, but there is still room for improvement.

15 - 18: You are an inspiring example, and probably have the best workers and a strong bottom line to show for it. E-mail us: info@theizzogroup.com

CHAPTER EIGHT

the expectation of community at work

"I believe that the ultimate in self-actualization is when a person is confused about the difference between employment and recreation."

– KEN BLANCHARD

"Welcome, recruits, and right this way please. Hope you had no problem finding our corporate headquarters. To our right, folks, just past the concierge's desk, is one of our fitness centers, and adjacent to it are courts for basketball, tennis, and volleyball. Out back is a driving range and horseshoe pits. Elsewhere on our acreage, we sponsor summer camps for employees' children, and employees can harvest herbs or relax on hammocks in our garden. The west wing holds a garage that offers free tune-ups and minor repairs to employees' cars. Upstairs, just beyond the hairdresser and nail salon, is our award-winning cafeteria, where a pianist serenades us as we eat our gourmet lunches. Between meals, of course, pastries, bananas, bagels, soup, and gourmet coffee are free — as is ice cream when the local baseball team is doing well.

"Speaking of food, we have barbecues and beer nights every Friday, as well as holiday parties for employees' children almost monthly. Last year, as you may have heard, we invited the entire town for a pancake breakfast and 20,000 showed up. We love celebrations, which is why we sponsor numerous parade floats and cookouts, too. Every employee's birthday is celebrated with teammates writing a personalized poem for the lunchtime party.

Which workplace offers all this, you may well ask. Are you sure it's a corporation, not an exotic country club and community center rolled into one? Does anyone truly work there in between all the distractions?

The "full Monty" we've just described may be fictional, but every component of it duplicates a real-life perk in an existing corporation. The point, of course, is to illustrate that businesses determined to woo the best talent today are metamorphosing into community centers, with both the recreational facilities *and* aspects of community spirit. An employee of one such enterprise, Wegman's Food Markets in Rochester, New York, (Number 1 in 2005 and number 3 in 2006 on *Fortune's* list of the "100 Best Companies to Work For") said, "I feel as though it's my second family."

Family? In this day and age of revolving-door employment, shattered families, and prolonged adolescence? Aren't we all free-agent robots, wired and workaholic, coming and going so fast that we hardly know ourselves, let alone one another? Precisely. Which is why an organization interested in winning today's workers needs to build a sense of unparalleled community and fun. When the hunter becomes the hunted — when skilled employees become so scarce that employers begin scurrying around to find new and better bait — the lay of the land changes. Workhouses become fun houses — specifically for the benefit of stars so inclined to work hard that they must be enticed to play. A study by the Society of Incentive & Travel Executives' (SITE) foundation found that incentive programs dramatically increase work performance by an average of twenty-two percent. We're not talking the entire work world, here — at least, not yet. But we are peering at a trend that the retention issue is helping to roll out.[30]

The fifth shift in expectations is toward a proactive sense of community at work. Of course, work has always served a limited function in this respect, and organizational theorists have long suggested that when people have a sense of community, they work harder and are more committed. But we are suggesting that there is now a definable shift in the magnitude of this expectation. Work is now seen as a major source of friendships, fun, mentoring, and connection — all matters once sought after hours. What has driven this change in expectation? As always, there are a series of influences. First, we spend a lot more time at work than we used to. With work taking up so much of people's psychic energy, there is simply far less time for finding friendship and community outside of work.

Second, younger workers often have "unfinished business" when it comes to community. Many of them spent a good deal of time alone (the latchkey experience) and with much less focused one-on-one time with their parents than previous generations. Hence, the hunger for mentoring and recognition are much stronger. Younger workers, the X and Net Generations, are also marrying later, thus making friendship the focus of their community in the same way family serves this function for older

[30] (ATLANTA, BUSINESS WIRE, Jan. 8, 2003).

workers. Fun, a sense of belonging, social life, leisure, and community-style caring are high on workers' "want" lists, and savvy business leaders are responding by sculpting the workplace to do double duty.

The workplace is demanding greater self-sufficiency of its workers, modern mobility is diminishing the traditional neighborhood and extended family, the new need for networking promotes shallow relationships rather than fulfilling friendships, and compressed production cycles leave little time for sports clubs or community work. Meanwhile, flexible work schedules, technology, and contract work disconnect the crowd once linked by water-cooler gossip. All of these trends have intensified the need for community. Bottom line: people expect work today to serve as a primary community center. Or as one CEO put it, to be "something between a college campus and a family."

is the expectation of community new?

One fair question is whether the expectation of community represents a shift at all. Haven't people always wanted to experience community at work? The answer is that while we may always have appreciated camaraderie at work, the focus on work as one of the primary sources of social fulfillment is new and represents an important and fundamental shift in how we see work.

In Chapter Six, we mentioned Arlie Hochschild's book (*The Time Bind: When Work Becomes Home and Home Becomes Work*) about dual-income couples seeking refuge from hectic home lives in longer hours at work. We postulated that workers enter into these long hours hoping work will provide a sense of connectedness. Individuals with stressful home lives are not the only workers looking for community between nine and five. A *Fortune* poll found that one of the main reasons people continue to work even when they don't need to financially is for social reasons — to connect with other people. A US Bureau of Labor study found that relationships were the No. 1 source of job satisfaction for women who work.

Ironically, friendships at work were unusual, and certainly not a common expectation, from the dawn of the Industrial Age right through to a few decades ago. A British study in the early 1960s (also referred to in Chapter Six) found that unskilled workers rarely discussed problems with their work peers, although some skilled workers did. Few workers felt involvement or ownership with their work, the company, or their colleagues. Even among the most affluent workers, a job was principally a means to an end — a salary to support leisure time spent with family and non-work friends. That is why membership in workplace social clubs was low and social networks tended to come from outside work — from the neighborhood, church, family, and so on.

There is, however, ample evidence that expectations of social benefit on work time have grown. For instance, where once employees eagerly anticipated retirement, today, fully eighty-five percent expect to continue with some kind of work and sixty-nine percent say they will work only because they want something to do, not because they will need the money. (A separate poll reports that forty-seven percent of senior citizens work because they need the money, eighty-six percent work because they like being with other people, and eighty-two percent work because they need to be productive.) The twin towers of learning and connecting with others stand out as primary supports of the "never plan to really retire" trend.

Somewhere between the post-war period and today, employees began to draw more on work for friendships and socializing, giving rise to 1950s- and '60s-style company picnics and bowling leagues. In the 1980s and early

1990s, amidst the re-engineering and downsizing craze, many companies deserted the company picnics and gatherings. While some, like PROCTER and Gamble, kept to old forms of building community, a counter trend has developed, with leading-edge companies sensing that a more intense style of community and friendship has become a major source of employee satisfaction.

It is often during the hiring process that a company begins to focus on the need for community. It is becoming more common for potential new hires to meet the team with which they'll be working *before* they accept a job offer. The rationale for this is that they will spend more time with these folks than they will with their families or friends, so they had better like them. Today's successful recruiter must be at least one part matchmaker.

Pete Makowski, former CEO of Citrus Valley Health Partners, says, "The biggest shift I have seen has been in corporate spirituality or soul. People are reaching out moreso now for a sense that the organization is a caring place that provides a sense of deep community. They want to know they are loved because of the hectic pace of their lives. They need a 'warm embrace.'"

In the sections that follow, we'll write a prescription for responding to this expectation for community.

it all begins with values:
the new company town

In a bygone era, there were company towns. For better or worse, the company and community were one, and the company provided everything from picnics to parades. The company was at the center of the experience of community. Some companies, like Procter and Gamble, have held onto that ethic. Let's explore P&G's successful, although some would say 1950s-retro, corporate culture, as described in *Built to Last*:

> New hires — especially those in brand management (the central function of the company) — immediately find nearly all of their time occupied by working or socializing with other members of "the family," from whom they further learn about the values and practices of P&G. The company's relatively isolated location in a P&G-dominated city (Cincinnati) further reinforces the sense of complete immersion into the company. "You go into a strange town, work together all day, write memos all night, and see each other on weekends," described one P&G alum. P&Gers are expected to socialize primarily with other P&Gers, belong to the same clubs, attend similar churches, and live in the same neighborhoods.

Now let's dance briefly back to the '50s ourselves: A 1958 *Mill & Factory* magazine survey of close to 300 organizations found that sixty-eight percent had organized off-the-job activities to help bond co-workers. More than half of employers said such programs helped cut turnover, while twenty-two percent of them said it helped cut absenteeism. Other benefits cited: better morale (thirty-four percent), easier recruitment (thirty-two percent) and increased productivity (seventeen percent). Only nine percent of the respondents reported that their off-duty programs had no discernible effects.

What goes around comes around. As we've already said, an increasing number of companies are now replicating these efforts, albeit in a less traditional manner than P&G. In fact, so many are beginning to resemble the facility described at the beginning of this chapter that the concept has been dubbed "the new company town." Here's Fortune magazine's comment:

> This new workplace is not just a place to work. It's a place to live. It's where you can eat, nap, swim, shop, pray, kick-box, drink beer, run your

*errands, start a romance, get your dental work done, wield plastic light
sabers, and sculpt nude models. It's where you can bring your whole self—
mind, body, and spirit   to work each day.Which is a good thing, because
you'll be here, if not from cradle to grave like the old company towns, then
certainly from dawn to dusk.*

Community and fun have become critical to worker loyalty. But how do
you put community at the center of the enterprise? AES boldly set a public
goal of "creating the most fun workplace since the beginning of the Industrial
Revolution." Southwest Airlines, the crown prince of companies with a rep
utation for fun, has declared fun to be a "serious management issue."

Employees of the Container Store are well-known for their over-the-
top loyalty. One responding to a *Fortune* survey wrote, "We grew up with
family values, and it's rare to find a company with the same values, philosophy, and foundation principles. Going to work is like going to a family
reunion every day."

Is having fun, building community, and encouraging camaraderie a central part of your company's strategic landscape?

creating a place where people feel connected

So how does an organization respond to this need for community? One
way is to create the leisure-style atmosphere we discussed earlier: pool
tables, volleyball courts, piano playing in the cafeteria, and so on. Whether
lavish or subtle, such amenities create inside the workplace the facilities and
ambience that people traditionally sought outside the workplace (when
they had the time!).

Of course, even companies without huge resources can work toward promoting community. They can do this through newsletters, celebrations of personal events (such as birthdays of staff members), and an onslaught of optional company events that, if offered frequently enough and made inclusive of employees' families, can't help but draw some of the people some of the time.

"Work feels a lot more like hanging out with your friends than going to work," according to an employee of Great Plains Software, a division of Microsoft, in Fargo, North Dakota.

Although workers' aspirations for community at work crosses generational lines, the companies quickest to respond tend to be those catering to younger workers. There are four dimensions of community as the Net generation sees things:

1. Create plenty of opportunities for co-workers to interact both intellectually and socially.

2. Tinker with the workplace design to ensure more social interaction. Executive floors, long hallways, and the lack of natural gathering points work against this aim.

3. Get creative about initiating opportunities for *quality* interaction, such as barbecues where workers of all rank mix casually.

4. Emphasize an open community by welcoming new members with vigor, and allowing "alumni" to come and go with ease, too. (Don't make them feel like turncoats; they remain useful industry contacts for your employees, and may even be persuaded to return.)

A community is also a place where people genuinely care for one another. Now that neighborhoods and extended families are less central, work can help fill in. In one company, maintenance staff came up with the idea of setting up an emergency fund for people who run out of workers' compensation. After they encouraged employees to donate one hour's pay per week into this fund, executives joined in by setting up a system that allowed employees to make their donations through payroll deductions. Those who did not contribute were still allowed to collect, which quickly converted them into the most enthusiastic proponents. Imagine the emotions at a Christmas party when one man who felt his life had been saved by this fund stood up to thank everyone.

Michael Hammer, author of *Beyond Reengineering*, foresaw the need for new workplace values to take the edge off increasing work stress: "Will a hunger for change produce a permanent condition of future shock? Will we face spiritual poverty even as we enjoy material plenty? Will never-ending organizational improvements inevitably produce a culture of tension and stress? Will it destroy our very humanity? Will intense concentration on customer demands usurp attention to family and community?"

As corporate leaders ponder these questions and open their hearts and facilities to help soften the edges of new-economy stress, grateful workers stay put long enough to contribute to and enjoy the fruits of community at work. Of course, the key to building community is found not just in amenities, but in the day-to-day actions of leaders.

At one management services company, the CEO has managers continually forward personal information about employees to the main office: anniversaries, deaths in the

> **AFTER THREE YEARS** on the job, store managers at San Francisco-based Jamba Juice receive three weeks of paid time off toward a sabbatical of up to two months (as well as a rentention bonus).

family, and so on. This helps the partners offer a more personal touch during conversations with employees, even those far afield.

Years ago, an executive sent a personal note to a low-ranked employee whose name had appeared in the local paper for winning the lottery, saying, "Warmest congratulations, but I sincerely hope this won't influence you to leave us, because we need you." She recalled this note with tears in her eyes many years later at his retirement party.

One executive told us that just one small change, such as asking employees to share something about themselves prior to kicking off a meeting or other work-related activity, changes the whole business environment.

Naturally, a more personal style is easier to achieve in a small corporation than a large one, which may be why surveys show that employees in companies with five or fewer workers are more satisfied than other employees (although the most-satisfied are self-employed). If community is harder to build in large places, all the more reason to have an intentional strategy for it. Little things can make a world of difference in helping to allay employees' suspicions that a company is all work and no community. A Petro-Canada franchise operator who can spend only thirty minutes per visit with service attendants recently changed tack from "How are things going?" to "Tell me one thing you did that was exceptional that I don't know about." This approach established a new kind of relationship and gave the franchisee a new outlook. When the operator learned, during the course of the more personalized conversations that ensued, that one attendant hosted a late-night talk show in his spare time, he made a point of listening in to that show and commenting on it during the next visit, a pleasant surprise to the employee.

This kind of personal community-building also builds trust. A thirty-four-year-old hotel worker told us: "Trust with my boss means him actually listening to me. Maybe once upon a time you could get by with an empty fly-by 'How are you doing?' without waiting for an answer. These days people see right through that!"

Charles Handy explains the need for this more personalized approach: "The more virtual an organization becomes, the more its people need to meet in person. The meetings, however, are different. They are more to do with process than task, more concerned that the people get to know each other than that they deliver. Video conferences are more task-focused, but they are easier and more productive if the individuals already know each other as persons, not just as images on the screen. Work and play, therefore, alternate in many of the corporate get-togethers which now fill the conference resorts out of season."

A great example of the personalized approach can be found in North Carolina-based Clarkston & Potomac, a fast-growing computer software consulting company. The majority of their three hundred staff works out of their own homes across North America. That's why the tradition of quarterly meetings involving the entire company has remained a priority even as the company has grown. At the one we attended, thirty new staff members took the time to tell their life stories to the gathered workers. And the four company founders have set a goal of every employee being on a first-name basis with at least one of the founders, no matter how large the company becomes.

Although leaders set the tone, it is the sense of community among co-workers that drives retention. Once inducted into a community, employees who value the warmth of that connection can find it difficult to leave. At a mid-sized information technology company, one professional cited co-workers' thoughtfulness and his manager's respect during the difficult birth of his child as the reason for remaining with the company.

As journalist Thomas L. Friedman has said, "There is still a deep hunger out there for that old-style, Main Street feeling, built on human contact.... The really successful [employers] in the Internet Age will be those who can combine the efficiency of cyberspace with the intimacy of the backyard barbecue." Okay, he actually said "retailers" where we've boldly substituted "employers," but you get the idea.

So, community-building doesn't necessarily entail massive restructuring or expensive new initiatives. A more personal, community-oriented approach wields considerable influence, including the use of symbols. A software company in Silicon Valley that was losing more than half its people when projects ended decided to institute a BMW lease program. Any employee moving to a new project while remaining with the company received a leased BMW, which they could keep as long as they stayed at the company. Retention suddenly skyrocketed, even though the value of the BMW leases amounted to less than pay raises being offered by competitors. Why did this program stem turnover? We believe that the employees suddenly felt part of a BMW "club," a community that had until then been merely a workplace.

Here are some more examples of community-building practices:

- Jack Harnett, the president of DL Rogers Corp. in Bedford, Texas, not only makes a point of playing golf with his managers and supervisors, he sends them birthday cards and drops by their homes to take them to dinner. He has even been known to help employees with marital or financial problems. "I don't think you can be totally focused on making money if you're worried about what's happening at home or at school with your kids. I want to help you," he declares. Harnett's managers stay an average of nine years, compared with the industry average of two.

- Total Systems Services, the world's second-largest credit card processors and a subsidiary of Synovus Financial, came up with an interesting way to help employees feel like part of a community. As mentioned previously, when the company built a new campus in Columbus, Georgia, it designed a river walk comprised of several thousand bricks, each of which bore the name of an employee. The message: When you work here, we create a permanent place for you, and your role in the community begins the first day you show up.

- It must be a Georgia thing, because Atlanta-based RTM, the world's tenth-largest restaurant company, puts your name on a brick when you become a member of the 2001 Club. That's a leadership organization into which employees and managers must be nominated, and through which one gets invited to an annual conference on strategy.

- HRH Prince Philip, CEO of Liechtenstein Global Trust, was recently asked why he underwrote a three-day gathering of 120 executives plus their spouses in Whistler, British Columbia. "It worked," he responded with a smile. "It started the process of bringing the company together."

- A&W Canada has formalized one of its values in the motto, "It's an enduring friendship that is the source of A&W's continued success across Canada." Lofty words, but when applied to a performance problem, they become more than corporate rant by ensuring the kind of tough love that pushes people to excel.

building community across rank

Just as true community at work cannot be achieved in an "us and them" atmosphere, joining hands across rank has proven to be a highly effective retention strategy. All the dimensions of community mentioned earlier must bear this hallmark: Opportunities for executives and staff to interact informally must become more commonplace, and workplace design must support this.

Getting rid of functional and hierarchical barriers is key to responding to this shift. Some companies tackle the challenge of breaking down the "us-they" feeling by having executives walk for a day in front-line workers' shoes. When Eileen Odum was CEO of GTE Northwest, she was known for riding along with telephone repair personnel. Images of this diminutive woman in a hard hat, and her decision to be accessible, built her reputation as someone who cared and was willing to listen to ideas. BC Hydro, also known as a progressive employer, went further. Company executives set a target for spending fifteen percent of their time talking to employees — an ambitious goal in any enterprise, but an effective one for companies endeavoring to respond to employees' heightened desire for community.

McKinsey and Company's Toronto office underwent a redesign to include brainstorming dens, video-conferencing rooms, team problem-solving spaces, and a three-story atrium for company-wide social events and announcements. "The old architecture was in conflict with what we wanted to be," explains a manager.

Following are more examples of building community across rank:

- In a move that emphasized how highly they value their employees, am AES annual report listed every staff member by name, even though this expanded the report by one-third, to ninety pages. Talk about meeting people's need to feel a part of something bigger than themselves!

- At Electronic Arts in Vancouver, Canada, former President Glenn Wong wandered the company's offices so often that he was on a first-name basis with most of nearly six hundred employees.

- Similarly, Synovus Financial CEO Jimmy Blanchard is known for being more likely to ask employees about family matters than about departmental goals.

making fun a priority

If there is less time these days for leisure, it certainly has not eliminated the need for fun and relaxation. The time and work crunch has simply forced individuals to find moments of leisure when and where they can. If "taking five" or having fun at work fulfills their leisure-time quotient without detracting from the quality of their work, all the better. Communal high spirits can only enhance productivity.

As mentioned earlier, studies have shown that until recently, a strong division existed between work and play. Employees worked in order to afford play and sought friendships elsewhere. More recent studies show that not only are workers increasingly inclined to blur these lines but North Americans with higher socioeconomic status and optimism about their personal finances are now *least* satisfied with the availability of leisure time. Could it be that the elite skilled workers so heavily in demand right now have forgotten how to play, and must be nudged in that direction by employers for the sake of retention?

Contemplate this: An in-depth Gallup study has tracked eight dimensions of satisfaction across time, asking the same questions forty-three times over two decades. According to the 1999 results of this survey,

Americans have never been more satisfied with their lives — with the exception of two readings, which show growing *dissatisfaction*. One is contentment with work and the other is "the amount of leisure time you have." These two criteria are now fifteen and twelve percentage points below their highest levels, recorded in 1969. And leisure time is the only dimension negatively related to income, education, and the shape of one's personal finances. (In other words, star performers are likely the most distressed by their lack of leisure time.) This insight makes the solution clear: Provide more relaxation opportunities through work facilities and the approaches we've discussed.

Companies have traditionally provided social events but most executives have not sensed how drastically the number of such social gatherings needs to be increased. In a recent survey, sixty-two percent of employees said their companies hold holiday parties and sixty-one percent said their firms hold occasional company picnics. Twenty-five percent named the odd dinner and theater event, sixteen percent boasted of lunchtime seminars. These are fine as far as they go, but when it comes to company socials, guard against tokenism at all costs.

community: it can't be left to chance

When employees saw work as a way to make a living, and when leisure time allowed for more sense of community outside of work, organizations could afford to leave most of the concerns expressed in this chapter to chance. But times have changed.

More and more companies have created departments or assigned new responsibilities to old ones to create community events. Yet being intentional about community ideally involves more than committees to plan social activities; it is also about focusing leadership attention on this dimension of work.

At Synovus Financial, leaders speak openly about having a "culture of the heart" and the "power of love." Talk to Synovus people and they will tell you about numerous acts of love and kindness, from helping people in a crisis to the day-to-day expressions of genuine caring that make employees fiercely loyal to this company. Where does such a strong focus on community come from? First and foremost from its CEO, who was chosen over thirty years ago because "lots of people could run a bank, but not too many could make people feel loved." Almost four decades after he came on board, the company's financial success and reputation for high employee loyalty has earned it much praise, but few Synovus people even know that a decision to focus on building community was at the genesis of their firm's success.

Profile
Craig Ritchie, Director of Human Resources
Verizon Northwest
Everett, Washington

Craig Ritchie is old enough to recall a time when employee surveys were administered annually, and young enough to be held accountable for the results of Verizon Northwest's (formerly GTE Northwest) now monthly surveys. As director of human resources for the three-state, 3,800-employee telephone service provider, Ritchie helps set new policy in response to employee input.

What has he learned from recent samplings, now taken by Internet and telephone as well as in written form? First, that maintaining and improving morale is a constant challenge due to increasing industry competition, and internal reorganizations.

"Employees have expressed a lower degree of trust and faith in senior management to represent their major interests. And people in our work environment are less apt to share positive stories and experiences with one another because a lot of radical changes, not all of them viewed positively, have transpired over the past ten years," Ritchie said, noting that Verizon Northwest workers tend to be mature and of long tenure.

The surveys have led to initiatives aimed at boosting morale and retention-turnover being of special concern given that approximately twenty-five percent of Verizon Northwest's technician workforce is eligible for retirement now. To promote better communication, the regional president recently conducted fifty visits with employee groups, answering their questions on the spot. "It really meant a lot to see the leader of our region not afraid to address tough issues, tough questions, and present herself as the honest and very integrity-bound person she is," Ritchie says.

To boost morale, Verizon Northwest reinforced and expanded its rewards and recognition program. Each major department surveyed its employees to gain a better understanding of what type of recognition was desired. Then, based on this feedback, each department designed several recognition programs and events. In addition, the region introduced the "herogram," cards with a fill-in blank for someone's name and deed worthy of recognition, which all employees are empowered and encouraged to pass out freely, whenever and wherever merited.

One of Verizon Northwest's biggest issues, however, remains employee development. First, past downsizing combined with a sudden, multi-industry demand for individuals with specialized telecommunications training has led to a dearth of well-trained, experienced people. "Traditionally, that has never been the case. We've always been the best. We're no longer the only game in town," Ritchie explains. He's responding with both expanded in-house training and overtures to outside community interests to partner in education and training.

But the challenge in no way ends there, he adds. Today's greater need for information-sharing has erased the line between "soft" people skills and "hard" technical skills, thereby changing the style and scope of training required. "Even people who have traditionally been in technical fields now must have good communication, people, and leadership skills. The bottom line is, if you're designing an application for a customer, you'd better be able to communicate effectively with that customer."

Yet another shift Verizon Northwest finds itself addressing is employees' need for community. Where once technicians drove to a facility and chatted with supervisors and workmates while picking up their day's assignment, today, technology allows some employees to check their schedule before leaving home and report directly to the job site. The result is more efficiency — at the price of less information-sharing with fellow field technicians, which adds up to less time for workplace camaraderie. The irony, as Ritchie sees it, is that on top of that, today's employees mostly reject traditional opportunities for socializing before and after work hours, due to longer working hours and correspondingly diminished family and free time. "We have people who bemoan the loss of the good old days, where people used to go out after work and bowl with one another and meet at the local pub and talk about the work day... and yet employee-association membership has been dwindling."

Fortunately, the company understands the dilemma, and is making efforts to help employees achieve an acceptable work/life balance. To this end, the company has policies that allow for flextime, telecommuting, part-time work, and job-sharing.

"Telecommunications is one of the fastest-growing industries out there. That means we're going to be continually challenged in recruiting, attracting, hiring, and training quality employees." The key, Ritchie adds, is administering and reading those monthly surveys — or keeping his finger on the pulse of what employees really want.

assessing your company for community

The statements below allow for an initial assessment of how your organization, division, and/or department is doing at responding to the employee search for building community at work. The assessment is meant to guide your thinking, not provide a definitive quantitative assessment of your progress. For each question below, answer how true the statement is of your work environment using the scale provided:

_____ Building community and having fun is a stated goal of our company ("Yes, it's on the books" scores one point; for "Yes, and this is a living, breathing mantra of our top people," tally three points).

_____ We have facilities on site that allow for social mixing and "fun" activities to occur while at work (one point if you have social gathering places that people use; two if facilities for fun activities exist and are used — e.g., volleyball, games room, aerobics, etc.).

_____ Our company uses "symbols" in a number of ways to make people feel a part of a community — e.g., bricks with employees' names on them, names in the annual report, pictures on the wall of people who have achieved a certain tenure, and so on (one point if these things are considered "real" by your people. Sorry, no points for empty symbols!).

_____Acts of kindness in times of crisis are frequent and leaders are role models in this regard (one point).

_____ Leaders walk around a great deal and take time to get to know people on a personal basis (one point if a fair number of leaders do this, three if it is so intentional that managers allocate time for it in their schedule).

_____We get people from remote locations together on a regular basis for "face time" (one point).

_____We have a "no dating" and/or "no nepotism" policy in place (Lose two points).

_____ Most people in our company or department are personal friends with several co-workers outside of work (two points).

_____TOTAL SCORE:

4 or under: Take a full week's management retreat for brainstorming policies that address these concerns.

5-7: You're beginning to look responsive.

8-10: You are above average in meeting today's workers' needs, but there is still room for improvement.

11-13: You are an inspiring example, and probably have the best workers and a strong bottom line to show for it. E-mail us: info@theizzogroup.com

CHAPTER NINE

the expectation of trust

"Honesty is such a lonely word,
but mostly what I need from you."
– BILLY JOEL

Once upon a time, security, loyalty, and trust were considered close cousins, a triad essential to building a long-term, profitable company. Job security built loyalty, which over time — and given good leadership — built trust. Trust, which could only be built over time, in turn nurtured loyalty and made security a two-way street. Inevitably, then, this threesome led to greater employee commitment and retention, an essential foundation for higher productivity and profits. Or so the theory went.

Then along came downsizing, rightsizing, re-engineering, and restructuring, all euphemisms for layoffs that were supposed to help firms survive the global marketplace (or, as detractors claim, cover up for decades of mismanagement), simultaneously inflating short-term profits for demanding shareholders. The jury has ruled on the long-term success of downsizing; earlier, we've cited examples of visionary companies that profited after resisting that trend, and opting to ignore bottom-line figures in the short-term to hire quality workers from their competition for longer-term gains. Certainly, no one argues with the fact that the unprecedented rate of layoffs severely wounded a sense of trust between employer and employee, shredded unwritten contracts about lifetime employment and two-way loyalty, and permanently altered perceptions of job security.

Since there is plenty of evidence that neither employer nor employee favors a full-scale return to security and loyalty (for reasons we'll discuss momentarily), attention to trust has suddenly intensified. Without trust, companies experience increased turnover, absenteeism, and internal theft — never mind the possibility of decreased employee commitment, productivity, and profits. Can trust, the last, battered leg of a three-legged stool, learn to support productivity all on its own? Why do employees crave trust even more now than before the rampage of downsizing? And how can today's leaders regain the workforce's trust?

They must and they can, as this chapter will prove, for trust is the workforce's sixth shift in expectations. But in this case, part of the challenge is that trust is far easier to build than rebuild, and unlike the other five shifts we've already explored, building trust is a reconstruction — as opposed to a new construction — for many companies. If security and loyalty are old-fashioned decorative pillars, trust is the retaining wall.

This last of our shifts may seem a bit retro. After all, this is the new century, "job security" has become a term belonging to stand-up comics, and most people have long since accepted that corporate loyalty is dead. Faith in institutions, from government and church to corporations, is lower than it has been at any time since North Americans began measuring such things. In many circles, a Dilbertized view of work has become the accepted vantage point: idiot bosses who care little for the masses of drones that work for them. And yet, in the midst of this cynicism, we suggest that while the expectation of security and loyalty is dying, the expectation of trustworthiness is actually growing. Why? Because senior management and employees operate more as partners now. When young women were first allowed to decline those who came courting, they gained new expectations of marriage: They wanted not just financial support but a trusting partnership. Now that the power balance of the employer/employee relationship likewise has turned more egalitarian, workers have gone beyond *hoping* for a trustworthy employer to *demanding* one, and leaving of their own free accord when such values are not there. The buyer's market allows this demand, and even encourages it; recent history lends it urgency. Employers have been slow to see the trust issue from this partnership perspective.

From those on the brink of retirement to those just stepping out of college, workers long for the very thing they feel they have lost: to work for an honest firm that will tell them the truth and live by an admirable code of ethics. Daniel Yankelovich, a leading pollster of North American attitudes for the past twenty-five years, confirms this new paradox: While people are more skeptical and distrustful of institutions than at any time in the last half century, underneath that skepticism resides a longing, a desire to believe. Any organization that bucks recent trends and gives employees a reason to trust again will win loyalty big-time from its people.

To understand this last shift, it is necessary to revisit our basic view of the workforce. For almost 100 years, workers have been depicted (perhaps rightly so) as an insecure mass, dependent on relatively few wealthy business owners and companies for meeting their basic needs. People traded their lives, literally, for at least the possibility of economic security. When the downsizing craze hit in the 1980s, that image of themselves as groveling dependants was driven home. Workers who lived through the beginning of the downsizing era, whether laid off or survivors, didn't like what they saw in the mirror. As luck would have it, shortly thereafter an unexpected power shift occurred. Today's economy has made small businesses the fastest-growing sector of the economy, and technology enabled small operations to compete with much larger enterprises in new ways. These changes allowed some of the downsized to sprout entrepreneurial wings, or work for those who did, which both nurtured their big-business resentment and channeled it into positive action. As we've mentioned before, eighty percent of workers are now confident they can find at least as good a job if they get laid off, and two-thirds feel quite confident that they have what it takes to be successful today. Despite seesawing economic times, characterized most visibly by the dot-com bust, which saw 200,000 jobs evaporate in Silicon Valley between 2000 and 2003, these events have broken downsized workers' sense of dependency, and with the help of demographics, allowed them to make their own demands. So what is it they want, anyway? We'll say it again: real trust, partnership-style.

the aftermath of downsizing

By now, the sad march of statistics and heart-wrenching human stories of the period from the early 1980s to the mid-1990s, and again during the dot-com bust in early 2002, are old news. We skim their surface and strum some of the numbers only to set the mood or remind readers of the scene from which workers have just emerged. We'd also like to remind readers that downsizing activity may have decreased, but it has neither finished nor reversed. What has tapered off is the shock value of layoffs, especially given that, by now, some workers have been laid off a second or third time. Below is a distillation of the brutal history of this era:

- Eighty-seven percent of North American organizations and eighty-six percent of companies abroad (especially in the UK, Germany, and Japan) downsized between 1986 and 1993.

- Between 1987 and 1993-the peak of the downsizing era-large companies like IBM, Sears Roebuck, and GE shed a quarter or more of their workforces.

- One-third of households contained someone who lost a job, and nearly seventy-five percent of all households experienced a close encounter with layoffs between 1980 and the late 1990s.

- On average, workers who lost their jobs but found work elsewhere earned fifteen percent less, and twenty-five percent lost their health coverage as a result of job dislocation.

In their book *Revitalizing the Workplace after Downsizing, Mergers and Reengineering*, Terence E. Deal and Allan A. Kennedy describe the process starkly:

> *The shock of permanent adjustments in workforce levels was further aggravated by the way most companies went about achieving the reductions. More often than not, reductions were orchestrated by teams of outside consultants hired by management under some popular rubric of the day, "reengineering" being a classic. Slogans about building a more productive future, eliminating waste, and "rightsizing" the organization rubbed salt into employee wounds. In effect, it blamed them for the company's underperformance. Ignoring the fact that most employees were working very hard*

indeed doing their assigned jobs, consultants, most of them young, had a field day. Without blanching at the levels of pay they themselves were earning, they produced charts and graphs and presentations that showed how most of the work being done was not only futile but was actually destructive to the company's competitiveness. Top management ate this up because it offered a quick and relatively easy way to solve problems they faced. Ordinary employees felt victimized because they had never been asked their opinions about what should be done, the rhetoric that accompanied the formal announcement of the consulting project notwithstanding.

Then the outplacement lists were drawn up, department by department. Despite claims that everything was going to be done analytically and based on reason, somehow the names on the lists did not seem to make sense. Too many of those tapped for outplacement were older. Too many of the bosses' favorites found jobs in the redesigned organization. This fuelled the perception that finger pointing was the primary basis for making decisions. Before long, the realization set in: The downsizing was arbitrary. It was mainly the luck of the draw as to whether you were picked to stay or put on a list to go. The end result: Trust was the first victim of the downsizing.

To be fair, however, most executives were good people striving to do a painful task demanded of them from many different fronts.

Let's take a magnifying glass to the shrinking levels of trust that resulted:

- Between 1988 and 1996, the number of employees who said that they often did not believe what management said rose from thirty-three to forty percent – this despite increasing company success over that period.

- Trust declined at three of four US workplaces in 1996 and 1997, dropping to a low point in corporate history there.

- Between 1995 and 1997, the number of workers who felt their company considered their interests in decisions that affected them dropped from fifty to forty-one percent.

- During a one-year period (1995 to 1996), the number of Americans who indicated confidence in the people running big business dropped from nineteen to twelve percent. At the same time, eighty-one percent said they believed that senior executives were benefiting from company profits on the backs of employees.

- In a survey of downsized firms, seventy-four percent reported that workforce morale was low and distrust of management high, nine percent reported an associated increase in absenteeism, and thirteen percent noted an increase in disability claims.

Finally, then, let's see where these results have left the current workforce. It's not a pretty picture, and many of the issues appear to revolve around rank, a situation that can surely be eased by the continued flattening of hierarchical management styles.

- Only thirty-seven percent of employees rate the level of honesty in their workplaces as high or very high, although ninety-five percent rate their own honesty level as high or very high.

- Only fourteen percent agree that "people trust each other."

- As we've mentioned earlier, fifty-four percent of senior managers think the level of trust between corporate ranks is good, while only twenty-seven percent of their employees agree.

- Sixty-four percent of employees believe management routinely fails to tell the truth, and forty-three percent believe that their managers cheat and lie.

• The level of trust is best between front-line workers and their immediate supervisors and worst between front-line workers and top-level
executives.

But surely, by now trust is beginning to show signs of recovery? Alas,
no. According to a 2004 by Office Team, fifty-two percent of executives and
thirty percent of employees believe a lack of open, honest communication
takes a heavy toll on morale.

Why is the level of trust between people and their organizations not
rising? The answer is twofold. First, perhaps many leaders have failed to
grasp the key practices that build trust in the new entrepreneurial age. We
attempt to help with that understanding throughout this book. But there is
another key reason for the robustness of this mistrust. Many times we have
referred to what we call "value imprinting," the idea that at a certain age,
an entire generation takes on a
world view based on certain sets of
events occurring around them.
Anyone born after 1967 or so came
of age during the downsizing era,
and that includes most of
Generation X and the Net
Generation. When today's college
graduates were ten years old, the
worst of the downsizing craze was

> **SIX WEEKS** of vacation time is
> standard at the German soft-
> ware firm SAP AG, and
> employees — who are
> allowed to accumulate time
> off — sometimes take months
> off after completing a project.

drawing to an end. It's highly likely that their parents or siblings experienced this mistrust directly. These children's images of the "greedy corporate machine" will die a hard and slow death.

As proof, we point to one person in that group, Murray Dobbin, author
of *The Myth of the Good Corporate Citizen: Democracy Under the Rule of Big*

Business. He kicks off his anti-corporate, anti-globalization tome with the following dedication: "To my father, whose downsizing by Eaton's after twenty-five years as a dedicated employee was the seed of my activism, and to my mother, whose unfailing sense of right and wrong have helped to guide it."

Connect the dots; contemplate the picture. Then build a strategy, pour on commitment, and groom patience.

new-style loyalty

Despite the stress and devastation that downsizing wreaked on the personal lives of employees, the process was not without its upside. First of all, years of hiring too many middle managers had been slowing down organizational efficiency, and quite apart from whether some firms overreacted or whether the process could have been conducted more fairly or humanely, observers agree that for many corporations downsizing was the salvation that enabled them to stay afloat in an ever faster-moving, more global economy. Further, survey after survey shows that despite the foul-tasting medicine, most surviving employees felt better about their jobs (although not about senior management) afterwards: The redesign of functions responded to their hankering for less supervision, more teamwork, and more cross-training or diversity of tasks. But most interestingly, despite underlying resentment and lack of trust, employee productivity rose or held constant in seventy percent of downsized companies. (Less surprisingly, *short-term* profits rose or held constant in eighty percent.)

How could this be? How could employers who restructured have reported adverse effects on employee workload (sixty-two percent), morale (fifty-six percent), and commitment (fifty-two percent), and yet an *increase* in productivity, service levels, and the competence of the workforce? The answer, in a word, is *fear*. Knowing that they, too, could be axed at any moment and that casualties were heavy as far as the battlefield stretched, surviving employees swallowed their pride and soldiered on. It may also be true that during downsizing, any adverse connection between commitment and productivity, any subtle acts of sabotage, any small increase in absenteeism or disability claims, may have been compensated for by the new efficiencies. (Acknowledging this is not the same as declaring the downsizing exercise an unqualified success.) And some of the resentment may have been watered down by employees' observation that almost all companies were involved, not just theirs, which implied external rather than merely internal forces.

The point is, none of these factors are decorating today's landscape. Rather, neighboring armies are roaming the territory actively soliciting recruits. Nor do employers *or* employees want a full-scale return to security and loyalty. Even if employers could offer these perks again, most employees would resist, and not just due to broken trust. Workers have long since realized that their best investment is in growing their own skills, not growing the company's profits. (Which is not to say that both groups would not welcome back a *degree* of renewed loyalty and security.)

Dennis Bakke, former CEO of AES, told us, "The security thing is a natural extension of the dependency thing. I just try to convince people that security is a false god, not something they should desire. Security is a horrible thing. What are the most secure places you can have? Prisons and Indian reservations. What happens in those kinds of places? All kinds of problems because you are treated like an animal, a kid, an asset. The line 'People are our best asset' is my favorite. What do you do with assets? Sell them, throw them away. The most irresponsible thing we can do is keep one extra person in a business when they're not needed. Some companies think they're doing a nice thing keeping them a little longer, but it prevents anyone else in the organization from growing."

And so we return to our one-legged stool and realize that trust is all that's left to support retention, engagement, and productivity. A sense of entitlement has replaced fear, thus eliminating any interference to the natural linkage between trust, commitment, productivity, and retention. Make no mistake: Commitment, productivity, and retention are increasingly influenced by the degree of trust coursing through the halls at work. Trust allows employees to speak up, take risks, and apply all their skills to resolving company challenges. Distrust influences them to contribute little and invest all their energy in keeping their rears covered.

"In a work world where post-boomers see few traditional rewards left for them, honesty on the part of employers about what they can offer is at a premium. Post-boomers have a completely unvarnished view of corporations, and of the world," says Barbara Moses, author of *Career Intelligence*.

So, too, do boomers. Middle managers of the downsizing era reflect the sharpest declines in morale, especially in areas that measure trust in the organization. In fact, only two percent of middle managers name dedication to their firm as the key to success. Instead, fifty-six percent cite individual ambition as the key. Similarly, a study of *Fortune* 500 managers found that those who survived restructuring focused more on their own careers and less on organizational goals.

People's new loyalty is to their professions. In other words, workers are less "IBMers" or "Microserfs" and more "software developers" or "systems analysts." In fact, workers seem to be staying in the same occupation longer now than in the past, even as tenure with a particular employer has declined sharply since 1993 (the length of tenure is currently at its lowest level in twenty years). All of which hearkens back to the days before the

Industrial Age, when most workers, from cobblers to fishmongers, were proudly independent. Although this situation stems from lowered levels of trust, is it all bad? Not necessarily. If professional rather than corporate accolades are what drives today's employee, employers can work with that, if only by trumpeting employees' professional standing and awards to their workmates. Certainly, it's something that insightful employers can support through training and "vertical" community-building even as they attempt to spin the wool that will re-knit unraveled corporate identity and trust.

But be aware that the demise of lifelong corporate careers has undercut the need for corporate loyalty. Individuals are now committed to the organization's goals out of self-interest. Loyalty to one's profession, division, colleagues, work team, or project is what should be encouraged, instead. Put another way, leaders must accept that there is only so much a corporation can do to re-sprout corporate loyalty or security — they'll be stumpy legs on the new stool regardless of retooling efforts. But trust is an entirely different matter. A work environment rich in trust and respect has been linked with less stress and greater productivity. Trust also minimizes in-house unethical or criminal behavior, which costs US industry up to $400 billion annually.

All of which begs three questions: What is corporate trust, how can one seed one's firm with it, and how long does it take to grow to maturity?

the ingredients of trust

We believe that Jack Lowe, chairman of TDIndustries, has summarized it best: Tell the truth, do what you say you will do, make decisions with people's best interests in mind, and hold to your code of ethics and values in day-to-day actions so that people can truly believe in them.

Frank J. Navran, a downsizing consultant and author of *Truth & Trust: The First Two Victims of Downsizing*, puts it more practically: "It is better to under-promise and overdeliver than to make promises that cannot be kept... You won't always win. You will not get them everything they want. You will not protect them from every inequity or injustice. It is sufficient that they believe that you are making a good faith effort and that your intentions are honourable. It is also quite acceptable for you to honestly disagree with your employees — to choose not to support a particular cause or to tilt against a particular windmill. But do so honestly, with integrity and full candor."

Co-author Pam Withers, while working as a middle manager in a publishing firm that had taken a financial turn for the worse, was offered a promotion and asked to "boost morale" among the ranks. Although the offer was tempting, she instead made a difficult decision to leave because she perceived that the tools for fixing the leaking ship were not on board, and the power to order them was not being given to her. She felt that a mandate to be honest with crew about the seriousness of the situation was not being granted, and her influence with fellow employees stemmed from years of being open and honest with them. In short, she ranked her personal values and industry reputation above the new title and responsibilities. As many a consultant has emphasized, it is this perceived values gap between company and employee that often ushers employees out the door. And yet, how often are corporate values discussed, how

NEW FATHERS and adoptive parents get six-week paid leaves at Republic Bancorp os Owosso, Michigan.
Source: *Your Money or Your Life: Transforming Your Relationship with Money and Achieving Financial Independence.* Joseph R. Dominguez and Vicki Robin (New York: Penguin Books, 1993).

clearly are they spelled out, and how closely are they guarded? How many leaders realize that although trust can come crashing down in an instant, it takes years to rebuild through daily, consistent actions and a dedication to extracting any weeds that threaten to choke its progress?

A colleague of ours was taken aback when a brand-new senior manager casually broke a long-held hiring rule to bring a crony on board. A member of the support staff said she felt sick when she overheard this boss tell one person one thing and — seemingly unconcerned that she was once again at his side — another person the opposite. Story upon story began to filter out about this administrator's lack of ethics.

"Watching him operate, I don't believe he has ever been schooled in right versus wrong," said one incredulous observer. Within weeks, this colleague noticed that other people in the department he had never before pegged as dishonest were trying out questionable political maneuvers. Morale plunged, old friends became wary of one another, work output slackened, and at least one senior executive threatened to resign. Meanwhile, everyone waited tensely to see whether the top boss, informed by a brave team of whistle blowers, would cover up or discipline this new executive. Sadly, a cover-up ensued.

"[Unethical] behavior will be mimicked by those who aspire to senior positions," say Terence E. Deal and Allan A. Kennedy. "The most difficult challenge in shaping a company's culture is recognizing that you have to put yourself and your beliefs on display all the time; otherwise you have little hope of influencing others.... Strongly held and consistently practiced beliefs give culture its power to raise human expectations and performance to truly extraordinary levels."

When whistle-blowers are treated as valuable reporters of problems that have gone undetected by other methods, rather than as liabilities, positive things happen. Organizations that have implemented procedures that encourage individuals to step forward say that company integrity and efficiency improve as a result.

eePulse, a weekly electronic reporting system developed by a university professor who specializes in human resources studies, has employees of organizations that sign on for the service answer a weekly e-mail questionnaire that gauges their "energy level." The questionnaire is designed to serve as an indicator of morale and an indirect measure of trust. Other products measure the culture for growth, customer enthusiasm and human resources effectiveness. The method is objective because employees submit their answers through eePulse, rather than to direct supervisors. The president of San Francisco-based Indus International, a software company that has used eePulse, has said, "Employees can voice their concerns and not worry about retribution. It helps management know what the issues are." He credits the system with fending off the poisonous results of personality conflicts that erupted during a corporate merger. "The problems were evident on the surface, but it would have taken months for it to boil up. This way, we knew right away about the problem and what to do."

As our colleague witnessed, distrust and dishonesty can spread as fast as one rotten apple spoils a barrel. "Trust and distrust create upward or downward, self-perpetuating spirals," confirms Sandra Robinson, a University of British Columbia lecturer often quoted on corporate trust.

Dennis Bakke, former CEO of AES Corporation, told us that he visited one of his company's plants once a month for five years and sat in the control room chatting for four hours at a time with the individuals on the night shift. "Not because I was trying to educate them about what we were trying to do, but to gain their respect and trust." Years later, when Bakke was faced with a financial crisis, he found that the union leader of this plant was willing to propose an alternative pay package, "because he believed he'd be treated like we said he would." The end result was that workers in a five-generation unionized environment agreed to be paid like managers.

"We don't spend a lot of time thinking about trust. We just try to live with integrity... Nothing matters but the willingness to give up power," Bakke says.

There's that reference to hierarchy again. As the old saw goes, it's hard to trust someone who has power over you. Or, as Daniel Oestrich wrote in *Driving Fear Out of the Workplace*, "Control seems necessary to people when they don't trust each other... The need for protocol stems from the lack of belief that I can trust others and myself to behave in the right way." Conversely, then, letting go of control and loosening protocol bequeaths a new sense of trust. Entrenched hierarchy is why surveys show that front-line workers are the least trusting of senior management. This is perhaps why progressive CEOs choose to woo them directly.

Not only does hierarchy depress trust but so, too, can an overemphasis on speed. As Edward Marshall said in *Building Trust at the Speed of Change*, "The sense of what is right and fair in work relationships seems to have given way to what is expedient."

Stephen Covey likes to say, "We're good at efficiency, but have you ever tried to be efficient at finding out what's bothering a troubled teenager?" There are times to slow down, times to heed a long-term commitment to build trust over shorter-term goals. Witness Tylenol's willingness to pull massive numbers of bottles off store shelves and engineer a new seal for them when someone poisoned a few bottles after they had reached retail outlets.

Researchers who studied seventeen million employees in forty countries found that people value eight distinct behaviors:

1. Treat others with uncompromising truth.

2. Lavish trust on your associates.

3. Mentor unselfishly.

4. Be receptive to new ideas, regardless of their origin.

5. Take personal risks for the organization's sake.

6. Give credit where it's due.

7. Do not touch dishonest money.

8. Put the interest of others before your own.

Business consultants tend to agree on the following five keys for leaders to create a trustworthy relationship with employees:

1. Create dialogue.

2. Ensure consistency of action.

3. Tell it straight even when the news is bad.

4. Accept criticism and admit when you're wrong.

5. Carry through.

Ken Lizotte, Chief Imaginative Officer of Emerson Consulting in Concord, Massachusetts, has three rules for building a trusting environment:

- **Listen:** "Let go of your ego and listen to what your employees are saying."

- **Tell:** Inform employees of changes and the rationale for your decisions. "It's slower and messier to keep everyone involved, but it helps create trust."

- **Act:** Don't just seek feedback from employees. If their criticisms or recommendations are justified, act on them. If you choose not to, tell employees why.

- **Be dependable:** Consistent behavior helps employees know what to expect from you.

For organizations that have lost trust, another step must be added: Determine if particular managers may have burned too many bridges, and if so, consider reassigning them so you can create an environment in which the new seeds of trust can germinate.

One way to think about building trust is to contrast the practices of leaders who lose trust with those who win it. How do leaders lose trust in the first place? A study has made that clear, too. They:

- act inconsistently in what they say and do

- seek personal gain above shared gain

- withhold information

- lie or tell half-truths

- are close-minded

- are disrespectful of employees

- withhold support

- break promises

- betray confidences

And how do they rebuild trust? Although it takes twice as long to build trust in a leader than to lose trust in one, here is the blueprint for a successful reconstruction:

- maintain integrity

- openly communicate vision and values

- show respect for fellow employees as equal partners

- focus on shared goals more than on personal agendas

- do the right thing regardless of personal risk

- listen with an open mind

- demonstrate caring and compassion

- maintain confidences

Different stages of a corporate cycle can also affect trust levels. On a scale of one to ten, a time of expansion ranks highest at 6.2, and a time of downsizing lowest at 4.7. In between are periods of acquisition, change initiative, re-engineering, mergers, and restructuring.

Trust is easier to build in a homogenous workforce than a diverse one. Diversity means sharply varying world views, work styles, and behavior patterns. And trust is earned in different ways in different cultures. North Americans tend to be quickly trusting, although with a "what's in it for me" layer. Overseas employees, or foreign-born employees, are often put off by the short-term profit orientation, youth emphasis, self-boastfulness, lack of understanding of nonverbal cues, and over-familiarity of North American managers, which work against the building of trust. North Americans, for their part, often become impatient with the lack of trust initially shown them, or the more laid-back regard for deadlines, thereby crimping the natural process of building trust. One observer found that Vietnamese workers, who comprised about forty percent of the workforce in one company, "were especially fearful of the team concept, which they likened to Communist work teams." As these and many more challenges show up in domestic workplaces as well as multinational work teams, it's time to break out some reading on the topic and/or indulge the workforce with seminars — whatever it takes to build workforce trust. For starters, we recommend *The Workplace Revolution: Restoring Trust in Business and Bringing Meaning to our Work*, by Matthew Gilbert..

Proactive caring is a less obvious but key ingredient of trust. We've talked before about the importance of preventing star performers from burning out. *Fortune* magazine recently related the story of Yolanda Perry-Pastor, a thirty-four-year-old customer service manager of a large plant nursery, whose entire life revolved around the company. She worked long hours, bought into the "we are family" pep rallies, moved to within a few blocks of the office, vacationed with co-workers, dressed her children in company-logo clothes, and didn't mind answering her pager at three a.m. or hauling her children to the company daycare center on weekends. Then a round of layoffs forced a more demanding workload on her. When she asked for a break due to health concerns, it was refused. At her doctor's urging, she took an extended sick leave.

> **AT EDWARD JONES,** most brokers qualify for twice a year, expenses-paid jaunts for two to places like Alaska or Pebble Beach.

"I felt betrayed," Perry Pastor said. "Now I see it so clearly. All that family stuff was fake. They were just using me to get that bottom line."

Did it need to come to that? Of course not. Years of investment in a loyal and hard-working employee were lost to the lack of a watchful leader, a proactive anti-burnout policy, a careless moment. Trust is not earned as much by company-wide policies as by the behavior and attitude of individual managers. This makes the process of creating a trustworthy environment more complex and dependent on a consistent pattern of driving a set of values.

Increasingly, trust today also entails resisting the use of technology to monitor employees, or setting policy for how it will be handled. Here, as we mentioned earlier, all the advances that a more democratic and open work environment seem to offer are on the line. Today's technology allows employers to eavesdrop on job applicants, employees, suppliers, and partners through any number of electronic means, from voice mail to the Internet. And as we related in Chapter Two, several British companies are discussing implanting microchips in employees to monitor their whereabouts and timekeeping. But in doing so, they risk felling trust faster than downsizing ever did.

The cynical executive will say, "We try our best to be trustworthy, and if the rank and file don't believe us, there's not much more we can do. Anyway, our first obligation is to keep up with market challenges and changes."

Precisely. Today's organizations must produce unparalleled amounts of change, from reorganization and new products to the day-to-day shifts that characterize business. All of this requires buy-in, and buy-in is facilitated by trust. Jack Lowe of TDIndustries put it succinctly: "Every change we have to make in business today is made easier by trust. When people don't trust you it takes so much effort to get people to go along with changes. They are always skeptical and wondering what you are really up to. Around here, people may ask questions when we say we want to go in a new direction, but not a lot of time is wasted having to convince people that we aren't up to no good. That's what happens when you have trust." It is not difficult to imagine the long-term financial implications of change implementation slowed down by mistrust.

Profile
Jane Graydon
Director of Human Resources
BC Biomedical

Some companies boast they have an open-door policy — that anyone can speak to top decision-makers. But BC Biomedical knew its employees took that seriously the day a staff delivery-boy passing by the boardroom during a high-level discussion decided to slip in and contribute his two cents' worth.

"He wanted to be part of a discussion on patients in other branches," recalls Director of Human Resources Jane Graydon, pleased that the employee knew he was welcome.

BC Biomedical, a privately owned partnership of pathologists in British Columbia, Canada, is a medical laboratory business. Established more than forty-six years ago, its 650 employees run forty-five patient-service locations — all of them buffeted in recent years by government health policy changes and budget cutbacks.

Despite such challenges, or perhaps because of how they've handled them, the firm has for three years running occupied the top spot on the Best Employers of Canada list, issued by Hewitt and the Globe & Mail's Report on Business.

When the government slashed its Medical Services Plan fee-schedule for lab service by twenty percent recently, BC Biomedical took it like a direct hit. "It was a huge impact, a revenue cut for us; it was putting at risk something that was working," Graydon says. But weeks before the decision went public, the firm ramped up its internal communication. It issued a weekly newsletter topped up with special news bulletins, and ensured that managers aired concerns.

"We're not afraid of sharing bad news," Graydon says. "Before the decision came down, we had been communicating everything we knew, so it was no surprise to our employees. We just kept saying, 'this is what we know.'"

Employee trust needn't suffer during a company's stressful times, Graydon says. "A long-term view, clear criteria, and consistency in decision making is what engenders trusts." That, and communication. "When you have an environment that's open, where people can ask questions — and when you have a common, well-understood set of values — you don't have a lot of second guessing going on. People will ask if something doesn't seem consistent. You don't find a lot of rumours."

To that end, BC Biomedical's managing director and CEO, Doug Buchanan, holds monthly, bear-pit-style sessions with supervisors. "Anything goes," Graydon asserts. "He uses those meetings to understand the pulse of the organization, and explain decisions."

To supplement that process, employee advisory groups meet every two months with Buchanan and the medical director. Minutes from the sessions are published for employees at large, and questions solicited beforehand. "Employees can ask questions about anything, and they do, from pay raises to the color of binders," Graydon reports.

BC Biomedical is also bullish on promoting a work/life balance. Given that a large portion of employees have to start work at the crack of dawn (to take blood samples from patients who've had to fast all night), the firm created many part-time and job-sharing positions.

Giving back to the communities in which they work is also high on the agenda. There's a push to hire employees who are underprivileged, and when it comes to building internal community, Graydon actively helps employees organize clubs for quilting, yoga, losing weight, and scrap-booking.

Then there's the annual general meeting, with its skits and lighthearted tone. No one is surprised when Buchanan shows up in a bow-tie, wig, and yellow polyester pants, and entices fellow managers to poke fun at themselves.

"They love it, and it sets the stage for open communication," Graydon says.

"The most important components of trust," she continues, "are authentic communication and a set of values with which you can align your decisions."

And trust, BC Biomedical has proven, can help hoist and hold a company's best-employer position.

Profile
Jack Lowe, Former CEO, Current Chairman of the Board
TDIndustries
Dallas, Texas

The year is 1992 and the setting is TDIndustries, the mechanical and electrical construction and service company in Dallas, Texas. Researchers are nosing around in preparation for the second edition of *The 100 Best Companies to Work for in America.*

"We were coming out of some difficult times — off life support but still limping," recalls Jack Lowe, former CEO. "They came to see us and spent the day talking mostly to front-line people; they didn't seem much interested in talking to senior executives. At the end of the day, they met with us as a senior team and said that there was obviously a very high degree of trust in our organization, and they wondered what we did to create it.

"I started talking about newsletters, communication, open-book management, participatory management. Finally, Ben Houston interrupted me and said, 'Jack, I know why people trust us. It's because we're trustworthy.'

"What he meant was that it wasn't the 'techniques'; it was the same things that make you trust someone in your life: You do what you say you will do. If you make a mistake, you tell them so and apologize. You give them the straight goods, and you care about their lives beyond simply what they can do for you. It may manifest itself in programs and things, but it is more about character, who we are as opposed to what we do." (When you meet executives at TDI, as we have on several occasions, it's hard not to see what he meant. Their very presence speaks of trustworthiness.)

At TDI-employee-owned since 1952 because Jack's dad decided it was the right thing to do — trust seems lodged in every pore, from the mission statement to strategic planning, even to layoffs. A few years ago, when TDI decided to sell off a few businesses because they did not fit in with company strategy, senior executives offered the employees involved a chance to buy them, which they often did. When employees declined at one of these businesses, however, TDI took the offers to these workers and asked them to select the best buyer. "They did not pick the highest bidder. The one they wanted was offering us twenty percent less, but we sold it to the one they felt good about. What we would have done if the difference had been millions of dollars, I can't say, but people knew we tried to do the trustworthy thing."

The same can be said for TDI's employee-development focus. "Our strategic thinking is to provide a place for people to retire at TDI." TDI is part of an industry in which turnover and temporary layoffs are taken for granted, so the company's focus on helping people stay employed creates a lot of goodwill.

"We do lots of cross-training so that if a particular part of the business slows down, people can do something else." The company, with 1,200 employees and $200 million in revenue, has seventy-five employees who have been with the firm for more than twenty years.

"How do you build trust?" Lowe asks. "You allow people to have peaks and valleys. You show that if they give you the extra mile when you need it, you'll do the same for them. Treat them with dignity — like there is more to life than work and that we know it. I think of a man who works for us who is a Muslim, who said he really appreciates the fact that he can take fifteen minutes out of his day at a construction site to say his prayers. A lot of companies would not make time for that, but trust is about honoring who people are."

assessing your company for trust

The statements below allow for an initial assessment of how your organization, division, and/or department are doing at responding to the employee search for trust. The assessment is meant to guide your thinking, not provide a definitive quantitative assessment of your progress. For each question below, answer how true the statement is of your work environment using the scale provided:

_____ When tough decisions are made around here (e.g., reorganizations, layoffs, etc.), people can count on hearing what's going on in an honest and timely manner (most of the time with some notable exceptions, one point; three points if you can't remember when it was last perceived that "management was up to no good").

_____ There are very few unmentionables in our organization. That is, people are fairly honest and straightforward across ranks (two points).

_____ Our company has a strong set of published values that emphasize ethical responsibility to customers and community (one point if these things are considered "real" by most people; three points if they are at the center of most corporate decisions and a topic of frequent conversation — sorry, no points for published values that draw mostly cynicism from employees).

_____ On a number of occasions in recent memory, the company demonstrated actions, putting the interests of its employees over near-term profits (two points).

_____ Our company makes a significant and consistent effort to avoid layoffs through cross-training, project shifting, and other means (two points if it has happened on a number of occasions; three if it is a religion).

_____ People who raise ethical issues in our organization are seen as adding value to the organization (two points).

_____ When there are rumors that our products or services are harming customers or the community in some way, there is a genuine interest in fixing the problem immediately (one point).

_____ Leaders are generally seen as saying one thing and doing something else (lose three points).

_____ TOTAL SCORE:

6 or under: Take a full week's management retreat for brainstorming policies that address these concerns.

7-9: You're beginning to look responsive.

10-12: You are above average in meeting today's workers' needs, but there is still room for improvement.

13-16: You are an inspiring example, and probably have the best workers and a strong bottom line to show for it. E-mail us: info@theizzogroup.com

Practical Applications For Your Organization

The Six Workplace Values & You

In Part one you were given an opportunity to read about current research and learn what great organizations are doing to support each of the six shifting values in the workplace.

Start with yourself. Read through each of the values shifts and based on what you have just read about the new expectations and values in the workplace allocate 10 points to the values that really matter to you at work. Distribute the 10 points however you want (all 10 to one value, 5 each to two values, and so on).

Talk to your team about each of the shifts. Give them examples and a definition of each and then share this exercise with them. Use it to create dialogue amongst your team members.

Value	Points	What does this mean to you in terms of your work? What would you like to change and do differently for yourself or your team?
Balance & Synergy		
Partnership		
Trust		
Growth & Development		
Noble Cause		
Community		

Practical Applications For Your Organization

Leadership Values Self-Assessment

You have had an opportunity to learn more about each of the six shifting values in the workplace and how they apply to recruitment, retention and engagement of employees.

By using the statements below assess your leadership in how you have responded to your team's search for each of the values. The assessment is meant to guide your thinking, not to provide a quantitative assessment of your progress.

The Expectation of Balance and Synergy

There is a desire for alignment between corporate and personal values.
Individuals are not willing to sacrifice their personal life for professional life or vice-versa.

☐ My team knows that they can come to me regarding their personal and work commitments and we will discuss it openly and try to resolve the conflict

☐ I never penalize staff for personal commitments or make it difficult for them to gain promotions and maintain their status

☐ I would support a staff member who asked me for a sabbatical to achieve a personal goal

☐ I try hard to monitor and make every attempt to ensure that my staff prevent work burnout

☐ I am involved in and support company social, leisure or sport teams and support my staff to be involved also.

Thoughts on how I could respond to this shift with my team: _____

_____

_____

_____

The Expectation of Partnership:

People want involvement and a stake in a company. There is little tolerance for hierarchy and meaningless processes

☐ As a manager I spend a great deal of time listening to employee's ideas, formally and informally

☐ I strive hard to create an environment that has limited hierarchy and where leadership decisions can be challenged

☐ I believe it's important to have an open book environment where strategic information and team performance is shared regularly

☐ I have a style of management that encourages people to take responsibility and authority with little micromanaging

☐ I tend to lead more by values and principles rather than by policies

Thoughts on how I could respond to this shift with my team: _____

_____

_____

_____

_____

The Expectation of Community at Work:

A need for connection with others, friendship and for work to be fun. There is an expectation for a day-to-day expression of caring from leaders. A strong interest in developing a support network that contributes to personal and professional development.

☐ Building community through social activities and having fun is a stated goal in my department

☐ I strive hard to ensure that acts of kindness in times of crisis are frequent and that I am a good role model

☐ I get out of my office and walk around my department with the intention of getting to know my people on a personal basis

☐ When I have team members that are in remote areas I try to get them together on a regular basis for 'face time'

☐ I encourage my team to become personal friends outside of work as well as at work

Thoughts on how I could respond to this shift with my team: _____

_____

_____

_____

_____

_____

_____

The Expectation of Personal Growth and Development:

There is an expectation of growth as a person and as a professional. There are concerns with maintaining employability and the development of a self-aware and compassionate individual that maintains high levels of competence and awareness. Exciting work is the best predictor of retention

- ☐ I routinely sit down with my staff every 6 months and discuss their development and the company's plans for their growth

- ☐ I support my staff by looking for opportunities for them to be part of task groups and to be involved in assignments outside their core job responsibilities so they can grow

- ☐ I support my staff by encouraging them to be responsible for their own career development by sitting down with them and discussing their career development plans so we can identify skills they want to learn and include them in these plans

- ☐ I don't create barriers for my staff who want to transfer to a new project, assignment, or division in our company

- ☐ During the first couple of years I am aware that I need to ensure that new recruits have been given opportunities for growth in doing interesting work.

Thoughts on how I could respond to this shift with my team: _____

_____

_____

_____

_____

The Expectation of Work as a Noble Cause:

People want hands on ways to be involved in worthy causes. There is an expectation for work to be more than a way to earn a living, and want to see it contribute to the community, the environment, and to feel their work makes a difference in people's lives.

☐ I support my staff's involvement in community service or volunteerism on behalf of the company

☐ My team has created their own vision statement that describes a deeper meaning of the products or services in the company that they are responsible for

☐ My team is fully aware and can name the corporate values that inspire them to act with higher ethics and to do the right thing

☐ I am involved in helping my company to develop a positive reputation in the community

☐ I am aware of how our products/services impact people not just profits

Thoughts on how I could respond to this shift with my team: _____

_____

_____

_____

_____

_____

The Expectation of Trust:

An expectation of corporate openness both inside as well as outside the company. Ethical and honest business practices where truth telling is the norm is what individuals are seeking. A place where people are aware of where they stand and where they feel they are always "in the know".

☐ When tough decisions have to made my staff can count on me to do this in an honest and timely manner

☐ There are few unmentionables in my department, I expect everyone to be honest and upfront across the ranks

☐ I always emphasis the ethical responsibility to customers and the community as prime importance in making decisions

☐ If at all possible I make every attempt to avoid layoffs through cross training, project shifting, and other means.

☐ I am not known as someone who says one thing and does something else. I walk my talk and can be trusted

Thoughts on how I could respond to this shift with my team: _____

_____

_____

_____

_____

_____

_____

Generational Reference Guide

You have had an opportunity to learn more about each of the six shifting values in the workplace and how they apply to recruitment, retention and engagement of employees. Use this list as a quick reference guide.

BABY BOOMERS	
Defining Characteristics of the Generation	• Gave all to corporation and perceive they got little in return. • 'My work is my life' • Wondering if *"this is all there is"* • Alternate between desire to drop-out & search for renewal • Severe tension around work-personal balance • Burned out on corporate life • Still want to believe in the company
Primary Driver	• The ability to be themselves at work • Harmony between life inside & outside of work • Balance of getting ahead and doing good • They want it to be fun again • Likes achievement-"live to work" • Loyal to the their chosen profession
Primary Values	• Balance & Synergy • Personal Growth & Development • Noble Cause
Key Recruitment Strength	• Life/work balance • *"Being themselves"* on the job • Being able to make a significant difference
Benefits	• Retirement benefits • Less business travel for balance • More interested in benefits than pay • Life/work balance benefits • Elder care benefits • Promotions to retirement sites (ocean, golf/desert)
Motivation Techniques	• Want to be change agents — to be involved • Expects recognition for their work & tenure • Likes an open door approach • Provide opportunities to lead • Desires to stay on top of trends

GENERATION X

Defining Characteristics of the Generation	• Watched parents and concluded that lifetime job security is not realistic. • 'My work allows me my life" • Have accepted that there is no job security except in their own career marketability • Seen as 9-5'ers because they value balance between life & work. • Dislike organizational politics • Little tolerance for authority & structure • Work should foster personal growth • Want to know WIFM
Primary Driver	• Community and sense of contribution • The ability to grow personally • Growing mastery as opposed to security • Value making a difference & "changing the world" • Traditionally 'work to live' • Family loyalty
Primary Values	• Balance & Synergy • Growth and Development • Noble Cause
Key Recruitment Strength	• Career growth opportunities • Making work fun • Describe diversity of skills & challenges of the work • Offer a compelling career experience • Provide competitive compensation
Benefits	• Educational reimbursement • Flexibility over work hours, methods of work (i.e. telecommuting). • More interested in pay than benefits • Health club memberships • Daycare facilities • Life/work balance
Motivation Techniques	• Task variety/ stimulating work • Attach rewards to performance • Provide opportunities to lead/advance • Allow room for creativity & innovation • Share all your knowledge not selected pieces • Doesn't want to hear "pay your dues" • Won't work where they can't grow

GENERATION Y	
Defining Characteristics of the Generation	• Indulged by wealthy boomer parents • 'My work allows me my life' • Has a sense of entitlement • Embraces cultural diversity • Believe in flattened structures • Corporate loyalty is in the past • Learned to fend for themselves at a young age • Very entrepreneurial thinking • Highly technologically advanced • Prefer to discuss via a series of emails
Primary Driver	• Want their opinions heard at work • Need mentors to support them • A sense of community and connection • Meaningful work that makes a difference in the world • Create partnerships at work • Work to live
Primary Values	• Balance & synergy • Community • Partnership
Key Recruitment Strength	• Social responsibility • Making work fun • Describe diversity of skills & challenges of the work • Offer a compelling career experience • Provide competitive compensation
Benefits	• Educational reimbursement • Health club memberships • Flexibility over work hours, methods of work (i.e. telecommuting). • More interested in pay than benefits • Life/work balance
Motivation Techniques	• Task variety/stimulating work • Work is their social environment • Don't misinterpret confident for 'cocky' • Doesn't want to hear "pay your dues" • Give regular performance review with substance • Attach rewards to performance • Work has to be challenging & interesting

Practical Applications For Your Organization

After reading each chapter on the shifts, scan through the quick reference guide for each generation. Write down how you believe these shifts have translated over to your work environment for each generation. Once you have identified how these imprints impacted work, you can then create strategies for change.

BABY BOOMERS	How These Imprints Translate to Work
• Time of optimism/job opportunity abundant	
• Civil Rights/women's movement	
• Corporate downsizing	
• Inherited old values — work hard — pay your 'dues'	
• Company loyalty a given	
• Raised by traditional family	
• Sparked the divorce movement	
• Healthiest and /wealthiest generation	

GENERATION X	How These Imprints Translate to Work
• Time of brutal recession/pessimism	
• Saw parent/sibling being downsized	
• Time alone, less with parents	
• Value making a difference & "changing the world"	
• Inherited most of old values — work hard	
• Marrying/children later due to economics	
• Consumer age lead to social conscious	

GENERATION Y	How These Imprints Translate to Work
* Few rules grew up as latch key kids	_____
• Internet, cell phones, 120+ TV stations, MTV	_____
• World problems (Global warming, ozone hole, war, terrorism)	_____
• Blended families	_____
• Tech bubble & burst	_____
• Delayed adulthood	
• College becomes High School	_____
• Techno savvy	_____

Three Generations: Communication and Training Tips

BABY BOOMERS

Communication	Training
• Respect their knowledge and experience in conversations • Don't use techno language unless necessary • Mix face to face and email • Use a participatory management style • Brainstorming & quality circles for team building • Use formal & informal methods for communication • Counsel respectfully and ask for their opinions of what they observe about their behavior • Don't be authoritarian/treat them as equals	• Provide technology upgrading skills • Limit online training • Supply informal workshops/seminar training • Increase formal education — Offer Executive MBA's • Invite involvement to facilitate programs • Encourage cross mentorship for skill development • Provide the ability to attend conferences as a participant or presenter • Acknowledge what they know

GENERATION Y

Communication	Training
• Wants discussion rather than top down approach. Dislikes hierarchy • Informal approach to communication • Want a direct say in what is to be, the steps to execute it & process involved • Expects a corporate culture that supports the individual person and their goals • Clearly define objectives and goals then give freedom to add to it • Will challenge authority. Encourage an open door approach with respectful communication • Expects timely, consistent feedback and performance reviews	• Provide blogs/Intranet discussion groups • Offer leading edge training programs • Shortened training programs • Wants a career development roadmap • Provide multi media training & multiple resources • Schooled in a experiential rather than role playing model. Created creative, strategic thinkers and problem solvers • Provide cross mentorship to across generations to exchange specialty skills • Promote lateral moves for skill development, projects based work • Use Gen Y skills to teach other generations about technology

GENERATION X

Communication	Training
• Outline and clearly define objectives & goals then give freedom to act on them • Trust they can do the job and get the results in their own way • Support the individual person and their goals • Use Gen X as a bridge with Gen Y & Boomers • Wants informal discussion not top down approach. Dislikes hierarchy • Will challenge authority. Encourage an open door approach with respectful communication • Expects timely, consistent feedback and performance reviews • Avoid dictating rules that aren't necessary. Concentrate on what is 'most important' and needed • Don't misinterpret confident as 'cocky'	• Wants a career development roadmap • Seeks role models • Give constant feedback that is timely, accurate & very specific • Want to be coached & mentored by highly skilled mentors • Doesn't want to hear "pay your dues" • Provide multi media training & multiple resources • Promote lateral moves for skills development, assign projects for learning • Provide blogs/Intranet discussion groups • Offer leading edge training programs • Shortened training programs

Practical Applications For Your Organization

Read through 'bridging the communication gap with open dialogue on the following page for ideas on getting started with your strategy. Review each chapter and the generational references guides.

Review the four steps for Getting Started on page 257. Follow the step below as a guide to building your people strategy

Strategy for Getting Started

Step one: Get the Leadership Team on Board

_____

_____

_____

Step two: Meet and talk about expectations around each shift

_____

_____

_____

Step three: Capture key points during your meeting about how to respond to each shift

_____

_____

_____

Step four: Create Commitments and Implement ideas

_____

_____

_____

Practical Applications For Your Organization

Here are a few ideas to get you started in bridging the generation gap. Share them with your teams, in meetings, training programs or when creating generational strategies.

Bridging the Communication Gap with Open Diaglogue

1. Leaders need to understand the key differences in approaches and become an example of reaching out first

2. Start to create a "flexible" culture, not one size fits all. Benefits, social gatherings, recognition programs, learning and development tracks need to be unique

3. Have dialogues across the generations — how we see you, how we think you see us, discuss what you need from each other and how you can support each other

4. Cultivate an understanding that value differences are simply "what is true" for each person

5. Ask question to clarify rather than assuming. Seek to learn from each other by actively listening with respect and without judgment

6. Provide a safe environment that practices open and honest feedback without reprimands

7. Practice transparency: share what you know, share what you don't know and if you know and can't say then share that too

8. Provide support for learning and growth that fits personally for each person as much as possible

9. Ask people what they need, how they learn, what motivates them, how

do they want to be coached and then wait for the answers

10. Show obvious respect for others values and differences as you would for your own

11. Encourage all generations to be teachers and to cross share their knowledge

PART
THREE

Getting Started

CHAPTER TEN

leading in the wake of the shifts

"If treated well, people are intensely loyal."
— STEVEN SMITH, CEO, FORMER CEO WESTJET

Years ago when John was giving a workshop for a corporate client, he noticed that participants suddenly started taking copious notes halfway through the morning. "The real workshop doesn't begin until they start taking notes!" he reflected ruefully.

Hopefully, you have been taking notes throughout the process of reading this book and identifying ways that you can put these insights to work in your company. For now, we will focus directly on a few simple questions:

- Where does one go from here?

- What do these shifts mean for an organization?

- How can a leader get started?

- How can this knowledge be tapped to increase retention and reduce turnover?

- And finally, are these shifts temporary, and if so, where are employee expectations headed next?

The decision of whether to act on the insights contained in this book rests on statistics we've already revealed. *Sobering statistic No. 1* is that the average cost of losing an employee is between 100 and 250 percent of that person's annual salary. So, if your organization employs three hundred people making an average of $35,000 per year, and has a turnover rate of 10 percent, the annual cost of that turnover is between $1 million and $2.6 million. Did that grab your attention? *Encouraging statistic No. 1*: Gallup found that businesses with the most engaged employees enjoyed 29 percent higher revenue, were 50 percent more likely to boast above-average customer loyalty, and were 44 percent more likely to turn in above-average profits.

Sobering statistic No. 2: Tight competition for good people, whether for front-line or high-tech positions, will continue for at least the next decade — a fact guaranteed by the sheer demographic volume of retiring baby boomers and reinforced by a growing world economy.

So, how does one lead in the wake of these shifts?

retention is a philosophy before it's a strategy

In most of this book, we have focused on what employees want and expect from work today, and what strategies leading companies are employing to win their commitment. To respond effectively, one must first realize that most of the companies we've held up as having creative responses to these shifts have at their core a *philosophy*, not just a set of tactics. Practices and benefits may entice employees in, but without a philosophical anchor for the company, the same employees will drift away with the next tide. Before your organization can start brainstorming its own innovative approaches, it must first believe in the employee-topped "inverted pyramid" we discussed in Chapter 1. That is, today's companies must be built around employees' wants, needs, and, ultimately, their expectations. To determine the strength of your organization's core philosophy towards people, ask yourself: Are employees regarded as an expendable resource or the gold mine of our enterprise? Is responding to their shifting values a priority or a nuisance to be dealt with by human resources? Does this organization care at a deep level about creating a great and fulfilling place to work?

A clear trend today is that the best workplaces are getting better; a few companies are leading the way in building entire enterprises around employees. How important does your organization feel it is to join these leaders?

One company we've men-

IN RETURN FOR completing a health assessment and attending a group counselling session on the results, employees at Fannie Mae receive a "Healthy Living Day" off.

tioned a few times in this book is Synovus Financial (and its subsidiary, Total System Services) in Columbus, Georgia. Years of consulting have made us a bit jaded about using superlatives in describing workplaces. After all, we've seen enough warts on the faces of supposedly leading-edge companies to breed plenty of skepticism. So when front-line people at Synovus started telling us how much they loved this company and how much it meant to them to work there, we were — well, skeptical! And yet, once John met and conferred with Jimmy Blanchard, the company's CEO for the past thirty years, he became a believer. Toward the end of their first meeting, John squeezed in the question, "Obviously, you have built something special here, something many leaders would die for. What advice would you give leaders who want to create the kind of loyalty you have?"

Blanchard replied unflinchingly, "I would tell them you have to want it. You have to wake up in the morning wanting to create a place where people love to work, and you have to care about that as much as you care about all the other things a leader must focus on-market share, sales, costs, and so on." John nodded, impressed, said his goodbyes, and was almost out the door when Blanchard added, "Oh, and you have to want it as an end in itself, not merely as a means to an end!"

Dennis Bakke, the former CEO of AES, echoed the same philosophy when he warned John about companies that respond to people's values merely to win them over: "That begins with the wrong premise."

These corporate giants understand the importance of tracking and respecting employees' values. They also understand that while retention may offer an incentive for building an organization around people's values, if retention is the organization's only motivation for doing so, the resulting changes will likely not run deep enough to have a major impact.

Synovus has coined the term "value chain" to describe how people and culture drive strategy and tactics, which ultimately drive performance and shareholder value. This thinking is squarely in the realm of philosophy. When was the last time your organization defined its core philosophies? And does the desire to make the company a great place to work keep leaders up at night?

One of John's mentors is Mark LeBlanc, a leading small-business strategist in San Diego, California. LeBlanc advises consultants to focus on something that keeps clients up at night. He built his own business around how to start and grow a small business because just about every owner of a small business loses sleep worrying about how to grow. Most executives of the companies featured in this book worry about creating an environment that people will want to work in, stay in, and give their very best to while there. Business leaders can apply this same approach: What keeps your management team anxious? How much time and priority is given to people issues?

Jack Lowe of TDIndustries, a construction company that has been on *Fortune*'s "Best Companies to Work For" list for several years running, is pretty clear about its people priority. Lowe says, "I want this to be a great place to work. This is the reason we are in business. This is our No. 1 goal." That commitment may explain how TDI has lowered turnover in new hires from 100 percent six to eight years ago, to 40 percent today — with total turnover at 15 percent (of which 10 percent is voluntary). If these figures sound high, rest assured that they are not for the construction industry. And yet, Lowe isn't finished. "I'm striving for 5 percent. Well, I don't know the exact figure, but I just want it to keep getting better. The shape of the [retention] curve has been very dramatic. We are focused on retention and on meeting the needs of our people."

Posted at the entrance to many a Zen Buddhist temple is a sign with three simple words: "Watch your step!" This is Zen masters' way of saying that paying attention is very important. In our experience, the business leader's most important role is to pay attention to the steps ahead of them — in other words, to prioritize challenges. Jack Lowe is focused on retention. Jimmy Blanchard is focused on the first link of the value chain — people. Before launching into a strategy around the values found in this book, re-examine your company's priorities, its root philosophies. We've seen many a corporate brochure that includes the platitude, "People are our most important asset," but winning and keeping people is not a public relations exercise. The companies winning at the retention game have been bold in actually making people a daily commitment.

will the shifts shift?

Before committing to new philosophies or strategies in light of the shifts we've discussed, some readers are wondering if, or when, those shifts themselves might shift. Where will employee values go in the years to come? Are these shifts an artifact of a red-hot economy, or are they more enduring changes? To know the answer is to understand where values come from in the first place. In much the same way basic personality gets stamped on our psyches early in childhood, cultural values — the way we see the world around us — are formed during our teens and twenties and tend to travel with us the rest of our lives, even as the world changes drastically around us. Values shift very little and very slowly, only a few times in each generation.

Consider John's grandmother, who was born in 1899 and died in 1985. She was a simple woman from Nova Scotia who settled in New York during the Great Depression. Raised in a farming community, she grew up in a time when loyalty was a core value, and she witnessed a world that went from horses and buggies to space shuttles. During her eighty-six years, the world around her changed immensely, as did her personal circumstances. She grew up poor, and although she never became wealthy, money was not a worry in her later years. Yet her values barely budged as her life changed. Years after the Depression, she would follow people around the house to turn lights off behind them, chanting, "Waste not, want not." And years after the Brooklyn Dodgers left New York, she remained a Dodgers fan, chanting, "I am no turncoat!" Having lived and sacrificed through two world wars, she would forever give both politicians and her country the benefit of the doubt. So she, like many of her age group, was slow to grasp younger people's disenchantment with the Vietnam War. She would chant, "America: Love it or leave it." Her values, from thrift to loyalty to politics, were forever imprinted in her psyche. As the world and her personal circumstances changed, her values remained stable.

So it is with the shifts we have identified in this book, and that is why we are confident that they will endure for some time. The boomers who "sold out" their flower-child heritage for corporate perks will forever have a soft spot for an environment that entwines a noble cause with one's livelihood. Gen Xers, who were initially blocked from the corporate world, and who watched older siblings or parents suffer the indignity of unanticipated downsizing, will forever doubt the corporation's loyalty and intentions. Netters who experienced parental divorce and precious little family time will as a generation always hold family a little dearer than most, and will forever seek the integration of their personal and work lives. And kids who grew up pressing the reset button whenever boredom threatened will forever expect, on some level, the world of work to meet that need for newness, instant growth, and excitement.

Exaggerations? Yes. Generalizations? For certain! But values do not change overnight, and the trends we've discussed will ring true long after the next generation's equivalent of a Dodgers exodus is over. Not only are these basic expectations unlikely to change anytime soon, but some will intensify. Here are our educated guesses as to how:

Balance

When the crunch of balancing family and corporate life hits Netters and Xers — who already have stronger values around time than boomers — the expectation of flexibility and balance will accelerate greatly.

Personal and professional development

As the new economy puts increasing pressure on keeping one's credentials up to date, and as Netters and Xers move into what we call the Peggy Lee phase of life ("Is that all there is?"), the desire to combine personal and professional development will grow. Both the aging of the population and the growing affluence of elite workers will accelerate this shift. Meanwhile, as the next wave of post-teens arrives at the workplace — a generation wowed by technology and newness since birth — the odds that they will be satisfied staying in one place without growth for long is slim at best.

Partnership

As more and more workers get a taste for being consulted in decision-making, and having a stake in the game, paternalistic management weakens. And the more educated people are, the more they expect to be able to make choices. Welcome to the new business world, in which there are more partners than employees!

Noble cause

There is growing evidence of a "green shift" in values among Western societies, as in Home Depot deciding it will sell only "certified lumber," and Nike's fall from grace over the childhood labor issue. As the world moves toward holding corporations accountable for integrity and environmental awareness, star talent will be increasingly inclined to pick and choose employers whose values appear to align with their own.

The A versus the B Team

An increasing number of people are drifting away from the influence of the retention craze discussed in this book. While star performers come to expect partnership, balance, noble cause, personal/professional development, community, and trust, workers less attractive to the new economy will struggle to find any work, let alone a meaningful or profound calling. The solution: Extend the same perks inspired by star performers' expectations to the entire workforce. Let janitors become millionaires through stock options. Let dishwashers enjoy the same free massage therapist as the top salesperson. Remember the business consultants who studied the US Marines for secrets to commitment? One recommendation was to take the time to bolster anyone who is floundering, in order to reinforce that individual's sense of belonging and promote an intense loyalty from everyone else. Breaking the chain breaks trust and dampens workers' belief in corporate support of partnership.

Diversity

Little has been written about the work values of newly landed North Americans, never mind the hundreds of thousands born, raised, and still living overseas who work for North American interests. As the working population grows more diverse and the more homogenous workforce retires, the need for organizations to attend to these differences will grow. Non-Westerners are, of course, "imprinted" with an entirely different set of experiences, based on what was happening in their culture as they came of age. The fact that workers throughout the world share a growing number of similarities will not greatly alter this imprint.

the first step: an honest assessment

Years ago, John met a salesman on a commuter flight. From the moment this man sat down beside John, he did nothing but complain — about his wife, his boss, the client he was going to visit, the airline, the weather, and anything else that crossed his radar screen. He even had a favorite phrase he uttered numerous times during the brief flight: "People are so stupid!"

As the plane drew near its destination, the salesman finally turned to John and asked what he did for a living. A somewhat peeved John replied, "I give speeches and workshops to corporations about the importance of being positive. I talk about how, if you live and work in a positive manner, great things will come your way." The man brightened and replied without hesitation, "It's so refreshing to sit next to a man who thinks like me!"

Years of consulting have convinced us that many leaders are as misled about themselves and their companies as that man on the plane. Undoubtedly, that salesman would slam shut this book and comment, "This is for other people, other companies, but not for me!"

So, to him and to anyone else about to pass this book along, we advise, "Do an honest self-assessment of how you and your company are responding to these shifts, before shrugging off the matter."

Begin by taking the self-assessments found at the ends of Chapters 4 through 9. Better yet, have each member of your leadership team (which, in truly non-hierarchical companies, means most employees!) fill out the assessment, then discuss the results as a group. Alternatively, assign the book to every member of your management team and have them meet weekly to discuss each expectation, how the company is currently addressing it, and what other measures could be introduced to enhance policy in that area.

A more thorough way to meet these challenges is to conduct a formal assessment of your current corporate culture and practices. The aim: to gain a clear picture of the vital few policies that must change to ensure that your company becomes an employer of choice. When meeting with prospective clients, John likes to ask leaders whether they know the two or three key issues they must tackle to win greater commitment and engagement from their people. Amazingly, many have no idea, or only a vague, intuitive sense of what those priorities should be. A formal assessment can start them down the road to greater things.

Several years ago, John was asked to conduct an engagement and retention assessment for a company considered by many to be a "good" place to work. Although the company's retention rate was above industry average, turnover had been increasing and recruiting new hires was becoming more difficult. Wisely, the leaders of the organization wanted to know why this was happening and, more importantly, what they could do about it. John recommended they conduct an assessment using both a survey and a qualitative focus-group process to determine how vulnerable they were to losing people and what would entice people to stay. John insisted on the qualitative study so that the leaders would hear the real stories and desires of their people — an invaluable supplement to the

EMPLOYEES of Amgen in Thousand Oaks, California can get free shuttle service to the airport, on-site car rentals, on-site childcare, and an on-site fitness center open seven days a week.

reams of reports on means and normative comparisons. John's assessment pointed to three critical issues that, if addressed, would cause retention to soar:

1. People wanted to feel that the company was concerned about their personal and professional growth; they wanted more opportunities for learning and expanding their skills.

2. People wanted to feel that the work they were doing was important, was making a difference in some tangible way.

3. They wanted more recognition from management.

Sound familiar? That's right: growth and development, noble cause, and community. (Presumably, this company already excelled at balance, partnership, and trust!)

Over the next year, John's client worked hard at communicating heretofore "hidden" noble causes, bringing in customers to talk to employees about the impact of the company's products. Executives crafted a new mission statement with greater input from associates. Leaders pondered the deeper meaning of work and began to talk about it with their people on a regular basis. They also initiated discussions on the need for greater partnership and personal/professional development. By the end of the year, the results were in: a 35 percent decrease in turnover, and a tangible new spirit throughout the company. What's the lesson here? Taking the time to ask and listen is critical. Surveys are helpful, but real conversations will tell listeners far more.

When was the last time your organization held frank conversations with colleagues as to why they stay and what would make them leave? What key values or needs are not being met at this time?

the second step:
transferring the knowledge

We have talked a great deal about demographics from the very beginning pages of this book. In Part One, we spoke about the different age groups and that they tend to have different views of what their ideal work life looks like. In Part Two we opened the door for leaders on how to respond to the six new shifting values in the workplace and offered ideas for higher retention and engagement of each generation.

All of these concepts are imperative, but for some of our readers they might be dealing with a demographic crisis spiraling downwards with too much workload and not enough employees. Many are wondering how to maximize the intellectual knowledge and experience of their workers that is laying dormant by not being moved along from generation to generation. If organizations are to remain fruitful and sustainable then the critical issue of knowledge retention must be addressed and for some, more quickly than others, if not then if will look more like a knowledge collapse.

One of John's clients in the USA has recognized for some time that there is a demographic crisis looming their way and that it has reached a critical juncture. Over the next decade over 60 percent of their workforce has plans for retirement. The burning question is how to ensure their leaders also see this sense of urgency in transferring knowledge, especially when one of the underlying beliefs is 'these kids haven't done their time". The stark reality is it's no longer about doing time. We missed that window long ago and the new generations, well, they abandoned that belief along with the mentality of staying in an organization cradle to grave.

Most organizations that haven't already developed and are acting on a serious knowledge transfer strategy are going to be out of time pretty quickly. Our suggestion is to begin as soon as possible.

where to start the knowledge transfer strategy

For starters, you need to dig in and find out the demographics landscape for your particular organization. Find out how many of each age group you have and what are your projected retirements lines are.

Be blunt with yourself. Ask what are the barriers in your culture that are getting in the way of a smooth transfer of knowledge amongst your departments.

Knowledge transfer is not just about burning information onto discs, gathering it onto your hard drive or in your file cabinet. You need multiply venue's to gather and pass along vital information and learning. Knowledge is hard to visualize, we tend to do it without thinking about the tasks. Find creative ways to take this knowledge and spread it around through various training methods.

Find where your greatest knowledge gaps are. Name what needs to be passed along from generation to the next generation. From this point, build your succession strategy by finding out who has this knowledge and how to tap into it. Start to recycle this vital information by creating coaches and mentors.

Bring the generations together in focus groups and ask them what the gaps are that are getting in the way of transferring this knowledge.

Ask how the younger generations would like to be taught in order to pass this information along. Different generations have preferred methods for training and development.

Pull together in-house networks of individuals with similar interests in the topics. If you want to pass information along quickly than you need to pick individuals who have a natural talent and interest in those areas.

Capture the knowledge into newly developed training programs. Restructure your training to be more tactile, hands on and less classroom oriented. Force the learner out into the field and out of the classroom, there you will get far better comprehension of the material.

Develop in-house Apprenticeship training programs. Use knowledge transfer programs and link them to career and promotional opportunities.

Create the position of a Chief Knowledge Transfer Officer. Assign them to a specific area such as finance, technology, systems, human resources, and operations. Make it there job to manage the transfer of information.

Put your top performers together and determine a priority of what is most important to transfer. From there create a system for retrieving this information from the generation leaving. Utilize your retirees as potential trainers and mentors on a part-time basis.

Lastly, you need to make a commitment to transfer knowledge both in time and financial resources. Build in the expectation of knowledge transfer as part and parcel of the manager's job role. Hold managers responsible for passing information along. Cover your entire basis by documenting important procedures, use multi media whenever possible, place people together for experiential learning, cross training, job shadowing, and job rotation. Keep going and don't look back, because the past is now your future.

imitation: the worst form of strategy?

Imitation may be the best form of flattery, but it is the worst form of strategy. It's tempting, of course, to simply imitate the examples of what other companies are doing to respond to these shifts. We can even hear a few readers thinking, "If informal barbecues create community, let's have a few. If giving work teams power spells partnership, count us in. And if bringing customers in to talk about what a 'difference' our products make illuminates noble cause, we'll bring them in by the truckload. In fact, let's just gather up all the best practices listed in this book and start checking off which ones we'll do. Will five within each category be enough?"

While the examples listed in this book are excellent for pre-strategizing inspiration, duplicating them en masse is not a strategy. Strategy requires focus, or knowing what the critical issues are for your particular enterprise. Before you adopt new perks, ask yourself which values your company has already responded to effectively and which need a new focus. Which practices are most likely to be enthusiastically implemented by the workforce itself and which might meet resistance? In the spirit of partnership-keeping in mind that partnership is one of the new expectations — ask your people for their own creative solutions to their own wants and desires — new policies that would make them want to stay. Again, asking is often as important as implementing new practices. Besides, imitation unaccompanied by a deeper pondering of your basic philosophy may lead to barbecues to which no one shows up, or flex time that no one dares take.

Nonetheless, assuming your organization's management philosophy and values are in the right place, the examples in this book form an excellent jumping-off place. Try discussing each expectation as a leadership team, exploring the practices listed. Using them as a springboard, brainstorm ideas more amenable or specific to your organization, department, or division. Above all, don't feel limited by the examples we've gathered together; use them instead as the foundation for your own creativity. Oh, and don't forget to send us your best solutions, so we can mention them in our next book! info@theizzogroup.com

getting started

Step One   Have the leadership team read each expectation chapter.

Step Two   Meet and talk about each expectation. Talk about how you understand it, what it means for your type of organization, and how you think your division or company is doing.

Step Three Using the examples for inspiration, brainstorm all the ways your organization or division could respond to that shift.

Step Four Identify a few new policies to get you started or to deepen your progress on that shift. Choose only as many as you can commit to implementing.

doing something is more important than waiting for perfection

We hope this book has stimulated lots of ideas about what your company can do to respond to the changing expectations of your people and to stoke the fires of commitment. The real danger is not a lack of ideas but the chance that those great ideas will never translate into action. In seminars, John often asks attendees to close their eyes and imagine they are stepping over a line between intention and commitment. At first, he worried that they would consider this exercise silly, but more and more came up after seminars and expressed how helpful it was and how often they intended to do things but never got around to them.

Why is it that we read a book like this and never act? George Leonard, a martial arts expert turned leadership guru, explains in his book *Mastery* that at the edge of any new path, we often stand for a long time waiting for the perfect plan and steps to emerge. Analysis replaces action, as we imagine that we can map out the journey in detail before taking a step forward. In reality, the best way to get started is to get started. Once we do something, those actions lead to self-corrections and then to other, more lasting practices. The point is, take a few moments and write down three to five ideas you can put into immediate practice regarding what you have just learned about changing expectations at work. How about purchasing a copy of this book for every member of your staff and have them create a grand list of ideas. Instead of worrying about whether these are the perfect ideas, just get started. It's more important to take some action based on what you've read, than to consign today's thoughts to that great stack of insights never yet passed on to commitment.

a final benediction

The kind of life we lead and the kind of workplace we create are never the product of one life-changing decision, but of thousands of decisions made every day. A few years ago, the entire workforce of the US Postal Service was told that it was now empowered! How important was that organizational proclamation? Not nearly as important as the small decisions leaders make every day. As in the type of decision a leader must make when people ask if they can attend their child's school play during work hours (balance). As in, the tone of daily conversations those leaders have on the meaning of work versus making the numbers (noble cause). As in, the times that leaders resist making a decision, handing it instead to people weary of having decisions made for them and then asking those newly delegated decision-makers to return and broadcast what they accomplished (partnership). As in, next Monday when you take the time to meet with some of your people, simply to ask how they are doing, or next Friday, when you make the effort to ask what they're up to on the weekend and then follow up by asking them how it went (community).

Stephen Smith, the former CEO of WestJet Airlines, told us, "One of the most important things a corporation can do is align the interests of the business with the interests of its people." This book has taken the first step in that process. Now that you know their expectations, the rest is up to you.

CREDITS

Opening quote, "To turbocharge retention...": *Harvard Business Review*, September/October 1999; page 152

Chapter One Credits

Seattle Post-Intelligencer quote: March 5, 2000; page G1; Unemployment is at its lowest rate in 30 years: *Economist*, January 15, 2000; page 25; Kinko's quote: *HR Magazine*, December 1999; page 8; Mark Sussman quote: *Megagtrends 2000*, page 221; 98% of population growth is occurring in countries without a strong education system: *National Geographic*, October 1998; page 4; Human resources issues have leapfrogged to employers' No. 1 concern: *Globe & Mail*, November 15, 1999; page D1; Number of voluntarily unemployed at 15%, highest in 10 years: *Fortune*, February 7, 2000; page 199; Average job tenure in information technology has shrunk to 13 months from 18 months two years ago: *Fortune*, February 7, 2000; page 199; Cost of losing and replacing an employee is between 50 and 150% of the salary of the leaving employee: *HR Information Matters*, September/October 1998; page B10; Taco Bell outlets with lowest employee turnover produced 50% more in sales: "Morale Boosters," *Marketing*, London, September 24, 1998; pages 36-38; A significant improvement in recruiting new talent can produce a 10.1% increase in a company's market value, and key HR practices can increase shareholder values 30%:, *HRDM*, March 2000: 510,000 full-time information technology jobs are vacant: Training & Development, January 1999; page 62; By 2006, half of all workers will be employed in information technology positions or within industries that intensively utilize information technology: *Fast Company*, March 2000; page 217; US Congress raised the number of visas from 1999 through 2001 for skilled technology workers by 142,500, a 73% leap: Training & Development, January 1999; page 62; National Manufacturers Association survey (48% unable to read and interpret drawings and diagrams): *Workforce* 77, March 1998; page 48# 004 17% of American MBA students polled by Stockholm-based Universum planned to leave their first position after one or two years: *Fortune*, March 16, 1998; page 167.

Chapter Two Credits

Angus Reid quote: *Shakedown*, page 310; Stephen R. Covey re: the new economy needs leaders in every rank: *BC Business*, January 2000; page 38; Half of women with small children work, 77% of women with children work: *Megatrends 2000*, page 217: Plante & Moran: (*Fortune*, Jan. 10, 2000 page 98); Claire Raines quote: *Beyond Generation X*, page 40; Plante & Moran: (*Fortune*, Jan. 10, 2000 page 98); Toxic handlers: Peter Frost and Sandra Robinson, "The Toxic Handler: Organizational Hero — and Casualty," *Harvard Business Review*, July/August 1999, pp. 96-106; Americans were exposed to six times as many advertising messages in 1991 as in 1971: *Fast Company*, March 2000; page 218; SAP-AG: *Industry Week*, August 16, 1999; page 106; CDW Computer Centers: *Fortune*, January 10, 2000; page 84; Stonyfield Farm: *Making a Living While Making a Difference*, page 13; Percentage of 20-somethings living with their parents has doubled since 1960: *Jobshift*, page 228; Half of Generation X comes from divorced families, and the divorce rate has shot up since they were growing up in the 1970s: *Rational Exuberance*, page 161; McCormick: *Fortune*, January 12, 1998; page 94; A recent survey of graduating MBAs showed that a large percentage of new graduates has vowed never to let their work life overwhelm their personal life, a clear backlash against an over-devotion to work: 1997 survey of 1,792 MBA students at 20 US and Canadian schools by Universum, a consulting firm in Stockholm; 40% of employees always have their resume up to date and 60% have taken courses to upgrade their skills in the last year alone: Royal Bank 2000 survey; Edward Jones: *Fortune*, January 10, 2000; page 83; Companies are lucky to keep an employee the current average of three and a half years (men, 3.8; women, 3.4): *Across the Board*, January 2000; page 17; The good risk-taker dwells for large parts of every day in ambiguity, uncertainty and vulnerability, and too much of this diet eats away at one's sense of character: Richard Sennett, *The Corrosion of Character*, pages 84, 85; Kinko's Inc.: *HR Magazine*, December 1999; page 88; 93% of corporate and human resources executives...: *Training & Development*, October 1999; page 12; People born after 1945 are 10 times as likely to suffer from depression as people born 50 years earlier, in a less materialistic era: *The Good Life*, page 144; Alcoa Inc.: *Industry Week*, August 16, 1999; page 45; Simon Zadek quote: *The Good Life*, pages 129 & 144; Two-thirds of experts at the Open University's Futures Observatory...: *Future Revolutions*, page 81; "Primary measures of success" chart: *Making a Living While Making a Difference*, page 3; Michael Hammer quote, "It is thrilling to be part of a revolution...": *Beyond Reengineering*, page 259; Direct democracy and personal happiness: *Economist*, April 17, 1999; page 122; US growth from 5% of total capital spending...: *Training & Development*, November 1999; page 38; Americans are working 163 hours longer per year than they were in 1969: *Fortune*, January 10, 2000; page 68; Just over one-third of Britons work on weekends, and 54% work into the evenings: University of Manchester, *The Times*, September 24, 1998; Americans are outworking the Japanese: *Fortune*, January 10, 2000; page 68; Internet chat group about "electronic leashes": *Fortune*, January 10, 2000; page 68; One in five American workers will telecommute by 2010: January 25, 1999 web site of IBM Advanced Business Institute, "Five Myths Regarding Leadership, Culture Change and Technology," by Patrick G. Brown & Robert M. Goett; Oracle anecdote regarding Intranets and employment perks: *Financial Post* DataGroup, March 6, 2000; Regis McKenna quote: "Technology's effects on us today are different...": *Real Time: Preparing for the Age of the Never Satisfied Customer*, pages 15, 16.

Chapter Three Credits

Barbara Moses quote: *Career Intelligence*, page 54; 20% of workers are non-white, median age will surpass 40 in the year 2003 for the first time ever, 48% women: Families & Work Institute web site, January 21, 1999; 44% of Generation X, 36% of boomers toying with the idea of starting their own business: *Rational Exuberance*, page 11; Ellen Gee information: *BC Business*, March 1998; page 26-28; PricewaterhouseCoopers' mentoring program, etc.: *HR Information Matters*; Boomers total more than 60 million Americans, etc.: *Workforce*, November 1999; games2train.com: *Training & Development*, November 1999; page 20; Boomer manager quote: *Civilizing the Workplace*, page 207; 54% of 18-24-year-olds highly interested in starting businesses compared with 36% of 35-64-year-olds: *Rational Exuberance*, page 11; Workforce tips for retaining Gen Xers: *Workforce*, November 1999; page 14; Unusual job titles at Play, the marketing agency: *Fast Company*, January/February 2000; page 172; 8 of 10 US adults trying to start a business are in the 18 to 34 age group. In contrast, only 2% of the Harvard graduating class of 1942 showed any interest in self-employment: *Career Intelligence*, page 49; One out of eight employees moonlights; between 35 and 57 of these own their own moonlighting business: Inc/Gallup survey of 1997; 19% of 50-plus crowd, 30% of under-30s are on-line, but users 55 and older spend more time online than their younger counterparts: *Fast Company*, March 2000; page 214; Young adults suffered an unemployment rate twice the national average for most of the 1990s: *Rational Exuberance*, page 11; By 2003, for the first time ever there will be more workers over 40 than under 40: *Fortune*, February 1, 1999; page 50; Computer ownership among individuals over 50 has grown 38% in four years: *Workforce* November 1999; page 29; 40% of over-50s own computer: *Training & Development*, November 1999; page 20; CEOs believe age 43 is productivity peak: *Fortune*, February 1, 1999; page 52; 46% of Gen Xers identify their jobs as an "expression of themselves," compared with 56% of boomers: *Rational Exuberance*, page 12; Trainers should change message or activity every 8, 10 or 15 minutes: *Training and Development*, February 2000; page 29; Three-quarters of college students say that making a difference in the lives of others is very important, and more than half say doing volunteer work is a worthy cause. Gen X volunteers more than any other generation in America: *Rational Exuberance*, page 16; One expert has said of the Net Generation, "They want spirituality incorporated into the company culture, more flexibility than even Generation X wants, and more information, more quickly": *Across the Board*, February 2000; page 55; Gender has more power to determine a pay gap than ethnicity: *HR Magazine*, February 1998; Human resources professionals believe minorities encounter barriers to career advancement, etc.: *Training & Development*, October 1999; page 12; 90% of attendees said they planned to start a family, and 78% of those said they would keep working: *LA Times*, March 6, 2000; Part E, page one; regarding UCLA's Anderson School conference; Most women return to work within six months after giving birth, according to Catalyst: *Megatrends 2000*, page 233; One-fifth of all complaints received by the Canadian Human Rights Commission in 1998 involved allegations on the basis of sex, and a disproportionate number of those concerned women who suffered adverse consequences when their employers learned they were expecting: *Worklife*, Volume 11, Number 4, 1999; By 1990, the number of women working outside the home had leapt to 57 per cent, and today, it stands at 61 per cent. Meanwhile, two-thirds of unmarried mothers with a child under three are now in the labour force, compared with just over half in 1995: *Economist*, January 15, 2000; page 25; While only 3%

of the most senior jobs in *Fortune* 500 companies are currently held by women, more than 400...: *Globe & Mail*, December 11, 1997; page A14; Women have taken two-thirds of all the new jobs in the information economy: *Megatrends 2000*, page 47; Ernst & Young's women's network and mentors: *Fortune*, January 11, 1999; page 136; "There are not nearly enough people with college degrees...": *Megatrends 2000*, page 48; 59% of working mothers would relinquish a day's pay for extra time off, while only 43% of fathers would do so: *Black Enterprise*, June 1993; Women like praise in writing, boomers like it more than they get it, and small companies are quickest to hand it out: *Inc.*, May 2, 1997; Women are more receptive to and appreciative of detailed feedback and assistance from others: *Across the Board*, January 2000, page 13; Women are more receptive to and appreciative of detailed feedback and assistance from others: *Across the Board*, January 2000; page 13; Female managers in organizations offering flexible work hours experience a significantly higher level of organizational commitment and job satisfaction: *HR Information Matters*, September 1997; page 3; Deloitte & Touche, well known as a progressive company, boasts at least ten part-timers who have achieved partner status: *Fortune*, January 10, 2000; page 90; No. 1 predictor of job satisfaction for women is the relationships they form at work: US Bureau of Labor study, 1996; David Thomas quote: "Effective management of a diverse workforce...": *HR Magazine*, December 1999; page 67; Companies with diverse boards reap greater market returns: Kinder, Lydenberg, Domini & Co., a New York-based investment research firm: *HR Magazine*, December 1999; page 68; Almost a third of the Silicon Valley's scientists and engineers are now Asian-born: *Economist*, April 17, 1999, page 69; Of the 36,000 Chinese students who have gone to the US to study, only 8,800 have returned since 1979: *Megatrends 2000*, page 201; Phyllis Swersky quote: *Megatrends 2000*, page 225; Alagasco's $500 prize for diversity suggestion: *Fortune*, January 12, 1998; page 95; Five approaches companies take...: "Valuing Differences at

Digital Equipment Corporation," *Diversity in the Workplace Human Resources Initiatives*; pages 119-137; 1993 article in *Advertising Age*: Regis McKenna, *Real Time: Preparing for the Age of the Never Satisfied Customer*, page 34;: Companies with greater diversity make better business partners and merge more smoothly with other companies, according to Amy Hillman, management professor at the University of Western Ontario's Ivey School of Business: *HR* Magazine, December 1999; page 69; Regis McKenna quote: *Real Time: Preparing for the Age of the Never Satisfied Customer*, page 35; Etec Systems anecdote: *HR Information Matters*, March 1998; "Minority-friendly companies tend to be superior performers": *Fortune*, January 10, 2000

Chapter Four Credits

"The key to *The Good Life* lies in balance and integration in all facets of our lives." - *The Good Life*, page 87; CEO's wife could tell lower-ranking corporate wives how to decorate their homes: *BC Business*, August 1998; page 22; American Management Systems: *Fortune*, January 12, 1998; page 87; Deloitte & Touche: *Fortune*, January 11, 1999; page 121; Workers willing to give up 21% of their work hours *and salary* to achieve more balance: 1996 poll by staffing services firm Robert Half International, Menlo Park, California; A lack of balance between work and personal life is one of the top six reasons why 65% of employees on flex schedules would have left the firm without the flextime: Ernst & Young, *Fortune*, November 9, 1998; page 250; 60% of men and women under age 25 with children say they would make "a lot" of sacrifices in money and career advancement in order to spend more time with their families: *Rational Exuberance*, page 12; 55% of 18- to 34-year-olds identify the freedom to take extended leaves or sabbaticals as a key workplace benefit: *Chips & Pop*, page 175; 1995 report of "the new work ethic" by Demos: *Chips & Pop*, page 176; Need to increase the over-55's labour participation by 25%: *Age Works*, page 124; AFLAC ill-

relative time: *Fortune*, January 10, 2000; page 84; Genetech: *Fortune*, January 10, 2000; page 90; Time spent on the job in a given year has increased by 163 hours in the last 20 years: *Beyond Generation X*, page 45; Jamba Juice: *Inc*, June 1999; page 42; 41% of British managers disappointed with work/life balance, 85% believe vacation should be compulsory, yet 48% feel guilty when they leave on time: *Management Today*, Work Life Survey, August 1999, UK; page 51; SAP-AG: *Industry Week*, August 16, 1999; page 106; Dr. James Maas, author of *Power Sleep*, advocates allowing workers to take power naps :"Sleep Deprivation," *Vancouver Sun*, March 17, 1998; pages D1-D2; Over the past five years, percentage of workforce sharing jobs has risen by 81%; number that work from home up 70%; 90% of large companies expect more to work from home; three-quarters predict more job sharing: 1997 survey by international management consulting firm Watson Wyatt Worldwide; Study of 800 employers indicates that 79% of employees have formal policies for regular part-time employment, and 38% for flextime arrangements. Another 34% provide for compressed work schedules and 26% have job-sharing programs.; Telecommuting programs are offered by 17% of employers, with an equal number considering or developing them: 1996 study of 800 employers by consulting firm William M. Mercer Inc.; By the year 2010, one in every five Americans will be telecommuters: Advanced Business Institute web site, "Five Myths Regarding Leadership, Culture Change and Technology," by Patrick G. Brown and Robert M. Goett, January 25, 1999; Job stress estimated to cost US industry $200 billion to $300 billion annually in absenteeism, diminished productivity, employee turnover, accidents, workers' compensation, and direct medical, legal and insurance fees: *Fast Company*, March 2000; page 219; Defining characteristics of Attention Deficit Disorder increasingly prevalent and perhaps due to environmental factors such as the information explosion: *Fast Company*, March 2000; page 219; Gemcom Services: *BC Business Magazine*, March 1998; page 28; A *Fortune* magazine poll of headhunters recently determined that the employees most likely to turn down job offers had flextime: *Fortune*, January 12, 1998; page 69;: Fannie Mae "Healthy Living Day": Fannie Mac Web site; Deloitte & Touche, well known as a progressive company, boasts at least ten part-timers who have achieved partner status: *Fortune*, January 10, 2000; page 90; Dawson Personnel Systems survey: *Inc.*, August 1999; Your *Money or Your Life* graph: page 282; DDC Inc and Medela regarding Mothers at Work program: PRNewswire, August 6, 1998; Republic Bancorp: *Fortune*, January 10, 2000; page 88; In 1935, the average working man had 40 hours a week free. By 1990, it was down to 17 hours: *The Sibling Society*, page 36; The number of managers working 49 hours or more a week has risen by 37% since 1985: Bureau of Labor Statistics 1998; 72% of British managers surveyed said that long working hours affect their relationship with their partner, etc.: *The Times*, September 24, 1998; Quality of Working Life survey produced by the Institute of Management with Manchester School of Management at the University of Manchester Institute of Science and Technology; Nearly one in five employed parents is single, 27% are men, and two-thirds of employed parents with pre-kindergarten children rely on partners and relatives as the primary childcare source: Families & Work Institute 1997; One of six primary-age children and two out of five grade-school children arrive home after school to an empty house: *The Sibling Society*, page 136; The majority of babies born in the US are placed in full-time daycare within a year; nearly half of babies today suffering from a lack of attachment to their parents: *The Sibling Society*, page 136; Nearly a third of the population suffers from a definable psychological problem depression in particular growing; may be due to a lack of deep friendships...: *The Good Life*, page 26; A company of 1,000 employees loses $1 million per year in stress-induced absenteeism alone: *BC Business*, May 2000; page 81; Amgen: *Fortune*, January 10, 2000; page 90; Edward Jones: *Fortune*, January 10, 2000; page 83; Family problems are one of the top five reasons that relocations fail: 1997 survey by Right Management Consultants in Philadelphia, Pennsylvania; *Beyond Generation X* quote: "Members of the X generation...have witnessed firsthand a work ethic that eats people up: page 46; Computer Associates International item: *Industry Week*, August 16, 1999; page 52; WRQ: *Fortune*, January 11, 1999; page 122

Chapter Five Credits

Corporate Celebration quote: page 101; Grand Metropolitan: *The Hungry Spirit*, page 166; Fannie Mae: Fannie Mae Web site; Lenscrafters: *Fortune*, January 11, 1999; page 136; Oxfam receives a constant stream of resumes from high-powered executives looking for a change: *The Hungry Spirit*, page 160; Volunteer work and Gen X: *Rational Exuberance*, page 16; 72% of corporate and human resources executives polled said their companies' values motivate them personally: *Training & Development*, October 1999; page 12; Bright Horizons quote: *Fortune*, January 12, 1998; page 92; The Body Shop item: *Megatrends 2000*, page 236; Environics International poll: *Across the Board*, January 2000; page 28; Associates III: *Beyond Generation X*, page 89; Every 100 pounds of product manufactured in the US creates at least 3,200 pounds of waste: Paul Hawken, *The Good Life*; page 129; The world's population nearly quadrupled between 1900 and 2000: *National Geographic*, October 1998; page 4; The world's income is now less evenly distributed than it was one hundred years ago: *Globe & Mail*, "Amazing Facts," April 3, 2000; page 2; Results of a survey of graduating MBAs: 1997 survey of 1,792 MBA students at 20 US and Canadian schools by Universum, a consulting firm in Stockholm; Even more recently, respondents responded marriage, health and ethics: *Making a Living While Making a Difference*; page 3; Pledge programs: *Making a Living While Making a Difference*, page 167; Dayton, Ohio flood in the early 1900s, and John Patterson: *Discovering America's Past: Customs, Legends, History & Lore of our Great Nation*, The Reader's

Digest Association, 1993; page 288; Medtronics: Fortune, January 11, 1999; page 136; IKEA's driving purpose: *The Natural Step for Business*; page 48; ICN Pharmaceuticals Inc: *The Mission Statement Book*, page 242; Johnson Wax: *The Mission Statement Book*, page 253; Borg-Warner: *The Mission Statement Book*, page 100; Pre-IPO stock pledges: *Fast Company*, March 2000; page 166; Pfizer: *The Mission Statement Book*, page 343; AES: *CMA Management*, October 1999; page 50; Jostens Inc: *The Mission Statement Book*, page 262; Shaklee US: *The Mission Statement Book*, page 384; Tandy Corporation: *The Mission Statement Book*, page 412; Patagonia: *Fortune*, January 12, 1998; page 86; Bell Canada item: *Making a Living While Making a Difference*, page 39; The Endangered Species Chocolate Company: *Making a Living While Making a Difference*, page 12; Placer Dome item: *Chips & Pop*, page 179; 90% of *Fortune* 500 companies have formalised ethics codes, and 30% of those have ethics officers or specialists to support their ethics programs. Canada alone employed 60 ethics officers in 1998, while another 60 Canadian companies boasted corporate ombudspersons: *HR Information Matters*, April 1998; page B5; *Fortune* magazine reporter and Container Store: *Fortune*, January 2000; page 76; DaimlerChrysler AG: *Industry Week*, August16, 1999; page 47; The Body Shop broadcasts: *Corporate Celebration*, page 100; Paul Hawken quote: *The Natural Step for Business*, page 202; Four companies profiled in *The Natural Step for Business*: pages 192, 193; Scandic Hotels: *The Dance of Change*, page 532; Coalition for Environmentally Responsible Economies (www.ceres.org), representing more than 80 businesses, non profits and public agencies: *Making a Living While Making a Difference*, page 56; David Packard quote: *The Hungry Spirit*, page 77; Michael Dell quote: *Fast Company*, December 1999; page 116; Nike Canada's P.L.A.Y. program: *Report on Business*, August 1999; page 22; The Body Shop item: *Megatrends 2000*, page 236; Worldwide survey of managers' values: Charles Hempden-Turner, quoted in *Corporate Celebration*, page 13; Psychotherapist Francis Hope quote: *The Good Life*, page 47 USA

Today survey: April 22, 1997; HB Fuller: *Fortune*, January 12, 1998; page 94; Homestead.com anecdote: *Fast Company*, April 2000; page 76; Bain & Co. anecdote: *Globe & Mail*, April 17, 2000; page M1;Computer Business Associates International Inc: *Industry Week*, August 16, 1999; page 52; General Mills anecdote: *Industry Week*, August 16, 1999; page 103; *Industry Week* quote: *Industry Week*, August 16, 1999; page 103; Marriott International: *Fortune*, January 12, 1998; page 87; Whole Goods Market: *HR* Magazine, December 1999; page 92; Finova Group: *Fortune*, January 10, 2000; page 84;Timberland: *Fortune*, January 10, 2000, page 90 and *Fortune*, January 12, 1998, page 90; Michael Hammer quote: *Beyond Reengineering*, pages 267, 268; Three parts of one's soul: Charles Handy *The Good Life*, page 127;Three factors common to *Fortune* magazine's 100 best companies: *Fortune*, January 12, 1998; pages 72-74

Chapter Six Credits

The Natural Step for Business quote: page 10; Kinko's Inc: *HR* Magazine, December 1999; page 88; 1968 study: *The Affluent Worker*; 3M: *Built to Last*, pages 157, 158; Net Generation's itchy feet: *Chips & Pop*, page 194: David K. Foot's four kinds of career paths: *Boom, Bust & Echo*, pages 61, 62; Foot quote: *Boom, Bust & Echo*, page 64; James Dyson anecdote: *Industry Week*, June 21, 1999; pages 42, 43; Sears Competency Transformation: *Network World*, February 21, 2000; page 66; Royal Bank of Canada survey: April 2000; Employer-sponsored training attracts recruits: Business Wire, September 7, 1998; *ComputerWorld* survey: *Technical Training*, March/April 1998; pages 16-19; 1999 Gallup poll: September 3, 1999 from Internet: Page 106: *Chips & Pop*: page 191; June 1997 survey of workplace benefits valued by Netters: *Chips & Pop*. page 175; 70% of companies believe that phased retirement offers solution to growing labour shortage, and three of four older workers prefer to reduce hours gradually: *Seattle P-I*, March 5,

2000; p G1: Page 106: Intel: *Fortune*, January 12, 1998; page 87; 1998 Watson Wyatt survey of employers: Strategic Rewards Survey of 614 US employers; 75% of higher performing companies linked training programs with strategic goals, compared with only 67% of other organisations: *HR Information Matters*, 1999; page 46; Employment in the information technology services sector is expected to nearly double between 1999 and 2005, from a current 1.1 million workers: *Training & Development*, January 1999; page 62; Technology-delivered training expected to account for 55% of corporate training, up from 20% in 1999: *Training and Development*, November 1999, page 38; Web-based training has produced 50% savings in time and cost: *HR Information Matters*, July/August 1998; page K8; Charles Schwab: *Fortune*, January 10, 2000; page 83; Design the training around the task, not the language: Kevin Kavanaugh, *Training & Development*, April 1999; page 15; Employee career development account: *Career Intelligence*, page 205; Mercer Management quote: *Fortune*, May 1, 2000; page 336; 86% of US employers surveyed found recruiting qualified workers difficult, and 60% reported problems retaining employees: *HR Focus*, July 1998; pages 11, 12; Motorola: *Fortune*, January 12, 1998; page 94; SAS turnover rate: *Fortune*, January 10, 2000, page 98 and *The New York Times Magazine*, March 5, 2000, page 82; Chick-fil-A: *Beyond Generation X*, page 89; Land's End: *Fortune*, January 12, 1998; page 88; David K. Foot quote: *Boom, Bust & Echo*, page 65; HB Fuller: *Fortune*, January 12, 1998; page 94; LifeCenter web site anecdote: *Fast Company*, October 1998, page 201; Wall Street firm: *Harvard Business Review*, September/October 1999; page 149; *The Harvard Business Review* quote: September/October 1999; page 146; Joan Mara and peer mentorship information: *BC Business*, November 1999; page 52; Up to 70% of employee knowledge is obtained informally on the job: Jack Stack, "The Training Myth," *Inc.* August 1998; *Fortune* survey re employees who had resisted headhunters' offers, as to why they had stayed put: *Fortune*, January 12, 1998; page 69; The Tandy Corp./RadioShack: *HR*

Magazine, December 1999; page 90; 1960s study in Great Britain: *The Affluent Worker*; A match of life and work interests is the most important of the three for long-term career satisfaction: *The Harvard Business Review*, September/October 1999; page 147; Silver Diner: *Nation's Restaurant News*, February 7, 2000; Paula Lawlor quote: *Inc.*, February 2000; page 78

Chapter Seven Credits

Charles McGrath quote: *The New York Times* Magazine, March 5, 2000; page 17; Kinko's quote: *HR Magazine*, December 1999; page 8; 61% of senior managers feel they treat employees as valued business partners; only 27% of employees agree: *Report on Business*, February 1999; page 3; Dyson Appliances: *Industry Week*, June 21, 1999; page 42; Schwab: Schwab Web site: Page 127: Donnelly: *Fortune*, January 12, 1998; page 94; Only 10 % of workers say they are part of a participatory environment: *Training & Development*, February 1998; pages 58-61; US employees rate two-way communication and individual recognition as highly important to job satisfaction, second only to salaries and benefits, but fewer than 35% frequently share opinions with top management: *HR Information Matters*, September/October 1998; page E7; Microsoft: *Fortune*, January 12, 1998; page 84; BrainBank anecdote: *Washington Post*, July 15, 1998, page C09; At Medi-Health Outsourcing, employees who pass on a lead that generates money can collect $500 to $1,000: *Inc.* February 2000; page 81; 3M: *Built to Last*, pages 158, 159; Best ways to engage workers: *Across the Board*, November/December 1999; page 52; *Megatrends 2000* quote: "People who are difficult to supervise...": page 223; Irshad Manji anecdote: *Risking Utopia* and *BC Business Magazine*, March 1998; page 26; Imagination Ltd.: *Fast Company*, April 2000; page 168; "Hungover" quote: *Beyond Generation X*, page 40; Noel Tichy & Ford: *Fast Company*, April 2000; page 148; Imagination Ltd.: *Fast Company*, April 2000; page 168; Kinkos: *Beyond*

Generation X, page 79; Teknion Corporation: *Globe & Mail*, March 3, 2000; AES Corporation: *CMA Management*, October 1999; page 50; Peter Senge quote, "Sooner or later, executive leadership becomes crucial...": *Dance of Change*, page 566; WL Gore: *Fortune*, January 12, 1998; page 84 & January 11, 1999; page 127; Marriott: *Harvard Business Review*, May/June 1999; page 117; Southwest Airlines employee quote: *Fortune*, January 12, 1998; page 84; Medi-Health Outsourcing: *Inc.*, February 2000; page 76; Harley-Davidson: *Industry Week*, February 1, 1999; page 6; Dallas-based Texas Instruments: *Fortune*, January 12, 1998; page 92; Continental Airlines: *Fortune 500*, January 10, 2000; page 88; Granite Rock: *Fortune*, January 12, 1998; page 86; Adrian Woodridge quote: *New York Times* Magazine, March 5, 2000; page 83; *Dance of Change* description of open-book management: page 181; International Harvester: *Dance of Change*, page 381; The Container Store: Container store web site; TDIndustries' monthly meeting: *Fortune*, January 12, 1998; page 84; Open books lead workers to see and understand the big picture: *Canadian Manager*, Summer 1999; page 27; Nordstrom Inc: *HR Magazine*, December 1999; page 87; Royal Bank study on employee attitudes: April 2000; 36 of 58 publicly held companies offered options: *Fortune*, January 10, 2000; page 83; "The new economy is about unlimited opportunity...": *Fast Company*, March 2000; page 166; Compensation pies: *BC Business*, September 1998; page 47; Pay-for-performance history: *New York Times* Magazine, March 5, 2000; page 46; AT&T, Blue Cross Blue Shield, and Owens Corning: *Fortune*, February 1, 1999; page 64; Whole Foods Market: *HR* Magazine, December 1999; page 92; Synovus: *Fortune*, January 10, 2000; page 1998; The millionaire clubs: Southwest Airlines, *Fortune*, January 10, 2000; page 82; Mary Parker Follett quote: *Report on Business*, April 1999; page 91; John Kotter quote: *Report on Business*, April 1999; page 92; Andrall E. Pearson quote: *Fast Company*, January 1999; page 73: Leadership business generates $15 billion US annually: *Report on Business*, April 1999; page 91; Task of today's leaders: *Fortune*,

March 6, 2000; page F9; The Container Store: *Fortune*, January 10, 2000; page 75; Robert Wright quote: *Megatrends 2000*, page 229; Four qualities that characterise effective leadership: *Harvard Business Review*, May/June 1999; page 111; Nordstrom Inc: *HR* Magazine, December 1999; page 87; US Marines study: *Harvard Business Review*, May/June 1999; page 107; Herman Miller: *Fortune*, January 11, 1999; page 142; Ingram Micro: *Fortune* January 11, 1999; page 140; Ernst and Young: *HR Information Matters*, September/October 1998; page E7; Whole Foods Market: *Fortune*, January 12, 1998; pages 87, 89; Vigilance: *CMA*, October 2000; page 51; Dyson Appliances Ltd.: *Industry Week*, June 21, 1999; page 40; Pfizer: *Fortune*, January 10, 2000; pages 88, 98

Chapter Eight Credits

Ken Blanchard quote: *Corporate Celebration*, page 65; Wegman's Food Markets quote: *Fortune*, January 12, 1998; page 85; 26 of *Fortune's* 100 Best Companies offer personal concierge services: *Fortune*, January 10, 2000; page 64; British study in the early 1960s: *The Affluent Worker*; McCormick: *Fortune*, January 12, 1998; page 94; 77% of employees get more satisfaction from time they spend away from their jobs than from work hours: Gallup, September 3, 1999; 85% expect to continue with some kind of work, and 69% say they will work only because they want something to do, not because they will need the money: Gallup, September 3, 1999; 47% of senior citizens work because they need the money, 86% work because they like being with other people, and 82% work because they need to be productive: *Training & Development*, June 1999; page 12; Amgen Inc.: *Industry Week*, August 16, 1999; page 46; P&G anecdote: *Built to Last*, page 132; 1958 *Mill & Factory* magazine survey: *SM's Roundup of Recent Research Findings*, August 1958; page 35; Amgen: *Fortune*, January 12, 1998; page 92; "This new workplace …": *Fortune*, January 10, 2000; Catapult Systems Corp: Inc 500,

1999; page 11; Southwest Airlines quote: *Accountancy* 121, February 1998; pages 40-42; PeopleSoft: *Fast Company*, January 1999, page 80; Container Store quote: *Fortune*, January 10, 2000; Page 158: BMC: *Fortune*, January 10, 2000; page 63; DeMarini Sports: *Inc*, June 1999; page 42; Great Plains Software of Fargo, North Dakota quote: *Fortune*, January 12, 1998; page 90; Four dimensions of community: *Chips & Pop*, pages 200-203; Maintenance staff emergency fund: *Dance of Change*, page 383; WRQ: *Fortune*, January 10, 2000; page 90; Baptist Health Systems: *Fortune*, January 12, 1998; page 94:; Marriott International: *Fortune*, January 12, 1998; page 87; BE&K: *Fortune*, January 11, 1999, page 136 and Fortune, January 12, 1998, page 89; Michael Hammer quote: *Beyond Reengineering*, pages 264, 265; Lawrence Management Services Inc: *HR* Magazine, December 1999; page 88; Empire Blue Cross and Blue Shield: *Journal for Quality & Participation* 21, January/February 1998; page 56; Employees in companies with five or fewer workers are more satisfied than other employees: Royal Bank of Canada Study of worker attitudes in Canada, April 2000; Petro Canada manager quote: *Chips & Pop*, page 202; Charles Handy quote: *The Hungry Spirit*, page 192; Four Seasons: *Fortune*, January 11, 1999; page 140; Thomas L. Friedman quote: *New York Times* service, *International Herald Tribune*, March 10, 1999; page 9; Jack Hartnett, the president of DL Rogers Corp.: *Inc.*, July 1998; page 64; Mountain Equipment Co-op: *BC Business*, April 2000; pages 47, 50; Peoplesoft: *Fortune*, January 12, 1998; page 86; Liechtenstein Global Trust, *Corporate Celebration*, page 9; MTW Corp.: *Fast Company*, December 1999, page 86; JM Smucker: *Fortune*, January 10, 2000; page 88; McKinsey and Co. quote: *Chips & Pop*, page 201; ObjecTime: *Chips & Pop*, page 203; Cisco: *Fast Company*, February/March 1998; page 56; Kingston Technology: *Fortune*, January 12, 1998; page 84; Kingston Technology: *Fortune*, January 12, 1998; page 84; SAS Institute: *Fortune*, January 12, 1998; page 84; SAS turnover rate: *Fortune*, January 10, 2000, page 98 and *The New York Times* Magazine, March 5, 2000, page 82;

Joe Demarte quote regarding Nordstrom: *HR* Magazine, December 1999; page 88; Leonard Berry quote regarding The Container Store: *Fortune*, January 10, 2000; page 78

Chapter Nine Credits

87% of North American organizations and 86% of companies abroad (especially in the UK, Germany and Japan) downsized between 1986 and 1993: Lisa Baggerman, *Industry Week*, January 18, 1993; Between 1987 and 1993, large companies like IBM, Sears Roebuck, and GE shed a quarter or more of their workforces: *Forbes*, April 25, 1994; One-third of households contained someone who lost their job, and nearly 75% of all households experienced a close encounter with layoffs between 1980 and the late 1990s: *New York Times* as reported in *Rational Exuberance*, page 148; On average, workers who lost their jobs but found work elsewhere earned 15% less, and 25% lost their health coverage as a result of job dislocation: *Revitalizing the Workplace after Downsizing, Mergers and Reengineering*, page 78; Quote from *Revitalizing the Workplace after Downsizing, Mergers and Reengineering*, pages 78, 79; Between 1988 and 1996, the number of employees who said that they often did not believe what management said rose from 33 to 40%: *The New Deal at Work*, page 238: Page 177: Trust declined at three of four workplaces: Manchester Consulting, *Management Review, July/August 1998 cover* story; Between 1995 and 1997, the number of workers who felt their company considered their interests in decisions affecting them dropped from 50 to 41%: Towers-Perrin Workplace Index press release, 1997; Number of Americans indicating confidence in the people running big business dropped from 19 to 12%, etc.: *Business Week*, March 11, 1996; page 60; A survey of downsized firms found that 74% reported that workforce morale was low and distrust of management high: US Department of Labor, *A Guide to Restructuring*, 1995; 9% reported an associated increase in absenteeism, and

13% noted an increase in disability claims: American Management Association Survey on downsizing, 1996: Page 178: Only 37% of employees rate the level of honesty in their workplaces as high or very high, although 95% rate their own honesty level as high or very high: Spring 1998 survey by the American Management Association reported in *Training & Development*, November 1999; page 16; Only 14% agree that "people trust each other": *Training & Development*, November 1999; page 16; As we've mentioned earlier, 54% of senior managers think the level of trust between corporate ranks is good, while only 27% of their employees agree: *Report on Business*, February 1999; page 3; 64% of employees believe management routinely fails to tell the truth: 1994 & 1996, US-based Council of Communication Management, *Worklife Report* 1999, Volume 11, Issue 4, page 6; 43% believe that their managers cheat and lie: survey by Mirvis & Kanter, *National Productivity Review*, Autumn 1989; The level of trust is best between front-line workers and their immediate supervisors, and worst between front-line workers and top-level executives: Manchester Consulting as reported in *Modern Machine Shop*, December 1998; 75% of executives say trust is declining, and only 15% believe it is improving: *Management Review*, July/August 1998; Netobjects CEO quote: *Fast Company*, January 1999; page 77; Murray Dobbin quote: *The Myth of the Good Corporate Citizen: Democracy Under the Rule of Big Business*; Employee productivity rose or held constant in 70% of downsized companies; short-term profits rose or held constant in 80%: American Management Association survey on downsizing, 1994, AMA, New York; Employers who restructured reported adverse effects on employee workload (62%), morale (56%) and commitment (52%), and yet an increase in productivity, service levels and the competence of the workforce: *The New Deal at Work*, p 126; Barbara Moses quote: *Career Intelligence*, page 74; Only 2% name dedication to their firm as the key to success. Instead, 56% cite individual ambition as the new key: *Training* , February 1992; page 74; *Fortune* 500 managers found that those who survived restructuring focused more on their own careers and less on organizational goals: *Strategic Management Magazine*, Journal 14, 1993; pages 161-179; Home Depot legend: *Harvard Business Review*, May/June 1999; page 110; Workers seem to be staying in the same occupation longer now than in the past, even as tenure with a particular employer has declined sharply since 1993; the length of tenure is currently at its lowest level in 20 years: *The New Deal at Work*, pages 134, 135; A work environment rich in trust and respect has been linked with less stress and greater productivity: *Worklife Report* 99, Volume 11, Issue 4; page 6; Trust minimizes in-house unethical or criminal behaviour, which adds up to $400 billion annually within US industry: *Canadian Manager*, Winter 99; page 23: Page 183: Frank J. Navran quote: *Truth & Trust: The First Two Victims of Downsizing*, pages 132, 133; *Sixty Minutes* & HB Fuller: Revitalizing the Workplace after Downsizing, Mergers and Reengineering, page 5; Arthur Andersen study: *Canadian Manager*, Winter 99; page 24; Terence E. Deal and Allan A. Kennedy quote: *Revitalizing the Workplace after Downsizing, Mergers and Reengineering*, pages 210, 211; Organizations that have implemented procedures encouraging individuals to step forward, say that company integrity and efficiency improve as a result: *Human Resource Management Journal* 7, No. 4, 1997; pages 5-10; Valour Pulse: *Management Review*, July/August 1998 cover story: Page 184: Dana Corporation: *Management Review*, July/August 1998, cover story:; Ciba Specialty Chemicals: *Management Review*, July/August 1998, cover story; Eight distinct behaviors, five leaders' keys to a trustworthy relationship with employees, and Lew Stern & Ken Lizotte mentions: *Management Review*, July/August 1998 cover story; How do leaders lose trust in the first place?: Manchester consulting, *Management Review*, July/August 1998; cover story; Mick Burkart quote regarding RailTex: *Management Review*, July/August 1998, cover story; Industry ratings for trust: Manchester consulting, Management Review, July/August 1998 cover story; One observer found that Vietnamese workers, who composed about 40% of the workforce in one company, "were especially fearful of the team concept, which they likened to Communist work teams": *Learning and Work*, page 27; Yolanda Perry-Pastor anecdote: *Fortune*, January 10, 2000; pages 65, 66: Netobjects CEO quote: *Fast Company*, January 1999; page 77; Jim Chesterton quote: *Management Review*, July/August 1998, cover story: "Hungover" quote: *Beyond Generation X*, page 40

Abrahams, Jeffrey. *The Mission Statement Book: 301 Corporate Mission Statements from America's Top Companies*. Berkeley: Ten Speed Press, 1999.

Bagby, Meredith. *Rational Exuberance: The Influence of Generation X on the New American Economy*. New York: Dutton/Penguin, 1998.

Barnard, Robert et al. *Chips & Pop: Decoding the Nexus Generation*. Toronto: Malcolm Lester Books, 1998.

Berry, Leonard. *Discovering the Soul of Service: The Nine Drivers of Sustainable Business Success*. New York: Free Press, 1999.

Bly, Robert. *The Sibling Society*. Reading: Addison-Wesley Publishing, 1996.

Bridges, William. *JobShift: How to Prosper in a Workplace without Jobs*. London: Nicholas Brealey Publishing, 1995.

Cappelli, Peter. *The New Deal at Work: Managing the Market-Driven Workforce*. Boston: Harvard Business School Press, 1999.

Cohen, Eli B. *The Leadership Engine: How Winning Companies Build Leadership at Every Level*. New York: HarperCollins, 2000.

Collins, James. *Built to Last: Successful Habits of Visionary Companies*. New York: HarperBusiness, 1994.

Covey, Stephen. *Seven Habits of Highly Effective People*. Salt Lake City:

Franklin Covey Co., 1989.

Darrah, Charles N. *Learning and Work: An Exploration in Industrial Ethnography*. New York: Garland Publishing, 1996.

Deal, Terence E. and Allan A. Kennedy. *Revitalizing the Workplace After Downsizing, Mergers and Reengineering*. Reading: Perseus Books, 1999.

Deal, Terence E. and M.K. Key. *Corporate Celebration*. San Francisco: Berrett-Koehler Publishers, 1998.

Discovering America's Past: Customs, Legends, History and Lore of Our Great Nation. New York: Readers Digest, 1993.

Diversity in the Workplace Human Resources Initiatives, ed. Susan E. Jackson & Associates. New York: Guilford Press, 1992.

Dobbin, Murray. *The Myth of the Good Corporate Citizen: Democracy Under the Rule of Big Business*. Toronto: Stoddart, 1998.

Dominguez, Joseph R. and Vicki Robin. *Your Money or Your Life: Transforming Your Relationship with Money and Achieving Financial Independence*. New York: Penguin Books, 1993.

Everett, Melissa. *Making a Living While Making a Difference: The Expanded Guide to Creating Careers with a Conscience*. Gabriola Island: New Society Publishers, 1999.

Foot, David K. with Danial Stoffman. *Boom, Bust & Echo: How to Profit from the Coming Demographic Shift*. Toronto: Macfarlane, Walter and Ross, 1996.

Friel, John C. and Linda D. Friel. *The Worst Seven Things Parents Can Do*. Deerfield Beach: Health Communications, 1999.

Goldberg, Beverly. *Age Works: What Corporate America Must Do to Survive the*

Graying of the Workforce. New York: Free Press, 2000.

Goldthorpe, J et al. *The Affluent Worker: Industrial Attitude and Behaviour*. Cambridge: Cambridge University Press, 1968.

Hammer, Michael and James Champy. *Reengineering the Corporation: A Manifesto for Business Revolution*. New York: HarperBusiness, 1993.

Hammer, Michael. *Beyond Reengineering: How the Process-Centered Organization is Changing Our Work and Our Lives*. New York: HarperBusiness, 1996.

Handy, Charles. *The Hungry Spirit: Beyond Capitalism: A Quest for Purpose in the Modern World*. London: Arrow Books/ Random House, 1998.

Hendricks, Gay and Kate Lickman. *The Corporate Mystic: A Guidebook for Visionaries with Their Feet on the Ground*. New York and Toronto: Bantam Books, 1996.

Hochschild, Archie. *The Time Bind: When Work Becomes Home and Home Becomes Work*. New York: Metropolitan Books, 1997.

Kaye, Beverly L. and Sharon Jordan-Evans. *Love 'Em or Lose 'Em: Getting Good People to Stay*. New York: Berrett-Koehler, 1999.

Klein, Eric, and John B. Izzo. *Awakening Corporate Soul*. Vancouver: Fair Winds Press, 1998.

Leonard, George Burr. *Mastery: The Keys to Long-Term Success and Fulfillment*. New York: Dutton, 1991.

Maas, James B. with Megan L. Wherry. *Power Sleep: The Revolutionary Program that Prepares Your Mind for Peak Performance*. New York: Villard Books, 1998.

Manji, Irshad. *Risking Utopia: On the Edge of a New Democracy.* Toronto:Douglas & McIntyre, 1997.

Marshall, Edward M. *Building Trust at the Speed of Change.* New York: Amacom, 1999.

McKenna, Regis. *Real Time: Preparing for the Age of the Never Satisfied Customer.* Harvard Business School Press, 1997.

Mercer, David. *Future Revolutions.* London: Orion Business Books, 1998.

Moses, Barbara. *Career Intelligence: Mastering the New Work and Personal Realities.* Toronto: Stoddart, 1997.

Naisbitt, John and Patricia Aburdene. *Megatrends 2000: Ten New Directions for the 1990s.* New York: William Morrow & Co., 1990.

Nattrass, Brian and Mary Altomare. *The Natural Step for Business: Wealth, Ecology and the Evolutionary Corporation.* Gabriola Island: New Society Publishers, 1999.

Navran, Frank J. *Truth and Trust: The First Two Victims of Downsizing.* Athabasca: Athabasca Educational Enterprises, 1995.

Oliver, Richard W. *The Shape of Things to Come: Imperatives for Winning in the New World of Business.* New York: McGraw Hill, 1999.

Promise of Diversity. New York: NTL Institute/Irwin Publishing, 1994.

Raines, Claire. *Beyond Generation X: A Practical Guide for Managers.* Menlo Park, California: Crisp Publications, 1997.

Reid, Angus. *Shakedown: How the New Economy is Changing Our Lives.* Toronto: Seal Books/McClelland-Bantam/Doubleday Canada, 1996.

Credits

Ryan, Kathleen and Daniel I. Ostreich. *Driving Fear Out of the Workplace: How to Overcome the Invisible Barriers of Quality, Productivity and Innovation*. San Francisco: Jossey-Bass Publishers, 1991.

Schor, Juliet. *The Overworked American: The Unexpected Decline of Leisure*. New York: Basic Books, 1991.

Senge, Peter. *The Dance of Change: The Challenges to Sustaining Momentum in Learning Organizations*. New York: Doublelday/Currency, 1999.

Sennett, Richard. *The Corrosion of Character: The Personal Consequences of Work in the New Capitalism*. New York and London: W. W. Norton & Co., 1998.

The Good Life. London: The Demos Collection Issue 14, Demos, 1998.

Wright, Leslie and Marti Smye. *Civilizing the Workplace: Corporate Abuse: How 'Lean and Mean' Robs People and Profits*. Toronto: Key Porter Books, 1996.

Dr. John Izzo, Ph.D.

As an author, community leader and one of North America's most thought provoking and inspiring voices, Dr. John Izzo has spoken to over a million people about the essential elements of *leadership* and how each of us can lead fulfilling lives while making the world a better place. His interests are *development* as it pertains to the individual as well at the company, *corporate culture* and the pursuit of creating places that support the individual as well as the corporate vision, personal well-being in the fight to balance work and life and our *social and environmental responsibility* to ensure future generations see and experience a preserved and sustainable planet.

Dr. Izzo has more than 20 years experience working in a wide variety of corporate settings. His clients include nonprofit organizations, Fortune 500 companies, Healthcare systems and mid-size companies. His appearance schedule has him presenting to Associations as well as National corporate conferences worldwide. He has become known as one of North America's most influential voices.

He is the author of over 500 articles, and is the co-author of the best selling book *Awakening Corporate Soul: Four Paths to Unleash the Power of People at Work* and its companion workbook. His second book focused corporate North America on the connection between the workforce's values and the rates of retention within the work world. *Values-Shift: Recruiting, Retaining and Engaging the Inter-Generational Workforce* (2nd edition) defines how and why our work ethic has changed by focusing on Six major *'values shifts'* that are occurring in the world of work. His third book, *Second Innocence: Rediscovering Joy and Wonder* was published in 2004 by Berrett-Koehler. It is a powerful book that blends personal stories with Dr. Izzo's thoughts on work, spirituality, relationships and daily life.

Recently, **The Biography Channel** and Dr. Izzo embarked on an adventure to learn from 200 Wise Elders across North America. The series, *The Five Things You Must Discover Before You Die* was filmed in Toronto at the John Bassett Theatre before a live studio audience and began airing in **April 2007** on **The Biography Channel**.

Dr. Izzo's environmental and pioneering corporate work has been featured on **CNN, ABC World News, the LA Times, Canada AM, CBC Radio, The American Medical Journal, B.C. Business, Fast Company, the National Post, the Wall Street Journal,** and the cover of **Association Management Magazine.** Dr. Izzo is the former president of Canadian Parks and Wilderness Society and a post board president of the Sierra Club. He continues to be a feature writer for the Globe and Mail career section.

Working with John B. Izzo, Ph.D.:

Dr. John Izzo speaks globally on topics related to life, leadership, spirituality and responsibility.

To inquire about his availability to speak at your upcoming event, please inquire at: info@drjohnizzo.com.

Contact information:
Office (604) 913-0649; Fax (604) 913-0648
e-mail info@drjohnizzo.com
Web site: www.drjohnizzo.com or www.theizzogroup.com

The Izzo Group

The Group of committed individuals that make up The Izzo Group Ltd., have all been in the personal, professional and organizational development industry for decades. We assist people in becoming happier, spiritually healthier individuals who feel their contribution to the world uses their gifts and talents fully. We also use our combined strengths to assist today's leaders in creating healthy workplace cultures where purpose, passion and profits are the pillars of success. Our work focuses on helping leaders create spirited, engaged teams and to assist people in finding more fulfillment and purpose in their own lives and work.

Products Available by Dr. John Izzo

Special discounts available for conference planners wishing to make these titles available at their conference:

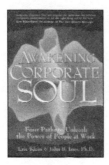

Awakening Corporate Soul:
Four Paths to Unleash the Power of People at Work

Awakening Corporate Soul:
Creating the High Performance /
High Fulfillment at Work:
the Workbook

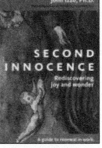

Second Innocence:
Rediscovering Joy and Wonder

Subscribe to our FREE Newsletter

...go to www.theizzogroup.com and register for his free newsletter. Please view our library as it lists back issues from the past three years.

Healthcare Newsletter

Renewing the Heart of Healthcare

Dr. John Izzo has created a Newsletter targeted specifically to healthcare professionals. If you wish to receive this newsletter please register online to be a free subscriber: www.theizzogroup.com

The Biography Channel • Series

The Five Things You Must Discover Before You Die

This unique series explores the things we all must discover before we die. Dr. John Izzo conducted 200 interviews with people aged 60-105 who were identified by others as having found wisdom.

This series features Dr. John Izzo before a live audience exploring the five themes that emerged from those 200 interviews. Through compelling stories, humor and practical ideas for change he explores the paths to contentment and purpose.

Pam Withers

Pam Withers has spent more than 20 years in the publishing industry, including stints in San Francisco, Seattle, New York City and Vancouver as a journalist, magazine editor, circulation director, associate publisher and consultant to magazine publishers. She is a regular contributor to business magazines and a recent finalist for a business-writing award.

Her writing credits include *The New York Times*, *The Christian Science Monitor*, *Your Money*, *Moneywise*, Profit, *Working Woman*, *McCalls*, *Equinox*, *BCBusiness*, *Workforce* and numerous airline in-flight magazines.

Born in Wisconsin, raised in the Dakotas, Pam studied English at Beloit College in Wisconsin. A longtime whitewater kayaker, she is also a former raft guide and teen camp coordinator. She now divides her time between editing business books, writing novels, and speaking at writers' conferences and schools.

Her series of five novels (Walrus press) are available in trade bookstores!

Working with Pam Withers

Pam Withers is available to author or co-author business books and articles.

She is an accomplished writer and has published five teen adventure novels.

Pam Withers
3835 W. 30th Ave.
Vancouver, British Columbia
Canada V6S 1W9
withers@intergate.ca
(604) 224-1194